It's All Good

Whether as a military medic, marathon runner, or Miss America contestant, I take life in stride

It's All Good

By Jill Stevens

SC

spring creek
BOOK COMPANY
Provo, Utah

ISBN 13: 978-1-932898-93-4
e. 1

Published by:
Spring Creek Book Company
P.O. Box 50355
Provo, Utah 84605-0355

www.springcreekbooks.com

Cover design © Spring Creek Book Company
Front cover photos by Studio West Photography of Cedar City, Utah
Back cover photo and interior photos courtesy of Jill Stevens
Title page illustration © Bryan Beus

"I Know He Lives" by Tyler Castleton and Staci Peters
© 2005 Diamond Aire Music (ASCAP)/Paulista Music Publishing (ASCAP)
Lyrics used by permission

Printed in the United States of America
Printed on acid-free paper

Library of Congress Cataloging-in-Publication Data
Stevens, Jill, 1983-
  It's all good : whether as a military medic, marathon runner, or Miss America
contestant, I take life in stride / by Jill Stevens.
     p. cm.
  ISBN 978-1-932898-93-4 (pbk. : alk. paper)
  1. Stevens, Jill, 1983- 2. Long-distance runners--Utah--Biography. 3. Beauty
contestants--Utah--Biography. 4. United States. Army--Medical personnel--
Biography. 5. Utah--Biography. I. Title.
  CT275.S6924A3 2008
  979.2092--dc22
  [B]
                            2008029933

Acknowledgments

For my family who helped make my life interesting.

For my mom, who believed in me from the beginning.

For Dorothy Dayton, who might as well be family and spent long hours translating some of my words into English.

For God, who gave me strength and continues to give me strength through it all . . . I offer my sincere gratitude.

TABLE OF CONTENTS

THE TENDER YEARS 1

WHY RUN A MARATHON? 23

FORGING MY OWN PATH 32

WE NEED A MEDIC! 62

SOARING AS HIGH AS A T-BIRD! 72

CALLED TO WAR 88

BOOTS ON GROUND 97

JILLYBEAN THE BAKING QUEEN 126

OUTSIDE THE WIRE 138

HOME AGAIN 161

ME IN A PAGEANT? 176

EMBRACING THE PAGEANT WORLD 199

OUT OF TOUCH WITH REALITY 212

MISS AMERICA 233

EACH HAPPY ENDING IS A BRAND NEW BEGINNING 269

About the Cover

The photos you see on the front cover will make you laugh once you read about what happened to me right before they were taken. Some people say that bad things happen in threes. On that particular day, I would have agreed.

Karl Hugh at Studio West Photography in Cedar City, Utah is a photographer that I know and trust. We've known each other for years, and I knew he would be a great choice to do the shoot for my cover. I drove down to Cedar City the day before the shoot, and I planned a hair appointment with my friend, Lizzy, that afternoon to do some last minute touch-ups. She offered to do my hair the next morning to have it ready for the photo shoot. That sounded perfect, and we scheduled the hair appointment for 8:30 a.m.

As I started to drive away after meeting with Lizzie, I noticed that my view in my rearview mirror was different. I was hoping that I had simply bumped my mirror, but it did cross my mind that a flat tire could, perhaps, also be a reason for the new view.

I pulled into a nearby parking lot and my speculation was correct—I had a flat tire. No big deal really. It just would take some time to fix it. I started getting out all of my tools and tried to loosen the tire's lug nuts, but they wouldn't budge. Luckily, a family saw me struggling and getting all greased up for nothing. (I like to get into my work.) They were a lifesaver as we got the spare tire in place.

The funny thing was that within a few hours I heard from my mom, asking me if I'd had a flat tire and I hadn't even told her about it yet. It turns out she'd heard from a friend, who heard from her sister-in-law, who had received a phone call from one of the kind women who had stopped to help me change the tire. Apparently after the good deed was done and we parted ways, she had thought to herself, "Wait, wasn't that

Miss Utah? I think that was Miss Utah!" And the phone calls began.

I was excited to be back in my old college town of Cedar City and even more excited to hit my usual 11-mile running route I had used in the past to train for marathons. I figured it would be a great way to start my day for my big photo shoot, and soon I was running in the crisp morning air. About eight miles into it, though, fatigue really set in. I suppose I was pushing it too hard and too fast, since I had just completed my 13th marathon only six days earlier.

I must not have been fully recovered, and my body was really dragging . . . literally, because suddenly I hit the pavement hard. This wasn't the usual hiccup-stumble most runners do where you quickly catch yourself. Instead, I skidded full-length across the rocky street. This wasn't just any street, but one of the busiest in Cedar City, right by a freeway entrance.

I grunted as I hit the pavement, but within a couple of seconds I was back on my feet running. It's embarrassing enough to actually fall down, so you gotta pop right back up as fast as possible, like it's really no big deal. I am no stranger to falling—this is a common occurrence for me. I seem to stumble a lot while running, but I had never hit the ground this hard before.

The best way I've found to get through the pain is just to keep running. If you stop and stare at what injuries you may have incurred, it will only hurt worse. So as I was running through the pain, I was checking out the damage from the fall. Blood was running down my right leg from my knee, and it looked like my left knee was starting to bleed as well. Abrasions covered my left thigh, and there was about a quarter size chunk of skin taken out of my left palm.

I was grateful to have been wearing long sleeves, but I could feel there were some scratches on my shoulder. Then all of a sudden I realized that my face hurt. My face hurt! "Oh no," I thought. "Of all days, this had to happen on the day of one of my most important photo shoots—the cover of my book!"

I could feel that my left cheek was scraped and bruised, and I was just praying the damage wasn't too bad. I stopped to look in a reflection of a business window and was relieved to see that make-up would be able to cover it up. The last three miles were tough to get through, but

I slowly completed the route. I was so grateful at that point that I had consented to Lizzy doing my hair that morning, since I would have been hopeless doing my hair with one hand.

I made it to the appointment, and Lizzy and I shared a good laugh as I told her about my mishap. But as she was working on my hair, the power went out in the salon. That was strike three! "That's just great," I thought. "Now I'll have my picture taken with a swollen face and only half of my hair done! What else could possibly go wrong?"

But Lizzy and I just laughed all the more. Luckily the power eventually came back on, and she was able to finish my hair.

The photo shoot ended up going a little bit slower than usual, but it was all the more fun as Carl and I joked about my battle wounds, especially the swollen cheek bone. It ended up looking like I put more bronzer on my left cheek.

I was relieved to see that in the final photos, my bruised cheek wasn't too noticeable. But I just I had to tell you about my memorable day.

CHAPTER 1

THE TENDER YEARS

I find it very fitting that I was born during the final episode of the TV show *MASH* on February 28, 1983, which is still the highest-rated program in the history of television. Maybe I wanted to see it too, because I was born five weeks before my due date. Consequently, I suffered some serious health issues as a newborn, but I fought through them.

I came into the family as the third child of David and Karen Stevens. My brother Brad was 3, and Tyler, age 2, was next in line. Just 13 months after my birth, my sister Janelle joined the family. We lived in Draper, Utah, at the time, but when I was one year old our family took off to Louisiana as my dad pursued some business opportunities. I was soon learning how to speak another language . . . Southern.

I attended pre-school at Honeysuckle Cottage, which had peacocks living under the building. My earliest memories include being chased across the school grounds by those birds, which kept life exciting!

I was a curious child who was always up for a challenge, and one day I decided to see if I could fit my body through the hole in the back of my chair. As my teacher kept talking, I slowly began this cool undertaking. I thought I was being very graceful, because nobody was noticing what I was doing. I would freeze whenever the teacher looked over at me . . . like she wouldn't notice.

"I'm so sneaky," I thought happily. I got my feet through, struggled a little to get my hips through, and then it came time for my head. It didn't fit as smoothly. "Wait, maybe I just have my head turned wrong," I told myself, but I was definitely stuck!

It's normal for kids at that age to have heads that are bigger in proportion to their bodies, but my head was abnormally large. I was even kept in the hospital a few extra days as a newborn because of it, but the doctors didn't find anything medically wrong. However, now there was something terribly wrong! My head was completely wedged into the hole of my chair.

I started panicking and making a bit of a ruckus. My teacher finally noticed my dilemma and came to my rescue, pulling me through. I was so embarrassed, but tried to act natural! I suppose it was just a little bit of my goofy side already starting to show through.

After living in Louisiana for four years, my parents decided to get a divorce. I moved with my mother and my siblings to Pinedale, Wyoming. To my parents' credit, I remember feeling happy and secure during this transition. I saw the move to Pinedale as an adventure, and since we had cousins that lived there, we had ready-made friends.

My kindergarten class often had dance parties, and the song "Wipe Out" was a favorite. My classmates would let loose, showing off their own dance styles. I came up with my own dance moves that I believed set me apart from the rest of my classmates. I would slowly work my way over to my teacher so that she could see my fancy dance moves. Every time she would tell me what great moves I had—of course, I already knew that.

Like most kindergarten classes, we had a designated time for "Show and Tell." One day, a boy named Isaac decided to take "Show and Tell" to a whole new level. As Isaac stood in front of the class, he pulled from behind his back a bottle filled with a clear green liquid. He said he had created a "shrinking potion." All the kids in the classroom looked wide-eyed at each other as this news sunk in. We all wanted to see the magic potion work, so before we left for recess, we put a big spoon in a bowl and poured the potion over it.

Recess just couldn't end fast enough for us. We all wanted to see if our friend had really done it. When we returned to class, we found that the big spoon was now the size of a teaspoon. His magic shrinking potion had actually worked!

I excitedly went home that day to share the news with my mom. I couldn't stop thinking about it. Then it hit me, "If he could make a magic potion, so could I!"

I soon began gathering every green liquid in the house that I could get my hands on. When I finished concocting my potion, it didn't look quite as clear as my friend's liquid had. My potion looked more like thick, green mucus, but I figured that meant it would be more powerful.

When I took it to "Show and Tell" the next day, I was confident it would work—even though I hadn't tested it at home. I went through the same routine with my potion as Isaac had, and then went to recess. When we returned to class, I found the same-size spoon was in the bowl. I was crushed! If Isaac could make a magic potion, couldn't I? I had thought that if I put my mind to anything, in the end I would accomplish my goal. I was five and I felt like a failure!

After that eventful kindergarten year in Wyoming, my mom found a place for us to live in Hilmar, California. You can actually smell the city before you can see it, because of the many dairy farms there, and it's also the home of a large cheese factory. That's quite a combination! At least that's what my Grandma says, since she has been a resident of Hilmar for more than 20 years.

I have a confession. Yep, I admit it. "My name is Jill Stevens, and I was a finger-sucker." Of course, the habit was understandable. Who knew that the index finger was capable of such quality taste? When I discovered its flavor, as an infant, I thought I had found happiness. The happiness soon turned to dependence, then a craving, and I knew I was on my way down that slippery slope of addiction. I was hooked, but I tried to hide it.

By the time I was a wise first-grader, I knew I needed to find a way to quit this finger-sucking obsession. So I did what any other 6-year-old child would do. I made a chart! I awarded myself a "star sticker" whenever I went a day without sucking my scrumptious index finger.

I thought it was going to be easy to overcome, because I was so determined to "throw in the towel" on this bad habit. I soon discovered, though, that I could barely make it three days before suffering withdrawals. During the day I had pretty good self-control, but the nights became my worst enemy. I knew I had to re-evaluate my plan of attack. (I was a natural-born soldier). Willpower by itself was not enough; I needed more back-up support. I decided to cover the tempting finger with a sock. I thought I was a genius!

I went to bed that night completely confident that I would be successful in my mission and be able to add another star to my chart the next day. Imagine my surprise when I woke up the next morning to find the sock still on my hand, but somehow I had chewed a hole through it to get to my finger. My plan had failed! All the same feelings from the failed "magic potion" incident washed over me again.

Of course, many people would have just given up at this point and surrendered to the enemy, but not me. "Why do I want to suck my finger so badly?" I asked myself. "Why had my plan failed?"

I decided it was because my finger was so tasty! To put the odds in my favor, I found a nasty-tasting cream to rub on my finger each night before I went to bed. Just to make sure, I even put a sock over it for reinforcement. Pretty soon, star stickers were filling my calendar, and I didn't even need to go to Finger Suckers Anonymous. I had accomplished my goal! I wasn't a magician, but I was a winner!

While attending church in Hilmar, I met and became good friends with a girl named Christie Stephens. I would play at her house every now and then. Coincidentally, her father and my mother started dating, and that dating led to marriage. It's not very often that one of your friends becomes your sister! My siblings and I thought it was funny that our last name didn't really need to change—Stevens and Stephens sounded pretty much the same.

After their marriage we moved to Turlock, California and I started second grade at yet another school. In my class we earned tickets for good behavior and completed assignments, then on certain days we were able to go to the "classroom store" to get small toys, candy or school supplies.

One day I had this genius thought: "If everyone at my table pooled all of our money together, we could divvy out the money in little bits and have more in the end . . . to buy more!" I expressed this vision to my tablemates and sold them on the idea. At first I thought it was a brilliant plan, but my business didn't last too long once they caught on that it didn't really change anything.

Taking a Song to Heart

Each Sunday my family attended The Church of Jesus Christ of Latter-day Saints, also known as the Mormon Church. My mom has a love of music, and she served as our church congregation's choir director for many years.

My siblings and I were each baptized as members of the church as we turned the age of eight, and at that time our mother would give us an incredible gift by writing a song specifically for us. Here is the song my mom wrote for me:

Let Your Light So Shine
By Karen Stephens

So long ago, there lived a man
He came to Earth as part of Father's plan
He was the light of the world
He lived his life so perfectly
He was the light for all to see
He was the Son of God
When He spoke to His disciples
He taught them how to love
How to glorify their Father up above

Let your light so shine to all the world
Let them see you serve the Father
Every moment everyday
Come and follow in my footsteps
And glorify His name
Let your light so shine

Not long ago, just like that man
You came to Earth as part of that same plan
I see His light in your eyes
And as you grow fulfill your destiny
Your light can shine for all to see
For you're a child of God
Though there may be times of darkness
Heed the Master's gentle plea
Let the light of Christ shine forth for all to see

Let your light so shine to all the world
Let them see you serve the Father
Every moment everyday
Come and follow in His footsteps
And glorify His name
Let your light so shine

Little did I know how much this song would become a strength to me and become a theme for my life.

By this time I realized I liked playing sports with the boys, and I held my own against them pretty well. It wasn't very often that you saw me without a baseball cap on my head. Boys couldn't wear hats in school, but girls were allowed to, and I took full advantage of that courtesy.

I was a fan of the San Francisco Giants, and I really liked Will Clark, the team's first baseman. Along those lines, collecting baseball cards was my big hobby. I was proud of my collection of over 2,000 cards and I learned a few "tricks of the trade" to acquire the top players' cards.

One of my prized cards was a "Bo Jackson, MVP" card, but it was taken from me during a trade in third grade when I wasn't paying close attention. I foolishly gave up my collection to my older brother a few years later.

During elementary school I also developed a desire to be a cartoon artist. I loved drawing, but that doesn't necessarily mean I had a lot of talent. My classmates thought I was pretty good, so I felt confident that I could get by as an artist if I kept at it. I had the ability to look at a picture and copy it almost exactly.

When I was in third grade, our teacher Mrs. Williams used the "ticket method" of compensation. So I decided to sell my drawings for tickets. It was great. I even sold paper "ninja stars" that my brother taught me how to fold. I was making the big bucks, and I felt pretty popular. I was the girl who could play with the best of them in kickball, running, trading baseball cards, drawing—you name it.

I was known as the fastest runner in the class—not necessarily because I was the fastest, but because I never walked. Most of the kids would lazily move around the track, but I figured if we were supposed to run, then I was going to run! I loved the feeling of being fast and was going to carry that title as long as I could. Life was good. Or so I thought . . .

One day Mrs. Williams announced that we were getting a new student. I was excited for a new addition! She told us, "He's just like any of us, but sometimes he acts a little strangely. Our new classmate has a condition called Turrets Syndrome."

She went on to explain what that actually meant and emphasized that we should treat him no differently. He showed up a couple of days later and looked just like the rest of us. Everyone in the class always kept a close eye on him to see if he would do anything unusual, but nothing ever happened.

One day in our P.E. class we were told to do a running drill around the field a few times. The class got moving slowly and soon I was at the head of the pack, leaving the rest of the students behind me. Then out of nowhere came the "new kid." He left me in the dust like it was no trouble at all. The whole class noticed and started cheering him on— and letting me know I was too slow to catch him. I certainly didn't like this feeling—I was losing. I backed off and played it cool like I didn't care. But I did.

Later on that week we had some free time in class, and I usually filled it by drawing. The new kid liked to draw as well and had an extreme talent for it. Soon our classmates gathered around our desks, moving back and forth to compare our drawings. I had drawn a sweet and gentle owl, while he had drawn an "Action-figure monster ready to conquer the world."

The kids were quick to notice the difference and made a point to tell me I didn't draw as well as he did. They had shattered my dreams. My spirits were low the rest of the day. I was one of the last students out of the classroom, feeling no rush to join the rest of the kids. But as I was walking out the door, Mrs. Williams called out, "Jill, you're still the best artist in the classroom to me." I gave a small smile, turned ten shades of red, and walked out of the room feeling elated! I was still an artist in her book, and right then that was all I needed to know.

I had a lot of respect for Mrs. Williams, and I always did my best to follow the rules. One day, though, I did something that made me worry I might get in trouble. One hobby in the classroom was "ruler flicking" where you hold a ruler at the edge of a desk and "flick" it to make a cool sound. Being third graders, we were intrigued by this and did it quite often.

On this particular day, I flicked the ruler a little too hard and snapped it. No one had noticed, and I quickly hid the pieces under my shirt as I pondered how to "dispose of the evidence." I nonchalantly walked past the garbage can and threw the pieces in.

As I returned to my desk, it dawned on me that others were going to see the evidence of my crime. I went back to the garbage can to throw away a piece of paper and buried the ruler pieces further in the trash. "No one will know now," I told myself.

As the class dragged on, my fear of exposure got the best of me. Someone was going to find the evidence . . . Mrs. Williams was surely going to find out . . . I was going to be kicked out of the school. The garbage can in the classroom wasn't adequate enough to hide my shame. I decided I needed to get the evidence away from the crime scene. I asked to use the hall pass and disposed of the ruler pieces in a bathroom garbage can on the opposite end of the school.

On the way home that day, my conscience began shouting at me again that I had done something terribly wrong. I hid in my room for a couple of hours, crying because of what I had done. I finally came to the conclusion that I must confess my action. I told my mom what happened and she just smiled. "MOM!" I cried out. "This is serious! What do I do?"

She suggested that we should talk with my teacher after school the next day. "We'll need to get a new ruler to replace the one you broke, and I'm sure your teacher will understand."

I felt a huge sigh of relief. After school the next day, I watched from a distance as my mom talked to my teacher, then I joined them to apologize and give her the new ruler. There was laughter and smiling! I must be okay . . . and I was.

My stepdad, Craig, had his own business of building houses, specializing in tile work. I liked to go on projects with him at times while growing up, and sometimes we would spend the night in the unfinished framed house. My dad would let me pitch in and help with some of the work, such as hammering nails and cutting wood. I loved the initial part of building—looking at the blue prints and seeing it come together in the wood frames. It was like a big fort to me and I enjoyed playing games within the walls and getting dirty.

It was about this time that my little brother Mitchell was born, on September 11, 1992. It was so much fun to have a new member of the family! A new school was finished that year, and I changed schools yet again. Then midway through the year, our family decided to move farther north to a place called Twain Harte in the California mountains.

I was realizing more and more that I really liked "being one of the guys." Sundays were the only time you would catch me wearing a dress. Pants from the boys section were my style. I wore my older brothers' "hand-me-downs" because I loved the feel of bigger clothes and hated anything that fit my body. If the sleeve of my shirt went above my elbow there was no way I was walking out the front door. If pants showed the outline of my thigh in any way, I felt they were too small.

There were a few reasons why I liked the bigger clothes: 1) it was the style then, 2) I liked that I could move in them easily when playing sports, and 3) I was a little self-conscious about my body and felt I could hide in them better. Who knew that one day I would stand confidently, although still a little self-consciously, in a swimsuit in front of millions of television viewers?

I definitely loved playing sports! Tackle football was my favorite. I was usually the only girl out there. I always tried to get in on some of my brothers' adventures of making forts out of tumbleweeds and playing night games. Some of the time I was able to tag along. I did do a bit of bike riding. We had some dirt fields around our house where I would go riding with my siblings.

I also liked baseball, but I was more of a hitter than a fielder. I had a decent arm but didn't have the best aim. For some reason, the more power I put into a throw, the more out of control it was and more likely to hit someone.

My awkward years

I guess I took being "one of the guys" a little too far. Being among boys so much, I was a little jealous of their simple hairstyle and decided to cut mine short as well. Yep, I had the famous "Bowl Cut." But I was my mom's first daughter, and she was really excited to have a girl and naturally wanted me to look like one. So we would take this hairstyle and curl it around my whole head. But this was never enough, so we would then fluff the curls. My head looked like a mushroom! Wait, it gets worse . . .

Now that I was 11 years old, my baby teeth were gone and I was suffering the consequences of my "finger-sucking years" with big spaces between my top teeth and a killer overbite. So attractive, I know.

It was now time to fix this matter, and I was told by the orthodontist that I needed to wear head-gear. I was ready for the bad news, but I was completely unprepared for what he told me next. Usually, people who have head-gear just have to wear it at night for a few months. Well, I was "special" and had to wear the head-gear 24/7 for a year!

So there I was with my nifty mushroom-fluff hair and head-gear permanently attached to my face. Just picture a young girl with that hairdo, sitting in class nibbling on metal, trying to chew off the coating on the wire just in front of her mouth. Go ahead and laugh.

My stepdad was really into wildlife and hunting, and I soon found it an adventure myself. There were even a few times where he actually didn't need to leave the house to go hunting. Living in the mountains in California, we were surrounded by animals. Often we would see deer in our yard and an occasional coyote. Snakes were common in our backyard, and we would catch them to keep as pets. I remember getting up one morning and hearing, "A snake is missing from the cage again," and not being the least bit scared about the idea of a snake being loose in our house.

Once, in the middle of the night, my dad woke us all up and said there was a bear in our front yard. That made me a little nervous! All the kids gazed out the upstairs window squinting through the darkness to get a glimpse of the bear. We saw something move in the yard, the dark silhouette moving slowly. Yep, it was definitely a bear. My siblings and I could hardly believe it.

After a few minutes, the bear walked off into the trees down the mountain. We all had a hard time getting back to sleep that night. It turned out the bear came back and decided to leave his mark. The next morning we found at least eight trash bags scattered across the front yard. We kept our trash in a fenced-off area on the side of the house to haul up to the dumpster every now and then, and it seemed the bear wanted to break down our fence and have a feast.

This bear didn't stop coming to our yard, and I soon started to hate the bear because we had to clean up after it before school started. We were getting annoyed and worried that the bear was going to do more damage to our property.

Finally one day my dad heard the bear in our yard again. (As a hunter, he had an ear for these things, and I was grateful.) It was during the Christmas season as we gazed out the window and saw the bear licking an eggnog carton, kicking back against the tree. We were all enjoying the show when all of a sudden, BANG! The bear rolled down the hill.

We screamed in fright and confusion about what we had just seen. My dad came up the stairs with a sheepish grin on his face and a rifle in his hand. It turned out he had received approval and a bear tag to get rid of the beast. We hung the bear over a tree later that day and started to gut it out—a stench I will never forget, but wish that I could. The skin and the skull are now part of the décor in my little brother's room.

Finding friends

There were about 800 students in our school that ranged from kindergarten through eighth grade. I tagged along with a group of girls and called them my "friends" even though we had very different standards. Friends to me, though, were simply people that I ate lunch with and hung out with at recess. It didn't really go beyond that. I was terrified to call people up and invite them over or ask if I could go to their homes. I always thought to myself, "Who would want to hang out with me?"

Moving around so much took a toll on me wanting to get close to people. I had a lot of fun with these girls at school, mainly being entertained by watching them and their "girly" personalities. I found it intriguing to watch people. I actually learned a lot about how I wanted to be, and especially how I didn't want to be.

These friends didn't have the most positive influence on me. Curse words were a big part of their vocabulary at such a young age, and they liked to play games like "puff, puff, pass" while standing in a circle, basically pretending to smoke a cigarette and passing it along. I was standing in a circle with them one day as they started to play. I got nervous wondering, "Am I going to look dumb for not taking it? Should I just take it? It's just a game, but that doesn't feel right."

My mind was whirling with these thoughts when the boy at my side imitated the "puff" and got ready to "pass" to me. Everyone in the circle was silent. The boy hesitated as I looked back and forth from his hand to his face, and then I took a step back. He just passed it to the next person. I did it! I just turned it down! No one was making fun of me. "I'm okay," I thought. "Actually, I feel even better for not playing."

My friends never really cared that I didn't do that kind of stuff, and they knew to leave me out of those types of games. I guess this game became reality for some of my friends, though.

While in one of my seventh grade classes, I was pulled out of class, along with another girl. We were told to bring all of our belongings. I was a little nervous and confused. I was racking my brain and couldn't think of anything I'd done wrong, but that didn't relieve the anxiety. The adults just stopped us right outside of class and said for us to stand back as they were going to search our things.

"What were they searching for?" I asked myself. Then they pulled out a pack of cigarettes from the other girl's bag. I couldn't believe what I was seeing! It turns out that someone complained of a "smoke smell" in the bathroom and talked to the school counselors.

My mom didn't like me hanging out with these friends because she felt their influence was going to bring me down. I tried to respect her concern and would sometimes eat lunch alone. Of course, my friends wanted to know why I stopped eating lunch with them, and I didn't really know how to respond other than to tell the truth.

They respected me for that, and later one girl came up to me and said, "Jill, I have noticed that you don't swear, and I really like that you don't get involved in the dirty jokes and games. I don't want to do that either. Can I hang around you more?"

"Uh... yeah!" I told her. I was completely taken aback. "Of course you can, that would be great!" That was a testimony to me that sometimes it is better to live by example than to force your standards and beliefs on others. Eventually others will respect you and soon may even want to change their own behaviors.

The move to Utah

After giving it a lot of thought, my parents decided it was best to move to Utah. There were several reasons: 1) most of the family was living there, 2) better job opportunities for my parents, and especially 3) a more positive environment for my siblings and me. I couldn't dance around the fact that I was really excited for the move, too.

Utah was love at first sight for me. The summer before we moved, we had visited my aunt for a few days. We didn't arrive there until about 3 a.m. I distinctly remember stepping out of the van and feeling awestruck, paralyzed by the beauty of the mountains. The moon was helping the mountains glow. I couldn't believe how big they were. It was an unforgettable sight!

Going to church in Utah was a different experience than what I was used to. The church building we attended was a couple of blocks away instead of several miles, yet it wasn't even the closest one to our home. There were a few girls my age that took me in as a friend and I couldn't have been more excited. I felt this was my chance to have some close friends, since I knew we were here to stay and not moving anytime soon. These girls knew everybody. I started eighth grade at Farmington Junior High and met so many great people the first few days. I didn't really feel like a new kid at all.

My new friends would call me to come over and hang out or invite me to go to different parties. I tried so hard to step out of my comfort zone and "be a girl." These girls had grown up together and I could see how close they were. But the way these girls talked, along with their body language, was so foreign to me. They would randomly sit so close to each other—or even on top of each other—so they could talk and giggle. In my mind, though, I would say, "Whoa, when did you ask her if you could sit on her lap? What makes you think you can do this and that?"

Looking back, I can see why I was never able to get very close to people. I was always too worried about what others might think. My worry soon turned into anxiety, and then into an obsession with the way I looked. For example, my hair had to have a certain amount in front of my shoulders with a certain amount behind my shoulders, always wishing my clothes could be the latest fashion trend. Even after getting into high school, I found myself imitating other people. It was always good people doing good things, of course, but they were also "cool" and "popular" things that I sought to do.

Several different junior highs funneled into our high school, so there were many more people to meet. Everyone had their "cliques" though. I soon became a "hopper" and would try to attend any party I heard about that was open to everyone. I met a lot of people that way. High school started out wonderfully and I felt my years were going to go smoothly, balancing school and meeting new friends. I also got my dream job working at Great Harvest Bread Company. I didn't consider it work at all, and it was a fun way to get me through high school and save up for college.

Although it appeared that everything in my life was wonderful on the outside, I still felt quite lonely. Some days were harder than others as

I wanted so badly to be a part of a group of friends, but I was also very ambitious and independent. I wasn't going to let the fact that I didn't really feel a part of any one group bother me or slow me down.

Taking my health on the wrong path

Growing up as someone who loved sports and anything dealing with health and fitness, I always tried to do the most good for my body. However, this outlook ended up taking me down a path that actually did my body a lot of harm. For some reason, I got into the mindset that to be healthy was to be skinny, and therefore I started losing weight the summer before starting high school. I never considered myself anorexic. Instead, I was doing a great thing for my body because I was going to be skinny, and for all I knew, that was healthy.

I started to establish extreme eating restrictions for myself. I felt I couldn't eat something unless my stomach had been growling for a certain amount of time—then I had earned the right to eat. I started to become obsessed with how I looked and would evaluate myself many times throughout the day. Whenever I passed a window or mirror, I would check to see how fat I looked. Standing up, I would see if my knees could touch before my thighs did. Leaning up against counters, I would see if my hip bones would touch without my stomach touching.

After months of comparing myself to so many other people, I felt I needed to keep losing weight. There needed to be more space between my thighs. My hip bones should be sticking out more. These were signs that I was healthier, right?

Along with eating less, I was also working out a lot as a member of the sophomore basketball team. After almost a year of this weight-loss routine, I was finally awakened to the harm I was doing to myself.

My mom picked me up from school one day and said she'd gotten a call from one of the school counselors. I was confused, trying to recall whether I had done something wrong. It turned out that a few girls on my basketball team went to one of the counselors in tears, concerned about my health.

"Take me to the doctor, Mom. I need help," I said after realizing that I must have taken it too far. The doctor said that I was lucky I had come in when I did, because if I had lost any more weight the damage to my body beyond what I had already done would have been irreversible, and I would have had to suffer the consequences the rest of my life. The current status of my health was that my body had shut down a few of its "systems" because of my lack of nutrients and calories, and the goal now was to rebuild them. I just wish it was that easy.

I was on the road to recovery, but my health habits were still a little extreme during my junior and senior years in high school. Once I could drive, I got a membership at a local gym. I would wake up at 4 a.m. every morning to work out from 4:30 to 6:15. That would get me home in time to blow-dry the sweat out of my hair, put on a little make-up, and use lots of deodorant. Who needed to shower? It's funny how I would get the best compliments on my hair on those sweaty days.

When it came to my eating habits, I was doing better, but I still wasn't consuming as many calories as my body needed. I would bring a lunch in a cooler full of pre-measured food that I packed the night before. Twelve baby carrot sticks and two slices of ham were one meal.

Two to three hours later, I would have sixteen Wheat Thin crackers and one cup of milk mixed with protein powder. Even outside of school, that is how most of my meals were, as I measured and wrote down all of my food intake so that I could calculate exactly what I was getting.

I did allow myself one "cheat day" a week, usually on Sunday. When that day came around, I cleaned out the kitchen! I usually made an unhealthy breakfast and would finish it off by making a great dessert for my family on that day. Come Monday, it was right back to calorie-counting and eating high amounts of protein. I gained maybe 15 pounds by the time I graduated from high school.

Finally, after adding 35 pounds and needing seven years of birth control pills to replenish my body with the estrogen it had quit producing, my body finally started functioning on its own. I still struggle with the "mental battles" of weight, but I try to keep focused on getting my body the right nutrients. I actually get nervous when my stomach growls because I'm afraid I am harming my body again.

I learned to really listen to what my body was telling me when it came to nutrition and fitness. I found that this trait came in handy as I took my fitness routine down a different path.

I've been known for never taking a serious picture. I guess this started at a young age. That's me on the right with my siblings at the beach. This became my signature smile known as "the Jill face."

Here I am with my siblings Tyler, Brad, and Janelle. During my pre-teen years, church was about the only time you would see me without a baseball cap. Being from California, the Giants were my favorite team.

The photo to the left was taken during my first time at a major league baseball game. I was pretty pumped about it.

WARNING! This photo of my awkward years could give you nightmares! This sums up my childhood in the California mountains fairly well— holding a deer head while sporting a bowl cut that my mom tried to style a little, with my headgear firmly in place.

This is me actually on a makeshift runway in my 6th grade year sporting the "mushroom" hairdo while with my little brother Mitch. Who would have thought that this girl would eventually walk down the runway at Miss America?

Working as a teenager at Great Harvest Bread Company.

My siblings and I in 2003.

Me in a daze trying to take my mind elsewhere during my first marathon, the St. George Marathon on October 6, 2001.

CHAPTER 2

WHY RUN A MARATHON?

After working out in the mornings at the gym for about a year, I felt a part of the "regulars" even though I was just finishing up my junior year of high school. I wouldn't really talk much because I was so focused on getting my workout in, but I would give an occasional smile and say, "G'mornin'."

I had noticed there was a group of people who would meet outside at 5:30 each morning and then go running together. "Why would anyone need to run outside when they have got all the cardio equipment they need right here in the gym?" I asked myself. "That's just silly."

I can't remember how it started, but I somehow got talking with a woman named Kim, one of the "groupies" that went running outside. She invited me to come with them sometime.

"Uh, I'm really not the best runner," I said. "I don't want to slow you guys down."

"Nah, you wouldn't at all," Kim said. "Come with us on one of our shorter runs and give it a try."

"Yeah, what might be a short run to you, might not be a short run to the rest of us," I said. "What are you guys runnin' this week?"

"We've got a four-mile run on Thursday," Kim replied. "You should come."

I agreed, figuring it would be good to try something new.

Well, my first run with the group wasn't the greatest. I felt I was a half-mile behind, just straining to keep close so I wouldn't get lost. I saw it as a challenge, and I started going on runs with them about once a week when their distances worked with my schedule. After a few weeks, I was keeping up with them and was joining their 10-mile runs.

The group was a hoot to run with. There were the faithful three runners who were like the "ring leaders" and then they would get random runners joining them, like myself. They were all fun to chat with, even through the heavy breathing while running. I would ask them all sorts of questions about their running careers and what it was like to do a marathon.

"You should run one with us," Kim said.

"Ha! There is no way. Why would you want to put yourself through that kind of torture? You guys are insane!"

My first long run

Not long afterward, Kim said, "Hey, we're doing a 12-mile run this Saturday. Are you comin'?"

I was intrigued. Pushing my body to a new extreme always seems to spark an interest. I said, "You know what, I think I'll join you. What do I need to do?"

"I would get some cold-weather running gear because it's supposed to snow," Kim said. "If you want water along the run, bring it, but one of us usually sets a bag of drinks out the night before so we have something at six miles. You can totally do it!"

On Friday night, I felt sick. I set out all of my gear, but there was no way I was getting to sleep that night. I was nervous about sleeping through my alarm, let alone running 12 miles the next day!

It was a cool, brisk morning with no heavy cloud coverage. I got to the gym at 5:45 to stretch, really only mimicking what I've seen other runners do, hoping it was going to help. There were six of us that showed up. We walked through the parking lot to the road and started to pick up a jogging pace. "I can totally do this," I thought to myself.

We hit our 6-mile point and I could feel it in my legs a bit. "It's just another 6-mile run," I encouraged myself. My legs were on fire the last three miles of the run, but I just kept going and finished it.

Of course, with my type of personality, when they asked me to take part in a 16-mile run on a cold Easter weekend, how could I turn it down? After completing that run, it hit me—it's just 10 more miles to complete a marathon. I soon found myself entering the lottery of the biggest race in Utah, the St. George Marathon. It was May during my senior year when I found out I had made it. The marathon would take place the following October during my first semester at Southern Utah University. I had just joined the military two months earlier in March. That year was the start of some big adventures.

Just one foot in front of the other, right?

When I was training for my first marathon, I felt clueless about what kind of running regimen I should do, or if there was a certain kind of diet I should be on. I started asking other marathon runners what worked for them and what kind of training I should expect.

After listening to them, I started doing what I felt would prepare me the best, and this soon became my regular workout regimen (even to this day). I did at least an hour of cardio a day (usually on the elliptical trainer) and weights usually four days a week. At least two of my cardio days were 90 minutes long, running one of those times. Yep, I only ran about once a week training for my marathon. Most marathon runners would gasp at the thought, believing you should be running everyday to adequately prepare.

I did one long run three weeks before the race. I was now living in Cedar City, Utah going to school at SUU, and I didn't have many running routes mapped out yet. I glanced up at the mountains and noticed a big "C" on one of them.

"Hmm, that should be a good run," I thought. I asked one of my neighbors how far it was to the "C" and they said it was probably around 10 or 11 miles. That sounded great, making a long run of at least 20 miles. Ha! If only I knew what I was really in for.

I ended up walking most of that day, since the first half was all uphill with some pretty steep climbs. As I was running/climbing my way to the top, an older gentleman drove by and waved. I happened to see him two other times during my run. Finally, when I was on my last four miles, he drove by and asked, "Are you lost? Do you need a ride?"

Part of me felt like screaming, "YES!" But the other part of me wanted to say, "No. I'm just really this stupid, and I like to put myself through this kind of pain."

"Nah, I'm fine," I replied. Which was partly true, because I was still walking. Even though I was in so much pain from having never run that long in my life, there was no way I was going to give up. I did wish I had asked him for some water, since I had run out. Wow, I sure had messed this one up.

At the end of the run I walked up the steps to my apartment on SUU's campus. My cousin Stevie happened to be my neighbor, and a look of shock came over her face as she caught a glimpse of me. I knew I didn't feel good, but from her reaction, I couldn't have been looking too good, either.

"What did you just do?" Stevie asked. "Are you okay? You're pale." I slowly made my way up the stairs, although the thought of climbing them made me wince. I explained to her what I had just done, and she loosely put her arm around me, and it made me laugh. I knew she was trying to help me, but also trying to avoid the sweat and dirt.

Hitting a "road block"

My arches were really bothering me on one of my runs, so I thought I must have "high arches" and needed more support. I bought myself these cheap inserts that came about halfway up the length my foot and figured that would solve the problem. In the middle of one of my runs, I could tell that this was a dumb move. I felt blisters forming on both my arches, so I decided to change my running stance a little to not feel them as much.

Bad idea. It turns out that in doing so, I was putting stress on different parts of my feet, creating another problem. I soon had trouble simply walking. I finally sucked up my pride and decided to see a podiatrist, since my marathon was only a couple of weeks away. I explained my symptoms and workout schedule leading up to that day.

"We might need to put you on crutches," the doctor said.

"Excuse me?"

He was serious. "For these next two weeks, you really need to stay off your feet as much as possible, icing them everyday and taking some anti-inflammatory medication. If you play it smart, you might be able to run the marathon."

I was crushed as I heard my prognosis. "This can't be happening," I told myself. "I have to run this marathon. I'll make it happen."

I really played it safe the next couple of weeks. The morning of the race came and I felt ready and sick at the same time. It was freezing at the starting line. About 20 bonfires lined one side of the road. Runners of all types were gathered around the fires as we started trickling in about 90 minutes before the race started. I had never seen so many Port-o-Potties before in my life! There were at least 40 of them lined up on the other side of the street.

I looked around nervously, watching what the other runners were doing to see if there was something I needed to do. I saw some of them running around to warm up before the actual race started. I thought, "Goodness, you've got 26 miles to warm up, no need to run more than that."

I met up with Kim and the others at a bonfire. It was great to see them as we shivered together. I couldn't help but think about the course ahead of me. I looked past the starting line, gazing into the dark, feeling like the road was mocking me with what I was about to do. I took a deep breath . . . bring it on.

The gun shots went off and the energy soared through my body from the excitement of the race, but we were hardly moving as 6,000 runners tried to cram through the entrance on the road. We shuffled across the starting line a few minutes later. Loud beeps were going off as runners crossed, activating the timing-chips on our shoes. We were moving comfortably through the crowd. My friends kept reminding me to hold back the first few miles even though I could run faster, because I needed to save that energy for the end.

I couldn't believe that this was it! All these months that I had been training now came down to the 26.2 miles ahead of me. I tried not to think about it and tried to focus on it being a "casual run." After about two miles, though, I became very aware of my full bladder. I tried to keep running and ignore it. I guess with my nerves, the water was going straight through me. I was seeing other runners pulling off the road and going behind some bushes—some didn't make it to the bush, though.

I was worried that I would lose my group if I took a break, and I tried to come up with a plan. I asked if they could hang out running on the left side of the road so I would be able to find them easier. They agreed, and I sped off to the nearest bush. I just had to laugh at what I was doing. I quickly made it back to the course, making a real effort to try and not fall as I ran through the desert weeds and dirt. After a few minutes, I caught up to them.

We soon hit mile 7 and looked ahead at the notorious "Veyo hill" that stretched before us. I saw Kim take one of her "energy gels" and so I did the same. "Where are you keeping yours?" she asked as we slurped them down running.

"Uh well . . ." I replied hesitantly.

"Do I really want to know?" she asked with a smile.

"Ha! They're in my sports bra," I muttered, because really, that was the only place I felt could hold something during the race. Kim just started laughing. Take a mental note, females. If you ever run a marathon, do NOT put the packets in your sports bra. The aluminum on them cut me up pretty good.

We passed a lot of people as we ran up the hill. Some were walking because of how steep and long it was. Hitting mile 11, I realized how much pain my feet were in, but not necessarily from my previous problem. It was the bottom of my feet that hurt from the pounding. The balls and heels of my feet were aching, and I still had 15 more miles to go. That wasn't a comforting thought.

Signs were posted along the course by friends and family members the night before to encourage either all of the runners or specific people. One made me laugh out loud: "How are the hemorrhoids doing, Jenny?" The signs became a great distraction to read along the course. We would talk every now and then to help the time go by faster, cracking jokes and so on. At that point, I had a burning question, literally.

"Why do you keep running marathons?" I asked. "What do you love about them?"

Kim and the others started laughing. One chimed in, "So I can eat more." They all agreed to that one.

Kim followed up, "I like the goal of always working toward a marathon. It helps me get out of bed because I know I have a race planned that I need to prepare for. It helps me stay balanced and actually keeps me sane." I felt I could relate to all of those reasons.

As the miles continued, so did the pain. Every now and then I would feel a twinge of pain in my feet. I would then try to focus on my foot placement to make sure I was doing it correctly. That is just one of the many great things about a marathon—you've got time to "recover" from an injury. Once I felt something begin to hurt in my body, I would work on changing up my running "focus" a little bit. Depending on what area I was feeling any discomfort in, I would do the following:

Hamstrings: I would focus more on bringing my leg forward with my hip flexor and thigh.

Groin: I would focus more on my outer hip and hip flexor.

Shin splints: I would usually just run through it because my legs just needed to warm up for a few miles, or I would concentrate on landing more on the ball of my foot.

Knees: I would land softer and glide through my steps while also focusing on my quads.

I found that changing my focus on different muscles while running had really helped my running career and especially helped me get through this marathon. I ended up taking my second energy gel around mile 19. Crossing the 20-mile mark gave me a little more strength mentally as I calculated in my mind that I just had a 6-mile route left to run.

"I've run 6 miles before, this is easy," I kept telling myself. It was a huge battle between my mind and my body. My body was screaming for me to stop putting myself through such torture, while my mind was telling me to not give up . . . the pain will be over soon.

As we came upon mile 23, crowds of people were cheering us on, and it gave me the biggest energy surge. I can do this! We rounded the corner on mile 26. "This was it," I thought, "just 0.2 miles left to go." That was the longest 0.2 I've ever had to do. That portion mentally plays a trick on you as you see the finish-line balloons in the distance. You glance to the side and smile to some of the crowd to say thanks for cheering us on. You think you are running, but when you glance to the side again and see the same people, you realize you aren't moving too fast.

Kim and I picked up the pace. "It's been an honor to have you stick with me this whole time," Kim said.

"Stick with you?" I asked. "You know I couldn't have done this without you." I paused to catch my breath and wince through the pain. I heard my name in the distance and turned quickly to see my mom on the sideline. "MOM!" I called out.

I lost her in the crowd as I continued forward. If I had stopped, I don't think I could have started moving again. Seeing my mom helped me pick up my feet that last hundred yards.

"Oh my gosh. Kim, this is it," I breathed out as we stepped over that finish line. Our timing chips beeped as we finished in 3 hours, 29 minutes. I just ran a marathon! Some volunteers were there to clip off my timing-chip. I could barely stand up, let alone lift up my foot. I grabbed one of their arms to help me stand up. I then shuffled through the line to get the "finisher's medal" . . . a crowning moment for a marathon runner.

Runners were crashed out across the lawn, stretching and eating the treats provided. I found my family, and I laughed as they gave me more of those "loose" hugs to not get dirty or contract my smell. The rest of the day I was in awe at what I had just done.

My family and I saw the movie *A Knight's Tale* later that evening. I guess the marathon had made me a little loopy, because I thought every scene was funny and I was the only one laughing in the theater. Every now and then, I would lean over to my mom and whisper, "I just ran a marathon!"

For the next week I was walking like I had aged 80 years overnight. Every time I came upon a set of stairs, I just stared. Going up was fine as I grabbed onto the rail, but going down was a whole new ballgame. Most of the time, I would grab onto both of the rails and lift myself off the ground and inch my way down the rails with my arms. If there were no rails, I would simply sit and slide down. I got laughed at a few times as I was doing it around campus at SUU, but no worries . . . I was laughing at myself as well.

Even though I was in so much pain and was walking really funny after the race, I thought to myself, "I've got to do this again!"

Another go at it

I learned some lessons from that first marathon, and I wanted to be more prepared the next time, now that I knew what I was in for. I signed up for the St. George Marathon again while I was actually at my Combat Medic training. I wanted to prove I could do better and felt my military training could really help me out in this regard. I got myself a funky pair of shorts that made a fashion statement by themselves, and I've been using them ever since. The shorts have seven pockets that go around them, and I strategically place certain items in each one.

In the front right pocket I carry my Ibuprofen to help me through the painful times. I always throw in a little extra in case there is anyone else that looks like they need some.

In my left pocket, I have my vitamins to help keep me replenished. In my two side pockets on each side, I store my energy gel packets. Then in my big back pocket, I sometimes carry a disposable camera to capture those painful, burning moments. In recent marathons, I've even been known to carry a cell phone to touch base with my family!

So as I tackled the St. George Marathon again, it was déjà vu being back at the starting line and meeting up with Kim and the others. As the race got started, a few miles into it one of our groupies, Don, started going ahead. I seized this opportunity to try and keep up with him. I struggled during part of the race but kept pushing myself. I would end up a few feet behind Don, just panting to keep up. I tried to see if I could go a little faster, but I also knew I needed to play it smart and not waste my energy too quickly. I was able to keep up with him.

At mile 9, I had my first gel and then at mile 18, I had my second. After 19 miles, I took my Ibuprofen and vitamins. I actually was feeling good. I don't know if it's mental or not, but taking those sure helped. Mile by mile, I kept pushing myself. It was getting painful and I tried to push through it. I thought, "I volunteered for this pain? I actually paid money for this?" And as I thought about it more, I felt, "Yep, that's right! If it was easy, I probably wouldn't be doing it."

I crossed the finish line that second time at 3:13:51. I couldn't believe I ran that fast! I was now a multi-marathon runner and this soon became a new hobby.

CHAPTER 3

FORGING MY OWN PATH

"Mom," I said hesitantly. I didn't really know how she would respond to my next statement. "I'm thinking about joining the Army."

My mom was a little confused by what she had just heard, since I didn't really grow up dreaming of becoming a soldier. I did, however, always have the burning question, "Could I hack Boot Camp?" I had wondered if I had what it takes to make it through.

One day during my senior year at Davis High School, I saw a booth set up in the commons area during the lunch break. It was for the Army National Guard. I started talking to the recruiter, asking simple questions to ease my curiosity about boot camp. I wanted to know if all of the horror stories I've heard and seen on TV were true.

The recruiter answered my questions and sparked up a good conversation that planted a seed of interest as I saw all of the potential benefits. It got the wheels turning in my mind. At first my family thought this was just a phase I was going through and didn't really think I was going to join. But once my mom saw that I was actually meeting with the recruiter, she decided to join me at the meetings.

"At Basic Training, they like to break you down and then build you back up to who they want you to be," answered the recruiter to one of my mom's questions about what to expect at Basic Training.

"That will be a huge mistake," Mom interrupted. "You want Jill just the way she is."

I was a little taken aback by what my mom had said. It gave me the courage to know that I could do this.

After my family members realized I was actually becoming a soldier, they thought, "Yep, this is Jill." I had always disciplined myself with how I lived my life and this just seemed to fit.

I joined the Army National Guard 1/211 Aviation unit on March 16, 2001, about five months after I first approached the recruiting booth. I hadn't joined immediately, because I really wanted to make sure this was the right thing for me. My mom and I would have a pad of paper set out so that whenever a question came to mind, we could write it down instantly and not forget.

So why would I sign my life away? I loved the idea of the National Guard because I could live the best of both worlds. I would still be a civilian enjoying the college life, as well as gaining the adventure and challenge of being a soldier. I was intrigued at what the Army could give me. I wanted to be a nurse, and I could get incredible medical experience for my nursing career. Plus, my education would be paid for, which was an offer that was hard to beat.

Above all though, the Army gave me a chance to give back for something that I felt so grateful for. I have always been very patriotic and loved this opportunity to serve my country. I grew up participating in service projects and I loved the fulfillment that comes from helping others. That passion has driven me in everything I've done in life. How could I not join?

Boot Camp

I wasn't scheduled to go to Basic Training (a.k.a. Boot Camp) until the next January. I decided to get one semester of college under my belt at SUU in the fall of 2001. Then January 4, 2002 finally came. I couldn't believe I was going to Boot Camp!

It was well before sunrise when I had to leave. All of my family had gotten up to see me off. It was an emotional moment, and I was a little nervous. This was going to be the longest time away from home thus far.

Upon landing at the airport in St. Louis, Missouri, the military personnel bused us to Fort Leonard Wood. Recruits from all across the country were on the bus. We all looked so different from each other and we each had our own story to tell, but that didn't matter anymore. We were united in our purpose, as well as in our anxiety.

Our travel on the bus was pretty quiet, interrupted by short comments here and there. I picked up on a few conversations with the "new recruits" in the back of the bus. Lo and behold, one of them happened to be LDS, a young man named Jason Weiss. I felt strengthened just knowing I was not alone in this adventure.

We were first taken to a part of the base called MEPS where we covered all of the paperwork, got IDs, uniforms, and so on. I was there for about a week. New recruits were coming everyday, and others were being bused out to begin training.

It was finally my turn, and we were bused to a different part of the base. It was then that it hit me—I was in a completely different world! Drill sergeants came screaming onto the bus demanding we get off and get into the building. There were a lot of them to handle the busloads of arriving "low-life privates" and it looked as though they were out for blood.

They pushed us into a gymnasium, yelling at us where we had to go. My heart was pounding. I was trying to make out the difference between their instructions and their yelling. I was trying to be alert to make sure I was doing the same thing everyone else was doing. If you are the only one doing something, you are wrong, even if you followed the right instructions. It didn't matter, because you forgot to inform the rest of your team.

We had to get into formation with our newly-formed companies. Of course, we couldn't do anything right, and the "correctional punishment" began (a.k.a. getting "smoked" because you are most likely going to be creating smoke from the burn your body was going to be feeling). The "smoking sessions" went something like this. They would make us get down and do push-ups, and then we would be called back to "attention." Of course, we weren't nearly as fast as they would like us to be, so it was right back down to "kissin' the dirt."

We were then taught, more or less, the famous "Front, Back, Go" that the Army is known for. When they yelled "front" it meant the "front leaning rest" position (a.k.a. the push-up). The "rest" in that position is obviously rather deceiving.

"Back" meant to quickly get onto your back for flutter-kicks to work the abs, and "go" meant simply to run in place or to a destination they pointed to. Such fun!

We also had to hold out our canteens at shoulder level for a while. No real reason—just because. One drill sergeant walked by and noticed my CTR ring. We weren't supposed to be wearing any jewelry. CTR stands for "Choose the Right" and I've worn it throughout my life to always keep myself in check.

"Private, what the !@#$ is this?" he shouted in my face. "Is this an engagement or wedding ring?"

"No, Drill Sergeant!" I said, terrified.

"Then get that !@#$%@ thing off your finger!"

"Yes, Drill Sergeant!" and I quickly buried it in my pocket. I was bummed I couldn't wear it. After an hour of "correctional punishment" the DS's were fed up with us. There were about 200 privates in my company, and they separated us into our platoons. My new friend Jason Weiss was not only in my company, but was put into the same platoon. I couldn't believe it! The Lord works in mysterious ways.

Trying to blend in

When we first arrived at Basic Training, we ran off the cattle trucks (our most common mode of transportation) not really knowing what to do, and the DS's just seemed to love that. They were yelling where each of the platoons needed to form up. We quickly learned that everything had to be "dress, right, dress" which meant basically, the same as everyone else. All of our duffel bags had to be laid *exactly* the same way, with the openings of bags in one direction and the handle on a certain side. It didn't really matter how it ended up, it just had to end up the same.

As some privates were still running off the cattle trucks and others were already in formation, the DS's would pick us apart on any detail we weren't paying attention to. Some soldiers were already drawing attention to themselves (which I knew NOT to do—thanks to some great advice I was given before I arrived) by either moving too slowly or being clumsy in their scurry. The DS's were not too happy and we were soon down in the "front leaning rest" position.

"Welcome to your new home, privates," yelled one DS. There were four platoons in my company, known as A co. 1/48 Infantry. Each platoon had two or three DS's in charge of them. We were lucky and had three DS's to "take care" of us.

This was now our home for the next nine weeks, and it wasn't too welcoming. It was a three-story brick building, with each level consisting of just a hallway with rooms and two bathrooms. The first level was for the females, while the males took up the second and third floors. Each room had about four bunk beds in it and eight wall lockers. They then explained where each platoon needed to go to get "acquainted" with their DS's.

My platoon's room was on the third floor. This was our "war room" where we would always meet together for PT (physical training) or other instruction. That first day we crammed in there with all of our bags. Not a word was spoken. Some privates were breathing hard, not only from exertion but from fright as well. After 10 minutes of us quietly sitting there, the three DS's walked into the room.

"At ease," we all yelled as we stood at "parade rest" with our hands placed in the small of our back, the standard protocol when any non-commissioned officer (NCO) that is higher ranking walks into the room.

The three drill sergeants just stared at us, two males (DS Barto and DS Geiger) and one female (DS Dixon). "Oh boy," I thought. I had heard the female ones are the worst. They yelled at us for a bit more, walking up and down our lines. There wasn't too much room for them to walk, since there was about 45 privates and all of our gear crammed into the room.

They had us do "over-the-head arm claps" because there wasn't enough room to do push-ups. I can't remember what we did wrong, but that soon became a common theme—no matter what, we were always wrong.

DS Dixon stayed in the room while the other two left with two males from our platoon, bringing back an empty wall locker. For the next hour, we were taught how to "keep up" our lockers. Our brown T-shirts had to be folded, rolled and tucked to six inches. Underwear was rolled to four inches. Socks were rolled and tucked to three inches.

There could only be a certain amount in each drawer, all placed a certain way.

All extras were in a duffle bag just to the right of the "three drawer set" in the locker itself. Hangers had to be two finger-widths apart with the uniforms in a certain order. The uniforms had to be completely buttoned or zipped up while on the hanger and must be facing the same way.

There was one section of a shelf for personal items and toiletries. Our towel was hung on the rack in thirds. We were given our bedding later that day and were also instructed on how it needed to be made every morning. The bottom sheet had to be tight with 45-degree angles at each corner. The next sheet and an itchy wool green blanket had to have 45-degree angles at the bottom corners, with a six-inch fold (the sheet and blanket folded together) 18 inches from the top, leaving room for the pillow. No creases were to be seen and the DS's were not supposed to be able to pinch or grab any fabric because it should be that tight. We were then told it had better be this way by PT (physical training) at 0500 the next morning.

After the DS's completed their instructions, we only had five minutes to drop off our gear and be back outside for chow formation. The rest of the company was already out there in formation, and we really didn't know what we were doing. Our formations looked horrible in retrospect and soon it was back to "kissin' the dirt."

They called us to attention and we all yelled, "ALPHA," as we were told to do during an earlier screaming session. One DS then called, "Stand at ease," and we moved to the "parade rest" position. I was trying to stay focused on keeping my eyes forward, because I learned that is where they always needed to be—except in the case of this command. It left my mind that this command also meant to turn your head to whoever was giving the command, because it meant they were about to give instruction and wanted you to listen. The DS started to give instruction and then stopped. The other DS's seized this opportunity and started to call out, "Hello! Do you realize he is talking?"

I felt bad for the private they were yelling at. Then as one DS continued yelling, I realized he was looking straight at me. "Where are your eyes supposed to be?" he shouted.

I just stared back at him, scared to mutter a word or even breathe. The whole company was silent with the DS's looking at me, waiting for my eyes to be on the DS who was in command right then. I felt sick. I was trying too hard to do the right thing. Ugh, I hated the feeling of being singled out like that.

I just turned my eyes to the other DS and the instruction continued, thank goodness. We then marched toward the chow hall. No cadences were called because the DS's said we hadn't earned our right to do so. When we got there, we were given a quick instruction on how things were handled at the chow hall. Not a word was to be spoken. When standing in line, we were to stand at the position of parade rest and as the line moved, come to the position of attention, take a step or two forward and come back to the position of parade rest.

As we shuffled in there and got in line, the DS's seized this opportunity to make us look like fools by asking us about our "chain of command" and other questions coming from our "SMART book" that we were given with our gear at MEPS. I was praying they would overlook me. Many of the privates were getting the questions wrong and the DS's were just getting more frustrated with us.

"Good *night*, privates! Good *night*," was one response a DS became famous for saying when he was getting fed up with us. "Good night" has forever become a part of my vocabulary because I became so used to hearing it.

Another DS yelled at his platoon, "You asked for it. Things are not going to be pretty tonight." Soon other DS's were saying what they were going to do to the privates in their platoon.

As I got my tray, I shuffled down the line as the cooks dumped food onto my plate. We didn't get a choice of what we wanted. Then we walked into the sitting area, but we weren't allowed to sit down. We had to wait to eat until the last private got his food and were told to stay standing until we ate it all!

"Ate it all?" I asked myself. I looked down at my tray and noticed the selection—spaghetti slop, canned veggies, and beets. I gagged as I looked at the beets. As I ate the rest of the food, I tried to go for the beets. I couldn't swallow them, but I was still trying to force them down because we weren't leaving until everything was gone. Weiss happened to be next to me and noticed (and heard) me trying to gag the beets down.

"I'll finish them for ya," he whispered without moving his lips (ventriloquism is a talent all soldiers soon take up). He very slyly scooted the beets onto his tray.

"Thank you," I muttered back, and we finished our meal.

It was a cold January night as we came back outside. I soon learned to hate winters in Missouri. When we made it back to the barracks, we did something wrong (who knows what) and were back into the push-up position. My arms were weak and my palms were getting bruised as they would grind into the pavement.

Afterward, we had to quickly change into our PT's (Physical Training uniforms), our only other outfits besides our fatigues. We had formation in the "war-room" for evening PT. After PT we were given more instructions and also told that 4th platoon would be known as the "War Lords" and were to yell that name every time we came to the position of attention as a platoon. War Lords . . . that wasn't a name I would have ever come up with on my own.

We were also told that there was a list posted at the end of each hallway showing the "fire guard" shifts for each hour of each night. Two privates had to "guard" each end of the hallway in hourly shifts, simulating what you would do in combat, where someone is always on watch.

After many more push-ups and sit-ups, it was finally time for bed. Lights had to be out by 2200 hours. It was already 2145 and we had to have everything ready and folded by 0445. This had been one of the longest days of my life.

"More PT, Drill Sergeant!"

The next few days were filled with more basic instruction as to what they expected of us, and of course, "smoking sessions" for everything we were doing wrong.

We had PT twice a day, at least on the schedule. It didn't matter that it was an on-going thing throughout the day. Mondays, Wednesdays, Fridays and Sundays were "muscle failure" days (literally), while Tuesdays, Thursdays, and Saturdays were "run" days.

I already had a lot of self-motivation when it came to fitness and getting stronger, and I loved the feeling of challenging myself. But this kind of PT took all the mental and physical strength I knew how to give. I am one that loves variety and changing things up, but most of our training for PT on "muscle failure" days consisted of wide arm push-ups, regular arm push-ups, then close arm push-ups, doing each kind for two minutes, 1:30, 1:00, then 30 seconds. It took everything I could muster to just hold myself up at the end of the workouts.

Then we would move to abdominal workouts. Doing sit-ups on the hard tile floor really bruised up my tailbone and back. "Yankee sit-ups" were DS Geiger's favorite, an exercise that worked the oblique muscles really well.

These workouts were a "love/hate relationship." I hated how boring they were and that there wasn't much to them, but I knew and loved that I was getting stronger over the weeks. I gave it my all during the workouts. Even if I was burning (and actually shaking just to keep myself up), I would still attempt to do push-ups/sit-ups if there was still time on the clock. As we were timed during workouts, I would see other privates give up toward the end. I fought through it. No matter what, even if I couldn't get out another push-up, I would still stay up off the ground. I wanted to show the DS that I was a hard worker and could be counted on.

Our first PT test was scheduled within our first week of arriving there. It was our diagnostic PT test to see where we were and how much we had improved throughout the training. A friend told me before I left for Basic Training that the DS had a reputation of not counting most of your push-ups or sit-ups, and that I should hold back anyway on the first PT test to make it look like I improved as we took other tests later on. When I heard this PT test was coming up, I understood why some people would do it that way, but *I* couldn't physically do it. I didn't have the heart to purposely not give it my all. It's just not my style to do things partway.

We lined up in three squads and progressed forward as our DS counted the push-ups of three privates at a time. We had the DS's of the 3rd platoon grade us. I moved up when it was my turn and got down on my hands and knees.

"Get ready," yelled one of the DS's. Those of us being graded moved to the "front-leaning rest" position. My arms already burned from the week of training. "Get set . . . GO!"

I started "knockin' 'em out" and feeling good but sore at the same time. I was trying to listen to the DS to find out what number I was on . . .

"Seven," was the number the DS had last said. WHAT? You've got to be kidding! I knew I had done at least 20. By the end of the two minutes, she only counted 11 push-ups. Sit-ups turned out a little better. She counted 35 and I maybe did 50.

Now it was time for the part where I knew they couldn't cheat my time—the two-mile run. We did the test on a track that wasn't too far away because it was snowing and they felt it would be a bit safer. Of course, they would never cancel the run. There is that famous saying in the Army: "If it ain't rainin', we ain't trainin'!" And that goes for any type of weather.

I love the two-mile run because I know I can do it, but I also hate it at the same time because it is like a sprint compared to what my body is used to. I ended up finishing in around 16 minutes. I was ticked! I wondered what had slowed me down. Was it the weather? The physical exhaustion my body was facing?

Even though that was a slower-than-average time for me, I still ended up as one of the top finishers, not only in my platoon but in my company. I was really surprised by this. I asked myself, "Weren't people who joined the Army already physically fit?"

I actually couldn't have been more wrong. For a majority of my company and many that I have come in contact with in the military, joining the Army was the first time they started working out. Many privates were getting injured within the first few weeks of training and put on a profile, meaning they couldn't do certain things in PT because of their injury. I vowed from the very beginning that I would *never* be one of those soldiers.

From my experience, if you are fit, you stick out in the military and are more respected because of what you can do. Being fit has definitely helped me in my military career, but I'm surprisingly in the minority by being fit.

Throughout the rest of the day, I guess the word got around about what I did on my PT test, mainly the run. No one did well on the push-ups and sit-ups because of how beat up our bodies already were. Our run scores determined how the DS divided us into our "run groups" for those PT days that we ran. There was Alpha for the "high speed" and Bravo for those that had a decent pace. Charlie was for those that weren't made for running, but were still made to do it.

Then there was Delta for the "broken" people who were on profile. If you were in this group for very long, you might as well start saying your good-byes. Most in this group were either kicked out and booted back to another company that started after us. That meant their training took a lot longer than the usual nine weeks.

I was the only female in Alpha for almost all of the training. Every now and then there were a few other females who would give it a try, but after a few days they would go back to the Bravo running group.

We had three more PT tests throughout the training to see how much we had improved. The final test during our last week was the one that really counted. If you weren't passing the test—or worse, not even improving—the DS's were furious and punished you all the more.

It was such a blessing for me that I was already fit, which made my time at Basic Training more manageable. As each PT test came along, I always tried to outdo myself compared to the one before. On my second PT test, I did somewhere around 37 push-ups, 75 sit-ups, and a 14:30 run. This was a lot better than the diagnostic, but nowhere near where I wanted it to be.

My DS's were noticing my improved performances, and so did the DS's of the other platoons. Some started to call me "PT" or "PT 5000" because I was scoring among the top. After our third PT test, I scored around 55 push-ups, 90 sit-ups and a 13:30 on the run. "That's more like it," I thought. Pushing myself during our PT hours and "smoking" sessions was really paying off. I knew I could do better, though, and I guess one of my DS's wanted me to do so, as well.

"Stevens, I better see 75 push-ups, 100 sit-ups and a 12:30 on your run for your final PT test, you got that?" DS Brito told me.

"Yes, Drill Sergeant! I'll do my best, Drill Sergeant."

Well, I almost did it. For the final PT test I got 77 push-ups,

99 sit-ups, and 13:08. I was proud of myself, but I was irked about the sit-ups being one away from hitting the triple digits. I got teased a little by the others, even by the DS, which didn't help me. I just tried to let it go in one ear and out the other, because I was already being hard enough on myself.

Some of my comrades struggled with the PT test and for a few females, the run was the hardest part. I volunteered to pace them when they were given another opportunity to pass the PT test. I loved being able to help in some way and encourage them. I didn't want the PT test to be the only thing holding these soldiers back from graduating.

It turned out though that those who seemed to excel in PT were made the "squad leaders" and "platoon leaders." I was put over the second squad after our first PT test, and Weiss was made Platoon Leader, although platoon leaders were just set up for failure. We went through a different platoon leader nearly every week.

"Taking it for the team"

You might think that being made a squad or platoon leader would be a position people would seek after, but not really. It might mean you have more responsibility, which can be fulfilling, but in reality, you just get punished a whole lot more for those you're over. If someone messes up, it is the leader's fault for not "squaring them away" and we had a few good "smoking sessions" on our part.

One session I will never forget happened when our platoon wasn't doing so well. We weren't being on time, cleaning our rooms up to par, and so on. There were a few of us who saw what was coming, but you can only do so much to motivate people to kick it in gear. But this time, instead of smoking the whole platoon, the whole platoon got to watch us, the leaders, get smoked for them. We were doing push-ups for a while (wide, regular and close arm) then DS Dixon gave each of us "ammo cans" that weighed about 15 pounds each. At first we just had one and had to stand there in front of everyone doing squats as we raised the ammo can to shoulder height.

As we were doing these push-ups and squats, DS Dixon was calling out everything we were doing wrong as a platoon, even if it wasn't the leaders' fault. She then gave us our "new" schedule. PT now started at

0445 (instead of 0500), so that meant we needed to be there at 0430, and PT extended longer into the evenings. "Fire Guard" shifts now had to have four soldiers each shift, dressed in "full battle-rattle" (ammo vest, Kevlar helmet, etc.) and so on.

She wasn't finished with the leaders yet. With these ammo cans, as she went on about what she expected of us, we had to go up and down six flights of stairs (three floors) 50 times. Down and up (since we were already on the third floor) was one time. And she wanted us to scream out what number we were on as we hit the top. The five of us walked out of the war room in silence because we knew we had no choice.

Down and up the stairs we went, having some conversations quietly, making jokes here and there, and venting as well. I just mainly listened as the others vented. Our legs were burning as we climbed. As we came up on 50, we shuffled back into the room, our shirts completely drenched in sweat. These kinds of smoking sessions became a common routine, not always just for the leaders, but for the whole platoon and company as well.

Wishing for a "smoke free" area

I especially hated getting smoked at first, because it meant that we were doing something wrong as a platoon, or that I had done something wrong. I actually cried one night during our first week because I hated that feeling.

As we marched to an area, DS Dixon wanted to teach us "filing by the ranks." She stopped us prior to reaching our final destination so that we could learn to do this properly. We had to pivot off a certain spot that she showed us with her boot.

I was the last one to file through, and as I pivoted off the spot, I pivoted off her boot as well. Yep, I stepped on a Drill Sergeant's boot. I would highly recommend NOT doing this during Basic Training. The shine on a soldier's boot is their pride and I might as well have just hit the DS in the face.

"PRIVATE!" screamed DS Dixon.

"Oh no," I thought, "please don't tell me I really just did that."

I nervously yelled back, "Yes, Drill Sergeant!"

"Do you realize what you JUST DID?"

"No, Drill Sergeant . . ." but of course I did. I just didn't want to believe it myself, and I was hoping maybe she wouldn't notice. Nice try.

"And where is your battle buddy when you are talking to me?" she asked. Soldiers always had to have a battle buddy of the same gender everywhere they go, especially when approaching a DS. I looked around to see who the nearest female soldier was. I felt bad for her, because I knew she was going to get smoked for something I did, and she wasn't necessarily the fittest one of the bunch, but I had to act quickly. DS Dixon told us we had to "bear crawl" (crawling on our hands and feet) to our next location. We would have to go down some stairs that way as well.

I found a quick way to bear crawl, but my battle buddy was struggling and I would have to wait for her. I tried to teach her the best way to bear crawl, but she couldn't get it. We arrived to the class a little late and snuck into the back.

Learning the basics

As Basic Training progressed, I was surprised by how much time we were actually stuck in classes, learning the "basics" of the Army. I thought we would be doing a lot more physical things. We definitely did plenty of those, but there were also a lot of classes, almost every day, learning about chain of command, marching commands, how to use a radio, weapons, tactical movements coming upon the enemy, and so on. The classes were probably the most difficult part for me because I got in trouble a lot!

I have a tendency to doze off in classes, because I am not being active and moving around. The DS's had no problem helping me out with that. When soldiers were caught nodding their heads during instruction, they were sent to the back of the room to do some PT to help stay awake. I found myself back there many times.

We had a variety of exercises given to us that would punish us but still allow us to listen to class. I assure you there is no way someone is going to fall asleep holding a folding chair at shoulder level for the rest of the class. Another fun exercise was to have us sit in a chair—only without the chair and with our arms raised at shoulder level.

There were other smoking sessions that are forever ingrained into my muscles. One time the DS took the whole company out to the "tar pit"—an area that had shredded rubber strips, dirt and rocks. We ended up being there for three hours doing different crazy drills, such as front-back-go's and jumping jacks. During these drills, a lot of dirt was kicked up and we were inhaling some nasty stuff. Many of us got sick after that session.

As the weeks went on, smoking sessions became more individualized instead of as a whole group, which gave our bodies a little bit of a break. I soon gained the reputation that if any girl needed a battle buddy when they were in trouble, girls knew to ask me because they knew I wouldn't mind. I would get questionable looks from some of the DS's because of the multiple times they would see me getting smoked. I figured I would be getting stronger and tried to make things as positive as possible.

One evening we were introduced to a new exercise when coming home from the range. Our DS's were unhappy about something we did. It had been pouring all day, and they made us do all of the drills in the mud. But this new exercise was called "sugar cookie" because they had us roll in the puddles and then in the dirt to simulate a cookie's cinnamon-sugar coating, although there wasn't really any dirt left because it was now all mud.

Super Bowl smoking

One night while *supposedly* everyone was either in bed or working on their wall lockers, a DS came screaming through the hallways telling us to get outside now! We had no idea what was going on. Some of us were in our PT gear while some had not yet had the chance to change all the way, so were wearing half fatigues and half PT gear. As we started to get smoked, the DS cured our curiosity—it turned out two soldiers had snuck out of one of the windows from the top floor to go get some candy bars. Another DS from a different company watched from a distance as the soldiers thought they were being sneaky. Our DS got a call while he was watching the Super Bowl and he was not happy, so we were smoked throughout the whole second half of the game.

Weiss and I ended up next to each other this night and we figured out how to make these sessions fun. We would always try to form up by each other after that so we could do different things to help the time go by faster and easier, like striking up a quiet conversation, making jokes or venting.

The main thing we would do was try to outperform one another. We both had some competitive blood in us, and we would always try to finish the drills before the other. It helped make horrible experiences into somewhat fun and bearable ones.

Light show

Fire Guard shifts were some of the toughest parts about Basic Training. When your body is so physically exhausted, you hit that pillow and are in the deepest part of the REM cycle within minutes. But after sleeping just an hour or two, one of your platoon members wakes you up. I remember thinking, "This has got to be a nightmare. It can't be time for my shift yet."

I could barely muster up the strength to open my eyes, let alone get out of bed. It was actually painful. After a few weeks of doing Fire Guard shifts, a female battle buddy named Stryker and I were grouped together, and we decided to change things up one night.

While on shift, we had our flashlights on us because we couldn't turn on any lights. The cool feature about a military flashlight is that it has interchangeable blue, green, red, and white lenses. We decided to take advantage of this cool feature and used other soldiers' flashlights (just borrowing them while they were sleeping), using different colors in each one. We laid down at our post and made our own "light show."

It was actually quite fun, and it felt good to laugh as we realized how silly we were acting. We then decided to do low-crawl races down the hallway. We received some weird looks from the females of the other platoons, but we knew they were just jealous that they weren't having this much fun.

It was then time to wake-up the next shift. I stood at the end of their bunk and climbed on some of the rails, shaking them and yelling, "INCOMING!"

Stryker got water from her canteen and started splashing it on their faces, saying, "Wet weather gear! Quick, get your wet weather gear."

We were laughing so hard. Other girls in the room started to wake up to see what was going on at 2 a.m.

"You guys are so stupid," Thacker said, half-asleep and partly laughing. Yes, we probably were, but we were having fun.

Building my reputation

Within our first week of training, other soldiers noticed that I didn't use profanity of any sort. I didn't go around telling others how to talk—it was more of just how I lived. I never have wanted to force my standards on anyone because we all have that freedom to express ourselves how we choose. However, the soldiers in my platoon soon would either apologize around me for "letting off some steam" or would even warn me. Even the DS's caught on—one in particular.

DS Geiger loved to share dirty jokes while in our war room, usually right around PT, and he had a pretty foul mouth along with it. He would get the soldiers laughing pretty hard. I would usually just turn my head in the opposite direction or look down to show no interest in what he was talking about. It got really hard to ignore sometimes because it wasn't like I had anywhere to go, and he soon noticed.

"Stevens, don't you think I'm funny?" he asked out of the blue one evening after PT.

"Uh," I stumbled, having been caught completely off-guard. "Yes, Drill Sergeant."

Other soldiers started to chime in, "She doesn't cuss and doesn't like dirty jokes."

"Oh, so you don't like my choice of words," DS Geiger replied. "You think I have a foul mouth?"

"Drill Sergeant, you can say what you want," I said, trying to be respectful. I was nervous about how he was going to respond, but it was cool to have other soldiers of my platoon look out for me without ever asking them to do so.

"Well, you might want to plug your ears for this next one," he replied. I couldn't help but smile as I plugged my ears. He never really let it go, though. One day at one of the ranges I was in a foxhole after shooting at some pop-up targets, and DS Geiger was supervising our foxholes nearby. He walked up to me and said, "Stevens, do you think

I'm going to go to hell because of my foul mouth?"

"Uh, I don't know, Drill Sergeant . . ." I hesitated for a second. "It's not my call."

"Good answer."

Phew! I thought he was done, but he continued, "But just say you were this Almighty Being for one day. Would I go to hell?"

"Drill Sergeant, it really isn't my call."

"No really, what would you do?"

"I . . . I think you could use better words," I nervously replied.

"All right, I'll give you that." As he left, I let out a huge sigh of relief.

The Warriors Tower

I am terribly frightened of heights. Yes, I know it's silly with how adventurous my personality is, but I just can't help it. Simply thinking about high places gives me a tingling feeling in my legs and butterflies in my stomach. But in order to pass Boot Camp you have to conquer the Warriors Tower, which consists of rope climbing and rappelling from about 50 feet in the air. (I know that isn't too high, but for me it might as well have been 1,000 feet.)

The night before our attempt at the Warriors Tower, we were learning how to put on our harnesses. I was sick to my stomach about it, and my whole platoon knew it. I was praying intently for a miracle, either in the form of strength from God to help me conquer my fear, or for rain to cancel the event!

The next morning, to my delight and relief, we woke up to rain. My platoon was upset, but I was ecstatic! It turned out that the DS's rescheduled the event. So I went back to my prayer plan, and the next time, it snowed! My platoon was really getting upset with me. They scheduled it for a third time, and it was too windy! I believe we might be one of the few companies out there that was able to graduate without completing the Warriors Tower. I didn't mind.

My platoon members told me, "Stevens, your God listens to you!" Ever since that experience, whenever other soldiers would catch me at my bed praying, they would come and whisper in my ear, "Hey, put in a good word for me, would ya?" It was great to hear that!

Becoming soldiers

The bulk of Basic Training is geared around weapons training and qualification. There were a lot of rules to follow while on the range, and if anyone was caught doing something different, even if it was safe, it was considered unsafe and you needed to prepare yourself for a lashing from the DS.

Many classes were focused on weapon safety and care, and I don't blame them. Giving a loaded weapon to hundreds of emotionally and physically weak soldiers is a scary thing and all precautions should definitely be taken. That's why we actually didn't get ammunition until almost a week of training on our M-16s. That allowed us to get the feel of our weapon and squeeze the trigger without the worry of someone making a mistake that could cost someone their life.

At first, I dreaded each day we had to go "check out" our weapons. It always seemed stressful. But after a week of having our weapons, these annoyances soon became comfort measures. I soon began to look forward to them—the smell of the carbon burst hitting my face as I squeezed the trigger, the kick of the weapon, and so on. At the beginning, my elbows and thighs would get cut up and bruised from being in the prone position, but soon they adjusted and it didn't hurt as much.

When I was first learning to shoot my weapon though, I was shooting the target very haphazardly. I was so frustrated because I was doing everything the DS taught me, but I wasn't delivering. I apparently wasn't the only one getting frustrated with my results, because DS Geiger ended up getting right next to me to watch my every move. Talk about pressure!

It turned out my technique was fine but when I aimed at the target, my left eye wasn't closing all of the way and I wasn't able to focus very well. The solution? They gave me a pirate patch and I've been using it ever since with much better results.

"Range days" always seemed to be a little bit more stressful, especially due to the cold weather. Our hands would freeze as we held the M-16, since we couldn't wear gloves. We started out on "paper targets" that had pictures simulating what the target would look like at those distances. Once I got my pirate patch, I loved it.

We soon progressed to practicing on the "pop-up range" where you had to move your weapon from side to side, not really knowing where the next target would appear. This one was a bit more difficult to master. I had to be constantly alert and find a comfortable position so I could easily shift. The closer the target was, the less time it stayed up, ranging from 50 yards (we called that one "fast Freddy" for being up only about a second) to 300 yards (up for about four seconds).

"Are you bulimic?"

Being so physically active and stressed beyond what I thought I could handle, my appetite increased quite a bit, although I had always been a pretty big eater ever since I got out of my anorexia phase. One day while at the range though, one of my good friends, Thacker, told me that the DS wanted to see me.

She offered to be my battle buddy, and I was confused as to why they wanted to see me. I ran over to talk to them in one of the holding tents. "What do you usually eat at chow?" asked one of the female DS's from another platoon.

I looked at her with confusion but quickly went on to answer as I gave her the basics.

"Is there a reason you don't eat the meat?" she asked.

"I do eat meat every now and then." Really, what it came down to was that I didn't trust the military meat and was very selective. I could tell this meeting really had nothing to do with meat and something else was really on the DS's mind. I was trying to figure out what they were leading up to.

The female DS got up, coming closer to me and whispering so the others wouldn't overhear. "Are you throwing up your food?" I looked at her in confusion. "Are you bulimic?"

"No, Drill Sergeant!" I couldn't believe what I was hearing.

"We have heard from a few different sources that lead us to believe you are doing something with your food," she said. "Anorexic or bulimic, we are going to keep our eye on you." I couldn't believe what I was hearing. "From now on you will get your food, show us what you have and sit in an area where we can watch you closely. Then we want to see an empty plate which is a 'happy plate' afterward."

From then on, at every meal, I had to show the DS what I had on my plate. It was all too weird and I don't know where they got their information. It lasted for about a week, then the DS themselves got sick of it.

It's not like I got much time to eat my whole pate, since we usually only got about two minutes to eat a meal. We definitely learned a few tricks on how to consume enough calories in so little time, such as finding what foods swallow easiest and in what ways. If we got five minutes to eat, that was wonderful!

Toward the end of training we actually started getting 15 minutes to eat. A lot of the soldiers were still in the mode of thinking that they needed to cram in as much food as possible—but with the longer eating time most soldiers actually gained weight during those final days.

Birthday bash

There were many types of ranges we went to as we learned how to use other weapons besides our M-16s. I will never forget going to the grenade range on my 19th birthday, although it wasn't as exciting as I had hoped, since we only got to throw two live grenades. We went through different obstacle courses, though, throwing duds at dummies. I hadn't realized how bad of an aim I really was.

I actually got a surprise gift for my birthday. The Sunday before my birthday, I was able to go to church. (The DS's allowed us to attend on some weeks.) I became close with some of the women that were there. On one of my first Sundays, they had us fill out a form so they could contact our families for us and let them know that we were alive and well. I was so grateful for that.

This particular Sunday, one lady got up and said, "We have a special surprise as we celebrate a special time of year for someone." She then said she would like to play a cassette that contained a special musical number for those females that were there.

As the song started playing, I smiled instantly. I not only recognized it, but it was also the exact arrangement of a song I would sing with my family: "Love at Home." It brought me so much strength just listening to it and thinking about my family.

"Sister Stevens, I understand it is your birthday this week," the woman said after the song. I nodded with a curious smile, wondering what was going on. She continued, "Your family has sent you and these other soldiers some Easter candy to help celebrate your birthday."

I just had to laugh when I heard that they had sent Easter candy. It was tradition on my birthday to give me Easter candy, since my birthday fell close to Easter and it was always my favorite candy.

As she passed out the basket of candy, she leaned over to me and whispered, "Did you recognize that song, and who was singing it?"

I looked at her, struck with amazement, wondering, "Was that really them?"

"It was. When I sent your family a card letting them know you were able to come to church every now and then, your mother got an idea and wanted my help. I could not resist such a creative gift."

"And priceless," I thought. I got teary-eyed as I thought about what my family had just done for me. I am so blessed to have them.

The girls and I in the church class weren't able to eat all of the candy, mainly due to time constraints. So I seized this opportunity to stock up on candy, loading it in my field jacket pockets. I just grabbed the candy and chocolate eggs that had no wrappers because that would end up as evidence, because our DS's keep a close watch on garbage. As I got back to my room, I snuck all of my battle buddies a handful of candy. They gasped at the sight and wondered how I got it. I was proud to tell them about my family's gift.

The famous "Confidence Course"

We soon were required to go through the Confidence Course. This is the obstacle course the Army always shows on their videos and commercials. Some of the obstacles were rope bridges (standing on one rope as you grab another) over a 30-foot trench, ladder drills, jumping over high obstacles (I struggled with those), and so on.

There were a few obstacles that really tested my fear of heights. I muttered something to one of the females standing by me, joking about my fear. I realized my stupidity when I saw that DS Geiger was right behind me.

"Stevens, are you scared of heights?"

"No, Drill Sergeant," I lied.

"You better hurry yourself up there then," he said.

I started the obstacle ahead of me. It required a lot of balancing high in the air. Finally I came to the last obstacle, a 50-foot-high tower. I gulped as I grasped the wooden ladder to make my way to the top. There was a little platform there, enough to fit about three people (according to my standards, I didn't think it should fit any).

DS Dixon was up there. The only way down was to hold on for dear life to the rope that arched its way down. As I reached the top, DS Geiger yelled from the bottom, "Hey DS Dixon, I heard that Stevens has a fear of heights."

"Stevens, do you really?" DS Dixon asked in a sharp tone.

"I'm fine, Drill Sergeant," I replied sternly.

"That's what I thought. You better get yourself down there."

I just concentrated on the rope that my life depended on. My forearms were burning as I made my way down. I held my breath, thinking that any other movement could make me slip to my death. I survived!

One of the strangest obstacle courses and training that I had to go through was with the bayonet attached to our M-16s. We had to low-crawl, run through different obstacles as we came up to these green dummies, having to stab them with our bayonets. Each time we stabbed them we had to yell "Kill!" at the top of our lungs. I felt so uncomfortable doing those drills. I'm glad those courses only took up a couple of days of our training.

Inspections

"You have an inspection coming up this Saturday," said one of our DS's. The whole room held their breath as we knew what we were in for. There were always the daily inspections of rooms, latrines and beds, but there were a few times throughout the training that we had full inspections of our wall lockers, uniforms, and dust in any corner of the room.

These big inspections took about half the day, as one DS would inspect at a time. This was a busy time for a squad leader, as we first inspected everyone to make sure they all got the same information and were doing it the same way. We weren't very squared away on our first inspection, though. We learned a lot (the hard way) about what the DS's expected, because they just told us generally that our stuff better be squared away and clean.

We also caught on quickly to the DS game of "setting us up for failure." As one DS would come through, he would search through the wall locker nonchalantly and while doing so, he would either "unbutton" one of our buttons or change something in the locker while we were standing at the position of attention, looking the other way. Then another DS would come through and smoke us for not having everything correct. We were confused at first, but we soon caught on to their game.

Failing inspections was the reason for a lot of our smoking sessions. After one of our first big inspections, our DS's were so upset that they told us to have our "three drawer set" up in the war room in 15 minutes to learn how to do it right. It was going to take some teamwork. Some of our guys were already living on the third floor so it was easy for them to just slide them in. But for us girls, it was a bit more difficult to carry them up six flights of stairs. The men really helped us out with that one. We were all in this together.

Homeless

When we got back from the range one day, the DS kept us in formation, declaring that our barracks had looked horrible when we left that morning, and we didn't deserve to live there.

"Privates, you've got 15 minutes to pack up all your belongings. You've got to find yourselves somewhere else to sleep tonight."

"This will be interesting," I thought, as we ran back inside. Some were trying to be organized about how they were throwing their stuff in their duffel bags, while others were just trying to grab everything. We did the best we could to have everyone look the same among the platoons, praying the DS would see the effort we were putting in.

However, we were smoked for awhile doing different exercises while the same DS yelled, "Privates! Did I not say *all* of your belongings? That means bedding too!"

All of the DS's were yelling at us as we ran back for our bedding. We were back out there in five minutes. The smoking continued.

Frankly, I was getting tired of this game of never being good enough. This continued into the evening for a few more hours as we had to run back in and scrub down the whole barracks—washing the walls, waxing and buffing the floors, etc. We were inspected afterward. Finally, after a couple of times of cleaning it, the DS then said we had to make our beds according to standard and be back outside in, you guessed it . . . 15 minutes (I learned to really hate that time frame). On and on this went as we had to unpack everything and be inspected. It was a long night.

Our final inspection during our last few days of training was the biggest one as they had our "Command Sergeant Major" (it might as well have been the President of the United States) come through and inspect us. If he didn't approve, we didn't graduate.

Everything had to be like it was brand new and never used by hundreds of privates before. Any metal (even on our ammo belt) had to be shiny, boots had to be like mirrors, weapons couldn't have an ounce of carbon left in them, and so on. We were all nervous for this one and it took a lot of extra preparation during the two days leading up to it.

As the morning finally came, in the middle of some small chat with some of the girls in my room, Thacker interrupted and said, "Would you guys want to say a prayer together?"

I had to smile. "Absolutely," I said as I motioned the girls to come together in the middle of the room and put our arms around each other.

"Stevens, you say it," one of them said.

I was proud to stand next to these girls—my battle buddies through these hard times.

My most embarrassing moment

The few days before we left for the field (the culminating event of all of our training) we were given a lot of instruction on tactical movements. One evening while in the war room, DS Geiger was explaining some different movements about coming upon the enemy. We were all sitting on the hard tile floor and I, being one of the squad leaders, was at the front.

My head was cranked back, since I was only about two feet away from where DS Geiger was towering over the platoon. We were all quiet and listening intently as he went on. Then out of nowhere, a little squeak broke the silence.

"What the @!%# was that?" DS Geiger asked, looking down at the front of the class. I turned about 10 shades of red as I realized that the squeak came from me. "Who did it?" he demanded.

I gulped, knowing there was no way to hide this one. I sheepishly raised my hand. Yep, I had just passed gas.

"Stevens!" everyone yelled. The squad leaders around me moved a couple of feet away and DS Geiger moved to the side of the classroom to teach the rest of our training. My face was a cherry red from how embarrassed I was, but I couldn't help laughing along with everyone else. I never lived that one down.

Surviving the gas chamber

Speaking of gas, one of my least favorite drills during my military training was the gas chamber. I understood why it was important, but ugh, I hated it! The day before our turn in the chamber, we got fitted for our masks. To get the right fit, you had to be able to create a seal on the mask against your face so no gas leaked through.

The gas chamber was a dark, smoky room. As we shuffled into it the next day, I was a little scared and didn't know what to expect. But I wasn't experiencing anything unusual, so I thought, "Sweet, I must have a good seal on my mask!"

Then the DS came around. He approached each soldier, and we had to break the seal on our mask by lifting it off of our chin and then reciting our name, rank and unit so they could see that we weren't holding our breath. They do this because you're only in the gas chamber for a few minutes and some soldiers have the talent of holding their breath for that long (I sure don't). But when you are in chemical warfare, you could be exposed to chemicals for hours, even days. The DS's want to make sure you learn to trust your mask so you are prepared to handle unexpected situations in the future.

When I lifted up my mask, I immediately felt a burning sensation on my skin and then felt the burn travel all the way down my airway into my lungs. It felt like they were on fire! I more or less just hacked out my name, rank and unit. After I recited everything I was allowed to reseal the mask. I still felt like I was inhaling the gas and I wanted to get out of there. We were allowed to leave the chamber, but if we were caught running out, we would have to go back in. I hoped that after that day, I was finished with the gas. Keep dreaming.

Field Training Exercise

It was time to begin our Field Training Exercise, known as FTX, and spend a few days camping out in the field. Those were the longest three days of my life! We marched about four miles to where the DS's had designated. It was very cold and was raining as we were marching in. We set up our "half-shelters" on the driest areas we could possibly find. We went through a lot of drills out in the forest, where different platoons would play the enemy and we had to take them on in our squads. Being a squad leader, I had to lead my team in and direct them.

This is where our training paid off, and the DS's wanted to see what we could do, especially what I could do as a leader. I tried to keep an open mind and hear input from all my squad. I had a great team and we should have taken the enemy down, but the DS said we were taking too long in our pursuit and so we had all been killed. Well, that was exactly my plan—to move slowly and unexpectedly. I thought patience was the key, but apparently not in our condensed training.

Our Battalion Commander happened to be out in the field with us as we were doing some drills. I was pulled aside later by one of the DS's saying that the Commander wanted to see me. Going through Basic Training, you establish a fear of any officer, but an even greater fear of those in high rank. It ended up being very brief. I was maybe with him (my battle buddy and a few DS's, of course) for a couple of minutes as he explained how he had been watching me throughout our training and had been very impressed with my leadership qualities.

My heart leaped inside me. I was actually being praised for doing something right! I kept my cool, of course, trying to show no emotion, as is typical of soldiers (I don't know why). He said if I ever considered becoming an officer that he would gladly recommend me. I was soon dismissed after that. I ran back to my platoon with a grin.

Nights were rough during FTX, as you had to pull "fire guard" watch with your battle buddy, only swapping between the two of you.

Most did about two hours on and two hours off. I didn't know which was worse—laying out in the prone position shivering and soaking wet, or in your sleeping bag shivering and soaking wet trying to sleep.

One morning though, we were awakened by a loud pop followed by a "Sssssss" which could only mean one thing—the DS's had just released a gas grenade a few feet from where we were all *attempting* to sleep. I quickly grabbed my mask (because it was attached to me, thank goodness) and put it on as the air got cloudy around me. In my haste I wasn't sure if I had sealed my mask well enough, and I started to doubt whether I was adequately protected.

I wasn't feeling anything yet, so I thought I was safe. But then my eyes started burning, then my nose, and I could see that the inside of my mask was getting cloudy and was blocking my view. I couldn't see where I was going as I ran blindly in the forest trying to dodge not only the gas, but the trees. I fell to the ground hard (because I'm a klutz) and as I fell my mask broke loose. I had made the situation a whole lot worse than if I had just stayed there, trusting my mask. My battle buddies actually had to drag me out of the forest, since I could barely breathe. That is one event I hope to never repeat.

The last hours of FTX were the roughest. We packed up everything, cleared the area and began our march home. Yet we weren't told how long it was going to take. We were already hurting after these last few days of training in the cold, and we were physically and emotionally exhausted. We were in "full battle rattle" wearing all of our gear. My body was aching. I could only imagine what some of the others were going through, knowing that these physical drills did not come as easy for them.

After a couple of hours, some were struggling to keep up and were passed by. They did have trucks following us for privates that were injured and couldn't make it anymore. Deep down we all knew those few probably weren't going to be graduating with us.

Some of my female battle buddies were struggling around me. One of them fell hard from exhaustion. I tried to help her up and grabbed her ruck from her to ease the load. Some others helped her up as we had to keep marching. The DS caught me carrying two rucks and told me to get rid of it, saying she had to do it on her own. I couldn't believe what I was hearing. I wanted to argue back, but I kept my mouth shut. I handed the ruck back to my friend as the DS saw and marched ahead. I stayed back to march with her a little while, lightening her load by lifting the ruck just slightly off of her while she carried it.

This march seemed to never end. Hours went by and we finally stumbled into an area after hiking about 12 miles. It was another range. But this range was different—*live-fire* was actually being shot at *us*. We were told that we had better be low-crawling to not get hit. In actuality, the shots were being fired probably 30 feet above us for safety, and it was more for the effect, but it worked!

The shots had tracers on them, meaning that you could see them in the dark really well. It looked like something out of a Star Wars movie as these traces of colorful light shot above us and loud explosions were going off everywhere. It really looked like a combat zone and I felt like I'd been through one.

Low-crawling with all our gear on this rocky, hard surface really tested my strength. I was in great pain as I inched forward, the rocks cutting into my skin. I tried to shift my weight to find a better way of low-crawling. No matter what I tried, it hurt.

The emotions were coming on strong, and I truly couldn't take it anymore. I'd had enough. My chest and throat were burning as I tried to hold back the tears. DS's were yelling at us everywhere, shots being fired, explosions going off—this was the night that separated the strong from the weak. After low-crawling a few hundred yards, we reached the other end.

Our Battalion Commander met us there to initiate us. Our whole company gathered there. We were an awful—but proud— sight. Some had tear stains on their cheeks, washing off some of the dirt we were layered with. Our uniforms were drenched with sweat, some with blood. We formed up to listen to our Battalion Commander. We were now soldiers.

Some soldiers that had started with us didn't make it, though. We started with 194 privates and graduated with 145. Most of those other privates were kicked back to other companies because they were either injured or lacked self-motivation. Some were kicked completely out of the military because of injuries, while others left by choice.

Boot Camp graduation

Graduation soon followed, and as we marched our way up the street to the auditorium up the hill—looking sharp in our "dress uniforms" and yelling our famous company cadence—we could hear our families cheering us on in the distance. Every soldier in that formation held their head high that day.

There was a big crowd gathered around as we came to a stop. When we were dismissed, the soldiers and families went wild trying to find each other. I found mine and tackled them at the sight. My parents and my little brother came, and I was so happy.

My mom and I embraced, and she said, "You did it Jill, you did it! I'm so proud of you!"

"I can't believe it, Mom," I said. "I really just survived Boot Camp! I made it!"

CHAPTER 4

WE NEED A MEDIC!

Soon after graduating Basic Training I was again saying goodbye to my family and some of my battle buddies, Weiss being one of them. A few in my company had the same Military Occupational Specialty (MOS) as me, so it was great to be bused to Texas together.

I have never seen so much junk food in my life as on that bus. Each of our families loaded us up with food that we had missed out on for the last few months. My family stayed true to the tradition of loading me up with more Easter candy. Did I mention that I have a sweet tooth?

The bus ride was long from Missouri to Texas, and I was feeling sick after eating all at that chocolate. I was thinking a lot about what I had just gone through. I kept telling myself, "I can't believe I'm in the Army! I just survived Boot Camp!"

Now it was time for my Advanced Individual Training (AIT). I really wasn't too nervous, because I figured it couldn't be as bad as what I'd just experienced in Boot Camp. Part of the reason is that this style of living is so ingrained in you that by AIT, it's more second nature. I was excited to get it started.

We arrived about 0430 at Fort Sam Houston in San Antonio, Texas. There was just one DS to greet us—definitely not as bad as 10. We had to get rid of anything edible (we filled up a few trash bags) and then we were off to complete a lot of paperwork. Following a few classes and briefings, it was time for formation with our new company, Bravo 232nd Battalion. We were the last ones to arrive among those who came from other training sites around the nation, such as Fort Jackson and Fort Benning, and they were already there waiting for us.

Those of us from Fort Leonard Wood were divided into our different platoons. As I ran by 1st Platoon over to 4th Platoon's spot, I glanced over to look at all of the other soldiers, and I did a double take at one of the soldiers. I knew him! Carpenter was his name, and we'd had a class at Southern Utah University together. We had hung out a little bit beforehand, both finding out we were medics in the Guard and leaving around the same time for Army training. We knew we were finishing up around the same time, but we never thought we would actually end up in the same company. These next sixteen weeks were off to a great start.

"Soldier Medic, Drill Sergeant!"

We were no longer addressed as soldiers (it's not like we had the title that long anyway). We were now referred to as "Soldier Medics." Whenever a DS came into the room or area, we responded with the same protocol of yelling "AT EASE!"

As soon as they would follow up with "As you were," (and that length of time depended on the DS's frustration level at us), we would have to yell back, "Soldier Medic, Drill Sergeant!"

Training began right away. We had to quickly be trained as an EMT-Basic and become nationally registered by the fifth week. The next ten weeks were focused more on combat medic skills, such as the types of injuries we would come upon in war, how to save a soldier with just the gear you have on if you have no aid bag, medications, and so on. I thought it was quite fascinating when we got to the combat training and all that we could possibly face. Our last week was filled with more FTX and putting all we had learned together.

When we would be out in a field next to our classroom, we would go through different drills to get the feel of what we might do at war. In these exercises, several of us would play the role of the medics while others would be the patients. I decided to spice things up a bit one time and make it as realistic as possible. So when it was my turn to be a patient, I made sure during lunchtime to save my cherry Kool-Aid from my MRE (Meal Ready to Eat).

As I was lying out in the grass during the exercise, I heard other soldiers moaning, acting like they were injured, but I just stayed motionless. As a medic came up to me, he did a quick assessment of my condition and as he went in to listen to see if I was breathing, I coughed up my fake "blood." Literally! I couldn't bear holding that sugar in my mouth much longer. It had instantly liquefied and I really had to cough it up. Red stuff was everywhere . . . even on the medic (which I didn't really mean to happen). It made for some good, and different, kind of training.

Singing cadences

One of my favorite things about being a soldier (okay, maybe there are too many to keep track of) is singing the cadences. We started singing cadences about the middle of Basic Training and that carried on into Medic training. It stemmed from pride—that pride you get when you feel the satisfaction of doing something right, especially when it was challenging. You hold your head up a little higher and sing out a little louder. And boy, did I sing out, especially when the DS called out some of my favorite cadences.

I even started harmonizing with the cadences. Who would have thought that you could harmonize with a bunch of yelling soldiers? I'm not saying it sounded good, but it was more of a hobby that kept me occupied.

I was lucky enough to be a part of the Alpha running group, representing the females in our company. As we were out on the road among the many other companies and battalions stationed at Fort Sam Houston, singing our cadences, the DS over the Bravo running group would yell out from the opposite direction, "That must be our company. I can hear Stevens!"

Wearing "Civies"

After a few weeks of training, our company earned the right to wear civilian clothes. Some soldiers had their families send them some, like I did. It was Friday evening and we were finally released for the weekend. Most of the males were already down in the company area, waiting for the females to come down so that they could go have fun in the city. A lot of friendships are made when you train together. The females were naturally taking a little bit longer, and excitement filled our barracks (we were all in one big room together) as this was our first time in months to actually feel, and especially look, like a girl. As we walked down the steps, I wished I'd had a camera to capture the men's faces as they saw our transformation into civilians. It was priceless!

Weekends were a wonderful break, and we looked forward to them just as any college student does. AIT was a lot like college, just with a few more rigid rules and different training. I loved that we were able to have snacks during classes. This helped me tremendously in not falling asleep. There was usually a snack truck available that we nicknamed the "Gut Truck."

Most soldiers spent their free nights in downtown San Antonio, which was only about 15 minutes away. I loved going to the River Walk. There were even a few times we went to a water park. Those free days really helped you stay sane during all of the soldier training, inspections, and smoking sessions.

Some of the females and males began "prank wars" against each other. Yes, this would lead to more smoking sessions, but most of them were worth every push up. Females would throw water balloons in the males' barracks, (as far as they could get into them without getting caught). The males returned the favor with eggs and powder. We had a special formation after some of the "wars" to get hosed off.

The "Odd Squad"

The standards I chose to live by during Army training always made me stand out, and the reputation I earned at Boot Camp was soon established yet again as soldiers and DS's noticed I didn't use foul language. One day as we were forming up after class, I was counting the soldiers in my squad who were present. DS VR (his last name was quite long, so he had everyone call him that) yelled from the front of the company for me to join him. I grabbed my battle buddy and ran over to him. He came up very close and talked quietly.

"I want to apologize if I have ever made you uncomfortable with my foul mouth," he said. "I know it can get pretty bad, but sometimes it's the only way to get through some of these privates' thick skulls."

I looked at him wide-eyed. "Thank you, Drill Sergeant. It's really okay."

"Well, I know you don't care for it, and I just wanted you to know that I've been trying to use different vocabulary."

"That means a lot to me, Drill Sergeant VR. Thank you." I was dumbfounded that he was saying this. It really did mean so much to me.

I guess not wanting to use rough language and do some of the other things that were common to many soldiers was unusual, but I wasn't on my own. There were two others who shared the same desire as we began our training, Carpenter being one of them. Yet by the end of training, other soldiers joined us. They were intrigued by the standards that we lived by—no foul language, no smoking, no drinking, and so on. During any amount of downtime, we would always be together. We developed a reputation as a group and were referred as the "odd squad" by the rest of the company. We had a lot of fun.

One friend in that odd squad, Jason Davis, decided to investigate the LDS faith and chose to be baptized. He asked me to speak at his baptism! I called my mom for some suggestions and moral support, and I also asked her to remind me of the words to my baptism song "Let Your Light So Shine."

The baptism was scheduled on Saturday, just two days later, and I told her, "Gosh, I sure wish there was a way for him to hear *you* sing it, but I'll just have to settle for reading the words to him."

Little did I know that the wheels began turning at home! My mom has a dear friend, Bonnie, whose husband works for Delta Airlines. Thanks to Bonnie's encouragement and creativity, by the end of the next day my mom had contacted one of my Drill Sergeants, used a buddy pass to get on a plane to San Antonio, and rented a car to drive to Fort Sam Houston—and I didn't have a clue!

When my mom got to the base, she found where she was supposed to meet the DS, but I'd gone off for the evening with my soldier friends to have dinner at the River Walk. So the DS decided to have a little fun. He called me and said there was a problem, and that I needed to get back to the base immediately. I was confused and a little panicked.

What had I done wrong? Even though I'd just ordered dinner, I called a taxi, grabbed my battle buddy, and headed back to the base. As I walked through the doorway, the DS stopped me and sternly said, "Stevens, where have you BEEN!?"

I tried to explain, stumbling a bit over my words, still wondering what I'd done. He cut me off and continued, "Do you have ANY idea how worried your mother has been?"

Right then, my mom stepped out from behind a door! I couldn't believe it! I couldn't have been more shocked and surprised . . . and happy! *My mom was at AIT!*

The next day, I spoke at Jason's baptism, and my mom played and sang "Let Your Light So Shine." It went beautifully and I was so proud to have my mom there.

An unusual FTX

Our field training exercise was supposed to last seven days out in the field—camping, setting up tents and hospitals, moving to different locations, simulating combat, etc. In our case, it was still seven days long but it just so happened that Fort Sam Houston and other parts of Texas were hit that week with one of their biggest rainstorms in decades. Some of our running routes had to be changed after the roads no longer existed, but soon we couldn't even run outside.

So our FTX took place in our barracks, and training was back in the classrooms. Even if we were done with our exercises earlier in the day, we were on "lock down" for the rest of the time, meaning we couldn't go anywhere around base. We had to treat this like we were actually out in the field, wearing "full battle rattle" all of the time and camouflage paint.

Each classroom represented a different drill we had to be tested on. NBC (Nuclear Biological and Chemical) drills took up a few of those rooms and comprised the bulk of our testing. We learned and practiced how to set up both clean and decontaminated areas, scrub contaminated patients, the protocol of shuffling patients through, and so on.

Our FTX was in the first week of July, and even with the wet weather we were hitting above 100 degrees wearing all of our chemical suits (MOPP gear) with the full battle gear. We were drenched in sweat underneath and covered in charcoal, a protective agent for chemical warfare.

Independence Day happened to fall during our FTX. We were lucky to be given the day off but still had to stay in the area. We were able to go to the field right next to our company area, so a few females and I decided to have some fun. We decided to get into our PT clothes (but wearing our company T-shirt), put on camouflage paint and challenge the boys to a good game of football in the mud (yep, it was still raining). That was one of the most enjoyable days I had while training. We were sliding everywhere. I actually felt like a civilian back at college. It was a good holiday.

We still finished off our FTX with a road march, but it was just around our running routes. The rain was starting to back off and we started to get decent weather.

My family was able to come out for my graduation again, but this time I was going home with them. I was excited to have them meet some of my close friends that I had made during training.

After seven long months, I was looking forward to being home and getting back to regular life. Watch out SUU, here I come!

Running through different drills out in the field, and enjoying some medical training.

"The Odd Squad" right before our ruck march to finalize our combat medic training. That's me second from the left, all "camoed" up and lovin' it!

This was an exciting day for me. After seven long months of training, I was now a soldier, a medic, and on my way home.

Drill Sergeant "VR" and I after graduation at Fort Sam Houston, Texas.

CHAPTER 5

SOARING AS HIGH
AS A T-BIRD!

Every senior gets excited about College Day. It gives you a taste of life after high school, and hints of bigger and better places. I was unsure during my senior year where I should go to college. Finally, College Day came around. Representatives from colleges and universities throughout the state of Utah came to Davis High School to provide us with information about the wonderful opportunities available at their school, and trying to persuade us to choose them. As seniors, we could choose three presentations to attend. I filled the first two slots easily— Brigham Young University and Utah State.

I had always dreamed of attending BYU, but as I got older, I heard a lot about other campuses, and was intrigued with Utah State as well. But what about my third spot? I didn't know who else I should look at. Then I remembered that my cousins Sheri and Stefanie were attending Southern Utah University. Now . . . where was that? I had never heard much about the school before. I decided to give it a go and see why my cousins liked it, because I trusted their judgment.

I liked what all three schools had to offer. USU and SUU offered a chance to visit their campuses, and I decided this would be not only fun, but would be a great opportunity to get the "feel" of college life.

I tagged along with a few of Davis High's student body officers and went on a one-day retreat to Logan, Utah with the USU ambassadors.

It was fun and I felt that USU was someplace I could probably go.

I later visited SUU in October 2000 with a few others who decided to sign up for an "Extravaganza" and get a taste of college life. We were assigned different Presidential Ambassadors (PA's) to shadow for a day, going to some of their classes, eating meals with them and then staying at their place that night. I was having a blast! From the many people I met that soon became my friends, to what I was learning about SUU, I soon fell in love and knew this was where I wanted to go. I felt like I was "somebody" on campus and I loved that feeling.

I also loved how much fun I saw the PA's were having and I wanted to know how I could be a part of that when I started at SUU. It turned out there was a whole weekend for potential leaders based solely on selection criteria: interviews, leadership opportunities, personality, and so forth.

March came around and I selected a "leadership weekend" to attend right after I joined the Army. Seniors from around the state came and I felt a little intimidated as most of these were class presidents, team captains, or student body officers—and then there was me. Was there anything really impressive about me?

For some reason I felt like I could prove myself. There was no one there from my high school, no one that had really known me, so I felt that this was my chance to start a new path and be that "Outgoing Jill" I had always wanted to be. I was wiped out by the end of the weekend because of how much fun we had with all of the workshops and games. I only came away wishing that I was starting college the next week instead of that fall.

I continued working at Great Harvest Bread Company through the summer to earn some money for the semester. I soon found out that my "leadership weekend" was a success as I was offered a leadership scholarship just as long as I keep a 3.9 GPA. (YIKES!) I was also offered a position as a PA! I was ecstatic!

I started looking into apartments right away. It wasn't going to be too difficult because I wasn't trying to go with other friends. I was excited about the prospect of meeting new people, even living with complete strangers and starting college life. I found that one of my cousins was going to be an RA (Resident Assistant) for some on-campus housing. I thought that would be a perfect situation. I was able to get one of the openings in her building and found out who my roommates were a few weeks before going down.

Moving away from home can be really hard for some people, but I couldn't wait. Now don't get me wrong, I love my family and have loved living at home, but I felt so ready to be on my own, to cook my own meals, to be in charge of my own schedule, etc.

I headed down to Cedar City, Utah a couple of weeks before school actually started because we had a "Leadership Retreat" with the PA's. The three-day retreat kicked off our goals for the year and got us assigned into different groups for leadership development and delegation. The PA's are just full of energy and I was so grateful to be a part of them, because now as my college days began, I already had friends and I was running into them everywhere.

As PA's, we had to be at most of the events on campus, helping out and directing people. It was fun to be "in the know" of things and I was having a blast at it because of the people I was doing it with. The first couple of weeks of school, there seemed to be so much energy. You could almost live off the free food that was being offered by different clubs wanting you to join. I didn't eat much of it because I was still somewhat of a health nut and didn't want to gain that famous "freshman 15."

I have heard of many experiences where people have tried the whole "unknown roommate" thing and it didn't work out too well for them. I was blessed with great roommates. We all seemed easygoing and willing to work with each other. We went to a lot of the parties on campus together and really made a lot of great friends with all those that were in our building.

My first semester was going great and I truly loved being an SUU Thunderbird. It was hard to leave for the next semester to go off to Basic Training and Combat Medic Training, but I knew I would be back at school the next fall.

After my training ended, I didn't really know where I was going to live and decided that I could move in with strangers again somewhere. I didn't want to live on campus anymore and started looking at other options. I was getting desperate when all of a sudden I got a call from my cousin saying she was going to take the semester off to work and wondered if I wanted her slot in her apartment. It turned out that all of her roommates were girls that had lived in on-campus housing my first year. I didn't remember most of them, but I figured it was going to be fun nonetheless. Little did I know it would be these girls that would change my life and help me discover my true self.

The day I discovered myself

Once I was re-acquainted with my roommates, I knew this was going to be a great year. One girl in particular, Lindsey Forbes, just made me laugh with her type of personality. She called herself Tinkles because, yes, when she gets laughing hard . . . I'm sure you can guess what happens. She would always be sharing her crazy stories about being a counselor at Oak Crest Girls Camp. She would teach us the weird songs and dances they learned there and we, of course, would perform these whenever someone was over. There were many times we would just be aching with laughter because of the silly things Lindsey would get us doing.

November came and we found out that one of our good friends and neighbors, Amy, was celebrating her birthday and was going to have a party. We were all looking forward to attending it. My roommates got a card and gift for her, and I was curious to find out what they got.

"Well," my roommate Katie said hesitantly, "we said in the card that she would get a birthday dance by the birthday bunny."

Lindsey actually had a mascot-bunny head. Random, I know, but that was Lindsey for you, and we loved it.

I started laughing, "HA! Who is going to do it?"

"Well, we were wondering if you would do it."

"Are you serious?" I was still laughing, "There's no way! Someone else would be better."

"No, you would be perfect and make it so much fun," Katie replied.

Were they really talking about me? I thought about it for a second and realized I didn't have anything to lose. "Oh boy," I muttered, "Why not?"

They screamed with excitement, then started helping me get ready for it. I put together an outfit that I felt would be perfect for the character.

I put on some rubber-ducky pajama pants with a yellow raincoat that I just happened to have. The other roommates found a song that would be hilarious to dance to. I called it "the armpit song" because it sounded like a bunch of armpit noises while someone yelled "Don't touch me!" during it. It was weird but funny all at the same time.

The party had already started, and we thought the timing would be perfect. My roommates headed over to check it out. Katie came back and said there were about ten people at the party. "That's not too bad at all," I kept telling myself. "I can do this."

My roommates staged the music and I came dancing through the door. As I was doing my little jig, I kept turning around and would just see faces everywhere. There were definitely more than 10 people there. I would guess at least 30. Katie had played it down because she knew I was hesitant. Those next few minutes were all a blur as I just kept on dancing and making an extreme fool of myself. I danced my way out of the apartment and quickly changed clothes.

I returned to the party five minutes later and just tried to act natural. "Sorry I'm late. I was caught up in some studying."

"Yeah, doing a project on bunnies, are we?" Everyone just started laughing as there was no hiding it. How did they know?

The night just got crazier from there. Someone gave Amy (the birthday girl) some of those "noise makers" and a few of us decided to make them our voices. We sounded like the Honkers off of Sesame Street. We went on for a good fifteen minutes making different sounds that made it seem like we were having a regular conversation using different emotions. It was hilarious. The night went well into the early morning as we were having so much fun.

I came home that night, feeling like I had just popped this "security bubble" around me. Previously I was the one that was always caring way too much about what others thought of me. It's very liberating to finally be able to just be yourself and not worry about fitting other's expectations of you. This night I felt like I truly discovered "me," and this was a turning point that set me on a whole new path in life.

I soon picked up the hobby of collecting costumes. I figured it would one day help me in my nursing career, randomly showing up some days with a costume on. Truly inspired by Patch Adams I guess.

Laughter is the best medicine. My roommates and I would come up with some fun stunts as I got more costumes. With my cow costume, we thought it would be funny to knock on others' doors and ask for a glass of milk. We knew the people we were visiting, but they didn't know who I was since my face was completely covered. My roommates would hide in the parking lot as I approached each door. Most would just close the door laughing with curious looks, but one guy watched me as I walked away.

As I walked down the stairs, I glanced out of the corner of my eye and noticed he was still watching. So I started skipping my way around the parking lot and then just plopped myself down in the middle acting like I was drinking it. I looked over at my roommates to wait for any signal and they motioned that he was still watching. I decided to get up and skip out of sight around the apartment buildings to be free of his stare. Our apartments just so happened to be by a high-traffic road and cars were driving by honking as they were randomly seeing a cow in the middle of the night. One car full of girls actually slammed on their brakes and one of them screamed out the window, "Look! A cow!"

I turned back to look at them and yelled, "MOO!" They started laughing, as did I. They ended up pulling into the apartments across the street and I rolled down the small grass hill behind a wall. Turns out there that was a birthday party for someone we knew across the street. Of course we went. My roommates met me behind the wall just laughing at the fool I was making of myself. This night was just getting better and better it seemed. We went to the party and I came in dancing as before to the same music, only this time as a cow and holding a glass of milk that I gave to the birthday boy. Oh, the college life!

My little brother off to college?

Many times throughout my college years my little brother, Mitchell, would come crash on my apartment floor for a few days when he had a holiday break from elementary school. The two of us set up a pretty fun tradition we called "movie parties" that became our thing to do together. We'd drag a large bean bag in front of the TV and each take a side, with treats galore surrounding us.

We also created a funky walk that we would do together around campus. He would hang out in the library or in my apartment until I was done with classes. I think he got more of a college life than I did! Me and my darn disciplined self still went to bed at a decent hour, even if there was a party going on in the living room. If it was time for me to go to bed, I would leave in the middle of anything.

When my brother was visiting, he would still stay up and play, such as going bowling some nights and staying up until 2 a.m. with my friends. An 11 year old (at the time) hanging out with college students! Gotta love my brother.

Getting involved

One of the many things that I loved about SUU was how easy it was to get involved with the student body, and being a Presidential Ambassador helped me do just that. Entering college and already being involved with an organization helped me easily transition into college life. My freshman friends knew to come to me to get information because, as PA's, we had to know everything about the campus and we were always helping out with the events going on. I loved it!

We had a PA meeting each week, which was more like a social gathering with an agenda. A lot of the meetings were very motivational, helping to build leadership skills in our "Personal Development" (PD) groups we were separated into. We were all given different opportunities to lead and teach. Sometimes our different groups would perform skits for each other. We would just be aching with laughter. There was one group in particular that called themselves "The Peanut Gallery" because they always cracked the jokes or muttered the sarcastic remarks, getting all the PA's laughing.

Our main role as PA's was to increase enrollment at SUU, give the tours on campus and travel around to different high schools around the region to share the benefits of what SUU can do. I was involved with the group for two of my four years at SUU.

We had a lot of holiday parties as PA's, but one in particular I will never forget. We had a Halloween party in the fall of 2003 that was a CLUE theme based on the famous board game. Our leaders wanted us to dress up like the characters—tuxes, gowns and all—because we were actually going to play the game. Students would draw their "character role" as they would come in. I didn't really know how I wanted to show up, other than I didn't want to show up in a gown. I wanted to change things up a bit. I went to Deseret Industries (a thrift store) to see what ideas I could fish out. I ended up taking a whole new direction that turned out better than I even expected. I decided to really play up one of the characters and got to work.

I showed up in brown slacks with a 57-inch waist and an off-white extra-large striped collared shirt. Suspenders held up my pants as I stuffed each leg with a comforter. Pillows filled out the tummy and buttocks area. To top it all off, I wore thick brown-rimmed bifocals with a mullet wig as my hair. Yep, I was "Professor Plump." It was beautiful!

I walked into the room filled with PA's who were dressed "to the nines." I started getting a lot of laughs. I tried not to laugh myself as I attempted to move through the crowd. There were so many people in this small room, standing and sitting, that it made the scenario even funnier as I tried scooting through the row of chairs as my "plump" self. I sat down on a few people to "rest" as I acted like I was overworking myself.

I then made my way to the food line. Crackers, cheese and fruit were being served. As I made it to the front, I grabbed the whole tray instead of just the small plates, rested it on my belly and started eating. The whole night was so much fun playing up the character. My costume collection was off to a good start!

ROTC Ranger Challenge Team

I connected with the ROTC department at SUU and discovered that they had an "elite" group of soldiers/cadets that were training extra hours for a big ROTC event called the Ranger Challenge Competition that took place each November. Over the course of two days, 30 teams from universities across the Western Region would compete at Fort Hunter Liggett, California.

I became intrigued as one of the leaders was explaining to me all that they do. I decided to test it out and see if I could make the team. It was a nine-man team, with one alternate allowed in case of injury. I thought I was going to be competing against just the men for the slots but it turned out that there was a new rule put out by Command that one member had to be female. I worked hard and got the slot.

We trained every Tuesday and Thursday mornings, as well as afternoons and some Saturdays. Most of our training consisted of practicing and perfecting each event. We usually got together at 6 a.m. I felt that since I was the only girl, I had to work extra hard so I wouldn't slow them down in competition. So I did cardio at the gym for about 45 minutes before we would get together in the mornings to really build up my endurance. There were seven events that we had to train for and very strict guidelines for each one:

Physical fitness test: This was the typical one in the military consisting of push-ups and sit-ups in two minutes, and the two-mile run. We would be scored according to the Army score card.

Obstacle course: This one came really easy for the men on the team, but I really struggled with this as it took a lot of upper body strength. One event I couldn't do on my own (and it ticked me off) was the monkey-bars. Goodness, I used to fly on those as a kid, but I lost the hang of it as I got older and really struggled getting myself across. In the actual competition, we figured out a special system. One of my team members that first went through would run back to have me stand on his shoulders for the monkey bars. I had to suck up my pride for this one.

In the rest of the course, there were a lot of balancing obstacles, as well as low-crawling, and rope climbing. The last obstacle took some great team work climbing a 10-foot slick wall. We finished the whole course in under six minutes in competition. We knew we could have done better with some of the things we messed up on, but after all the universities went through it, the closest team was more than a minute behind us. We were surprised, but obviously excited, at the results.

Weapons qualification: We practiced only twice on the range before we went to the competition. We realized afterward that we should have practiced a bit more on certain techniques . . . we didn't do so well. We only had nine rounds of ammo to zero our weapons, and then 20 to shoot each target twice.

Written land navigation test: We practiced this in the classroom in the afternoons, going over our map-reading skills. There were about 30 questions on the actual test about the basics of map reading and also how to find points on a map given us.

Rope bridge: This event took a lot of strategy and was an intense few minutes as we had to make a bridge out of one really long rope between two tree poles about 50 feet apart. Each of us made our own "swiss-seats" out of some short rope and was given a carabineer. We all had very specific jobs and each one was critical as each second counted if you wanted to end among the top finishers. We usually practiced this at an area just off campus. We would blast rock music from a car to really get us revved up. "All Night Long" by AC/DC became our theme song.

For this event, the long rope was laid out in a precise manner as one cadet would count out certain feet and curve it a certain way on the ground. The rest of us would go to our specific places around the rope. The team captain would yell, "Count off!" and we each would yell our different numbers according to our job. As the ninth one counted off, silence would fill the air as we would wait anxiously for the grader to yell "Begin!"

Instantly, each cadet began working furiously on their position. One was counting to help us stay on mark, one ran off to the other poll across the trench (one of the only two allowed to do that, it was a penalty if anyone else touched the middle ground), others were tying knots, gathering the slack of the rope, assisting others in tying our end of the bridge, getting it as high as possible so no cadet touched the ground as they zipped across.

Within 20 seconds we were ready to hoist the first soldier up to be clipped to the rope and pull himself across, hanging by the carabineer from our swiss-seats. One by one, the remaining seven of us would zip across the rope bridge, using our arms to pull us as quickly as possible to the other end. There, we would be clipped off, making sure we are out of the way when the last cadet untied the other end and brought the rope with him. We had to make sure the rope was free of knots and was completely on the other side once our captain yelled, "TIME!" The graders then stopped the clock. All of this was done in under two minutes.

It was intense and cool to be a part of it all. These five events ended the first day of competition. Our team tried to rest up and prepare for the last two—and most difficult—events the next morning.

Land navigation course: Each team was given about 25 locations (known as points) to find in the woods and mountains. It was some hard terrain to be running in. We split our team into groups of two or three people and divided up the points. If we did our calculations correctly, we were supposed to find a six-inch stick in the ground that had orange paint sprayed at the tip. Each point had a code written on the stick which was to help the graders make sure you found the right one, instead of just writing down any stick you came across out there.

Each cadet ended up running about eight miles to get to the different points spread out across the range. There were some steep areas, hiking up them to hopefully get to a point and then sliding back down to get to another point. We did not do too well. We just couldn't seem to be doing it right and must have been orienting ourselves all wrong with the map and the actual terrain, which is the biggest key to staying on course. We were worn out as we made it back to the starting line as the time limit expired. We had 30 minutes to doctor up our wounds (i.e. blisters, cuts, etc.), grab our rucks that we packed the night before and head to the final event.

Ruck-march: There were a lot of rules with this last event. We had to run as a team in "full-battle rattle" along with a 40-pound rucksack (military backpack), and carry a weapon through a 10-kilometer course in the mountains.

There was a list of items that needed to be with us, and we divvied out the items, giving the heavier items (i.e. radio and antenna) to the stronger runners. Each cadet had to have certain things in our ruck and it had to weigh 40 pounds, even if the equipment they listed didn't equal that much weight. We ended up having to put some rocks in our rucks to make weight, since they were weighed at the end of the event to make sure we followed the rules and we didn't ditch any items to lighten the load.

There is just something that makes you feel good and stronger as you run with that ruck. It's an attitude of "bring it on." This was one of my stronger events, but it wasn't necessarily so for some members of my team. So we would tie ropes onto the back of our rucks so our teammates could grab on and we could pull them along to take off some of the load.

When were about four miles into the event, I suddenly found myself face-planted in the dirt. I groaned and tried to get up, but I couldn't do it. I had muscle failure from all of the events, along with my ruck and weapon being on top me. The saying "I've fallen and I can't get up" totally applied to me here.

My battle buddies had to actually pick me up. When I looked ahead and saw that the rest of my team had stopped as well, I started yelling at them, "What the heck are ya stopping for? Keep running!" as I had blood running down my hands and mud all over my face. I guess I'm a little competitive.

After crossing that finish line, I felt like I had just run a marathon. My body ached all over from what I had just put it through, but it was a good feeling at the same time, knowing I had challenged myself. After all was said and done, we took first place in the "Small School Division" and fourth place overall. Not too shabby! I competed on the team in both 2002 and 2003 while at SUU.

Nursing school

While I was finishing up my prerequisite classes in the spring of 2003, I decided to apply for nursing school. SUU didn't have their own program at the time but had a program set up through Weber State University. To my great surprise, I was accepted and would begin nursing school that fall. I was so excited!

There was a lot more work involved, because I was essentially attending two different universities—paying WSU's tuition and fees as well as some of SUU's, and communicating with both schools. Thankfully, it had been done for years and there was an established system.

The semester got off to a great start. I was still a PA and training with the Ranger Challenge team as well as training for my fourth marathon. I had run in the Deseret News Marathon during the summer and was training for St. George again. I finished around 3:30 for both of them, which seemed to be my average time. I wasn't able to put in as much training as I would have liked, because of how involved I was. I was named President of the Student Nurses Association at SUU and got right into the thick of school throughout the fall. I also met the "man of my dreams" at the time and started dating him exclusively. We couldn't have been more alike, and we had so much fun together.

Thanksgiving break arrived, and I started driving home to Kaysville to spend the holiday with my family. Although I was very busy with many activities stretching me a bit thin, I felt like my life was on track and everything was fitting into place. But during that drive home, I had a phone conversation that threw me for a loop and altered the course of my life forever.

Above, my roommates and I are enjoying a girls night out. (Top row from left: Camilla, Ann, me, and Miranda, with Lindsey, a.k.a. Tinkles, and Katie in front)

At left, I'm off to have some fun with my friends.

At the "Clue" Halloween party dressed as Professor Plump.

Joleen and I cheering the T-Birds on at a football game.

My best friend and little brother, Mitch, getting a taste of college life with me.

Chapter 6

Called to War

I love the holidays, and I was looking forward to spending that Thanksgiving with my family . . . baking with my mom, breaking out in song with all my siblings while working in the kitchen, and playing in the family Turkey Bowl. It was going to be a nice break.

However, I got a call from my section sergeant while on my four-hour drive home. The call wasn't unexpected—I received one every month to let me know about our drill schedule. Our next one was planned for December and was going to be our Christmas party.

But the sergeant didn't sound too cheerful. "Um, sorry Stevens, plans have changed," she said. "You have to be up here in a couple of weeks. We're going to Afghanistan."

Silence . . . I couldn't talk. I actually couldn't really breathe. After a moment, I realized I needed air. I breathed out as what she had said hit me. "Okay, have a happy Thanksgiving," I tried to croak out.

I was alone in my car, and I tried calling friends and family with the news, but no one was answering. Emotions started rising. I needed to talk to someone. During the next few hours, I ended up having a good one-on-one chat with God. "What is going on?" I asked.

I had everything going for me: I was already in the middle of nursing school, and I'd found the man of my dreams and planned on getting married the next spring. This couldn't possibly be right. "What good could possibly come from this?" I thought.

Then the words of a song came to my mind, and I believe God was really trying to tell me something. (I call those "brick moments" because the answer can feel like a brick hitting you in the head.) It was written by my mother, comparing our lives to a tapestry. Sometimes we are only looking at the side with all of the knots, strings and entanglements, but what the Lord is looking at is something far more beautiful on the other side.

I knew that I needed to place my trust in Him; "Faith and fear cannot exist at the same time, one must depart." It should bring comfort to all of us, knowing that our Savior is in control of our lives. And now I know why the Lord needed me over there—to learn what I needed to for myself, and then help others through their hard times.

My Tapestry of Love
By Karen Stephens

My life is like a tapestry with threads of every hue
A fabric interwoven with Christ's love
Such trust was placed in me, to create this tapestry
So I weave with care as he guides from above

Sometimes the colors seem to be so dark and dull and gray
Will there be any beauty when I'm through?
Is there purpose and design, to this tapestry of mine?
Or am I alone in what I'm called to do?

Chorus:
I do not know the pattern or design of what I do
Nor the end of this great work that is for me.
Still I weave with care each day, every color on my way
 And trust He'll guide what only He can see
This Masterpiece of love, my tapestry

I wonder what the other side will be when it's complete,
When I have finished weaving and can see
The Savior's gentle love, in the view from up above.
Will it be as He intended it to be?

Will my fabric be of use to those who cross my path of life?
Will it's strength be such to serve my fellow man?
Will I realize in time, that its purpose was divine?
Will I see in it the touch of the Master's hand?

Chorus

Father, can you help me?
If only I could see it from above.
Father, will you guide my hands,
As I labor in this Masterpiece of love?

Chorus

As time went by during the drive, I was able to process some of my emotions before I was finally able to reach my family. It worked out well in the end so that I could be strong on the phone for my mom as she let out her emotions. When I arrived that evening, it was a solemn greeting. It ended up being an emotional rollercoaster for my family that day—my sister got engaged, my brother announced that his wife was pregnant, which would be the first grandchild of the family, and I was going to war.

As my family was gathered around playing games and eating treats later that evening, I snuck off unnoticed to my room. I had to be alone as it sunk in that I was 20 years old and going to war. I was terrified! I started crying uncontrollably. What was going to happen to me? I was heartbroken to be leaving my family and especially the man I was dating seriously at the time, because I knew deep down it wasn't going to last.

Preparing for deployment

After finals were over, I moved everything up north to Kaysville during the second week of December and prepared myself for some long training days. We were in a rush because we had less than four weeks to have everything inventoried and packed up. I didn't realize how much stuff we had just in the medic section alone, and every little piece had to be typed up on a list, down to the last Band-Aid. Each list had to be signed and we gave that task to Hamilton (a.k.a. Hammy).

After a couple of weeks, this was getting old and so I tried to keep an "up-beat" attitude while going through the same motions . . . singing songs and such. Well, as I was handing each list that we had so far inventoried off to Hammy to sign, I said, "Hey, I need your George Foreman on these."

Hammy looked up slowly, a little confused.

"What?" I asked. "Isn't that . . ." and I trailed off as it hit me that I'd just said the wrong name. I knew I needed to say a famous name (e.g. John Hancock) but I guess the name of a heavyweight boxer that sells cooking grills on infomercials was the wrong one.

Hammy started laughing really hard, and by the end of the day everyone knew about it. Even in Afghanistan, that "blonde moment" seemed to carry strong and was never forgotten.

I was trying to soak in all I could of what little civilian life I had left, while trying to keep a cheery holiday spirit about me. Goodness, I was treating my situation like I had cancer or some life-threatening disease. I tried to remind myself that my life was not over and there was still so much to be had. My neighborhood threw me a "going away party" with great gifts to help me prepare for the "longest camping trip of my life." That New Year's Eve was a hard one to take as I realized that as 2004 was just beginning, I wouldn't be home again until mid-2005. That thought sunk deep.

On January 4th, families and friends gathered at the military hangar in West Jordan, Utah to send us off. We were headed out on buses to Fort Carson, Colorado for training. We didn't know how long we were going to be there, but it ended up being until mid-April.

After leaving and being on the road for not even an hour and a half, a good portion of my busmates were already drunk! My seat was in the midst of it all, and I was trying to listen to some music to drown it all out. Thankfully, my good friend Dallas Wilkerson told me about another seat up front. He knew I didn't want to be any part of it, and I ended up sitting by Shawn Flanagan and watching the movie *Mr. Bean*. It was nice to know some people were looking out for me. I just hoped I could return the favor.

Journal entry on January 4, 2004: *A whole year and a half. Ya know, sometimes that just sounds so long and yet not, at the same time. Right now it seems really long but I'm gonna have fun while doing it. Might as well, right? You always got to make the best of any situation. I have mixed feelings about this whole experience that lies ahead. I'm excited! I really am, it's just a long time to be gone. I hope I can hack it. I don't want to let my soldiers down. They are counting on me to save their lives. If one dies, it is my fault. Our motto as a medic is, "Bring 'em all home." I hope I can live up to that and not let my country down. That is the only thing I'm nervous about.*

Let the training begin

We arrived to Fort Carson in nineteen below zero weather, which wasn't the greatest welcome to the start of our deployment. We settled into old barracks that reminded me too much of my Basic Training days, but with a bit more freedom and room, of course. I had only one female roommate (Kotter) during my stay at Fort Carson.

Our training began right away. Classes, classes and more classes on Laws of War, Rules of Conduct with the enemy as well as Enemy Prisoner of War. This definitely wasn't SUU anymore. I found the information actually intriguing. We also learned the different types of bombs that had been used in the war: what they look like, how they work, what types of explosion they create, what triggers them, how they have been disguised, and so on.

Growing up, I never dreamed I would be attending classes that talked about bombs and rules of engagement. This was all too cool. I also learned how to use NVGs (Night Vision Goggles) and got to go for a test run. You can't beat a night of "off-roading" in a humvee with no lights using some cool equipment. The soldier life is too fun!

Quite a few days were spent at the Soldier Readiness Program (SRP), making sure that each soldier had everything squared away medically, financially, emotionally and physically. It is quite a process. As we were getting bused there one day the song "Stand by Me" came on the radio and the whole bus of soldiers joined in, belting it out at the top of their lungs. It was hilarious seeing a bunch of men singing like that.

The bulk of our training was spent going to weapons ranges (no surprise) but most of the ranges that I had been to before had dealt with an M-16 and firing at targets 50-300 yards away. We did go to some of those, but the bulk of our training was spent at different types of ranges made specifically to help train soldiers in this new type of warfare—how to enter a room, tactical signals, crowd control, etc. These ranges made it seem all too real about what we might run into in Afghanistan. Even though our unit was Aviation (Apache, attack helicopters) and we would most likely be sending our guys out to the trouble, we still had to be ready and trained for any type of circumstance.

Keeping your eye on the target

One of the new ranges that we went to was a close-fire range, where we were only about 25 feet from the target. Instead of lying on the ground and shooting, we would go through different walking/pivoting motions, simulating combat and then facing our target. I figured this was going to be a piece of cake with the target that close.

I went in a group of about 20 soldiers where we stood in a line in front of 20 targets. We would walk this way and that way, and then pivot around to come up to shoot, modeling a real combat situation. We would shoot three shots and then would check out our targets. I ran up to mine with all sorts of excitement, thinking I just nailed that target—and found there was not one hole in it.

"You've got to be kidding me," I thought. "I'm about to go to war and I can't even shoot something 25 feet in front of me?"

I would check the soldiers' targets next to mine and they were actually hitting the paper, but were still way off from hitting the actual silhouette. Then I looked at my friend Hammy's target, which was just next to mine. I saw three holes grouped together right in the chest. Okay, maybe he had an advantage because he just happened to be a member of the SWAT team in Utah for his civilian job, so he had some prior training!

"Hammy, share the wealth," I pleaded as he saw my results. "C'mon, give me some pointers. I'm going to be fighting along next to you."

He agreed to help me out, and gave some advice. Then we started the next drill, taking a few steps and bringing our weapon up to shoot. I checked out my target and saw three holes grouped together right in the head.

I did a complete double-take and yelled "Woo hoo!" while doing a little victory dance. To the soldiers down line, I yelled, "Check that out! Good thing you've got Stevens on your team. Watch out Taliban!"

All of the soldiers were just shaking their head and smiling, but Hammy was busting up with laughter. I figured he must have been so proud of me, but then he continued laughing and that just didn't seem right to me. He should be congratulating his newfound apprentice, not laughing at me. Once he regained his composure, he said, "Stevens, I'm sorry, but that was me shooting at your target just to see your reaction. Man, was it worth it!"

"You didn't!" I fired back. I cringed at those words. Please tell me he didn't just say that. So I responded, "Yeah whatever! Prove it!"

So we decided to both shoot at the same target, Hammy aiming for the right shoulder and me aiming for the left. The results? Let's just say it's a good thing I'm a medic and not in the infantry. Talk about going from an all-time high to an all-time low in just a couple of minutes.

MEDIC!

For nearly a month I was the only medic to take care of almost 300 soldiers. What a task. The other four medics were off at school updating their medical skills. I had already had the training, but it had been a year and a half earlier. The Army changed the combat medic training after the others went through it, so they needed to get the update. I was jealous, because I wanted all the medical experience I could get.

I was kind of nervous to be a medic. I had confidence in what I knew, I just needed to know more. I had to keep up on sick soldiers, transporting them to the nearest clinic, chasing others down to follow up on immunization records, assigning combat life-saver bags, among other duties. I had to be very proactive and make some pretty quick decisions. I actually kind of liked it. I was the youngest (in rank and age) attending all of the command meetings.

This same month when I was the only medic just so happened to include our 15-day Field Training Exercise where we were tested on all of our missions. We set up tents out at the hangar to be by our aircraft at all times. The first week was to practice, receiving more training and preparing for validation that took place the second week. Once we were validated, we would get our mobilization orders telling us when we would go to Afghanistan.

I found a little room that I made into an aid-station so people would know where to come if they needed anything. I usually slept on the floor there to have a medic around at all times. I asked another soldier, Jenkins, to help me out with medical tasks as I wasn't able to handle it all. A medic needed to be on all of the missions (convoys) while one needed to also stay back for base support. I couldn't possibly do it all. It sure kept us busy with both of us either being tasked on a mission or back in the clinic.

My new battle buddy, Jenkins, was a great example to me. Our first morning working together, Jenkins says, "How about a Medic Prayer?" So we knelt down in the middle of the room and I offered to say it. What a great way to start the day!

The last week or so of FTX was filled with convoy after convoy. I went on most of them. It was good training. I learned a lot and felt more prepared for Afghanistan. One convoy was to simulate a rescue for a "downed Apache." We were out there for hours with the evaluators. I got evaluated while working on one of the pilots simulating a head injury. I passed!

Another Apache was supposed to fly out to help complete the scenario the evaluators had laid out but after waiting a couple hours, we heard on the radio that it wasn't coming. This mission was taking quite a bit longer than anticipated and all of a sudden I was becoming very aware of my very full bladder.

I'd been holding it for some time knowing that we would be leaving soon . . . but things didn't go as planned. I was praying that I would be able to make it as we packed up to head back (about a two-hour trip). The humvee was really bumpy and the pressure of my body armor on my bladder wasn't helping.

After about 30 minutes of four-wheeling out in the middle of nowhere, I couldn't take it anymore. I told the driver that we had to stop. Of course, he needed to know the reason. He smiled at the others in the humvee after I told him. We were trying to brainstorm our options besides stopping, but it all came down to: 1) I was female, and 2) I was in a vehicle full of men. They said that they could radio the front vehicle to stop and without hesitation I yelled, "YES!"

"Pirate one, this is Pirate niner, we have an emergency with a soldier and we need to pull over."

"Do we need a medic? What vehicle is the medic in?"

"Actually, it is the medic . . ." a moment of silence, "Uh, she has to pee . . . and it's an emergency." I could hear men chuckling on the other end of the line.

The convoy slowed to a stop and I hopped out, darting down the side of the mountain. There was a couple feet of snow on the ground so it made the trek quite fun and difficult at the same time. Well, after the business was done, I hiked up the hill and the evaluators were waiting for me at the top. I just smiled as they said, "You stopped a convoy to pee . . ."

"We've been out here for . . ." I started to explain.

"You stopped a convoy to pee," they interrupted and just shook their head smiling as they walked off.

Yep, I didn't live that one down for a long while. I became a great joke for the unit.

Journal entry on April 16, 2004: *"Cause I'm leavin' on a jet plane. Don't know when I'll be back again." And that is so true. It says a year on my orders but it sounds like it will be a for-sure 18 months. But you really never know until the day they send you back.*

I am flying World Airlines right now and we are just about to take off. We will first have a fuel stop in Maine then off to Germany. We will then move on to one of the "-stan" countries.

Well, it ended up being Kyrgyzstan. There were around 295 in our group, but they can only move 100 soldiers into Bagram one day at a time. So we were broken up into different "chalks" (groups). I was in Kyrgyzstan for a little over two days until I was finally able to depart. This was it . . . I was going to war!

CHAPTER 7

BOOTS ON GROUND

As our C-130 was descending, excitement washed over me. I couldn't believe I was actually going to be landing in Afghanistan— a combat zone! Shouldn't I be scared? Yes, there were some nerves, but I saw this as a great adventure, one I was lucky to be a part of.

The C-130 landed roughly and soldiers were holding on tightly inside. One by one, we shuffled out of the aircraft and our boots hit the pavement of the runway in Bagram. This was now my home for the next year.

We were directed into a building made out of quarter-inch plywood. I soon found that almost everything was made out of it. ROE cards were issued to us after we were given instructions on the "Rules of Engagement" and they had to be on us at all times. A lot of rules and regulations were given to us. Weapons were to be carried at all times. This was definitely not a place to be wandering around and sightseeing.

Bagram, in and of itself

We were taken to our assigned camp where we would be living. Bagram was broken up into different camps, each specific to its regiment: Special Forces, Military Police, Hospital, etc. We, of course, were taken to the Aviation division, Camp Albert.

I was trying to soak in all my surroundings as we were walking over. There was one main road named "Disney" that had each of the entrances to the different camps on it. About a mile of this road was paved and I learned later that it circled around, making the perimeter of the base. Twelve-foot high and three-foot wide barricades lined the streets. I glanced in the entrance to each camp and saw bunkers and "B-huts" (basically wooden tents) lined up everywhere. I felt like I was a tourist as one soldier was telling us where everything was.

"On your left is the hospital," he mentioned. I peeked in as we walked by and got excited just looking at the area. "I can't wait to check it out," I thought.

We finally made it to Camp Albert. Our camp looked much like the others. Rocks about the size of softballs covered the ground. They were placed there when the first soldiers arrived in Afghanistan to help keep the dust down from all of the wind. I knew right away that twisted ankles were going to be a common injury seen in the Aid Station. Rows and rows of tents and unfinished B-huts, as well as some completed ones, filled the camp. It looked like our homes were getting an upgrade to be more stable.

My "hooch" (as our homes were all called) was in the outermost row. They put all the single enlisted females in our unit together. There were six in my hooch. My room was an 8x8 foot space which soon became my sanctuary. There was a wood platform about one foot off the ground on the opposite wall that had an old beat-up foam mattress on it. This was obviously the bed that the previous soldier had quickly made. I got started unpacking right away. Kotter and I left for the PX to see what was available and what we could get.

The PX was about a half-mile away and was about the size of a gas station. It had various items that a soldier cannot live without: hygiene products, some snacks, drinks, and a few household items like fans, coffee makers, water boilers, plastic drawers, pillows and bedding. Some army paraphernalia was also there so that you could send some souvenirs back to family, such as clothes, cups and mugs. I was a little surprised to see those items.

There were some snacks there that I soon learned were put on the shelves and quickly gone within the day. A few soldiers and I had a system to inform each other about the coveted items so we could get some before they were gone. Chocolate was a rare item there (due to the heat it wasn't shipped that often at first) and would vanish quickly off the shelves, as did soda pop and chips. During the first part of our year, the PX struggled to keep the shelves stocked, but by the end we usually were able to get what we wanted (of what they offered, at least).

There was a lot of construction taking place outside because more hutches were being built, and also inside the soldiers' rooms themselves. Some soldiers got really creative and made fancy beds and desks. Some would build shelves in such a way as to make it look like a personal "home theater" system in their room where they would set up their laptops and speakers. Little by little, I would add certain things to my room to make it more like home.

Journal entry on May 9, 2004: *Well I have now been here three weeks tomorrow, and truly . . . Bagram is fantastic! It's got a gym to work out at, a PX to buy a few army supplies and local Afghanistan stuff, a decent chow hall, an MWR building (Morale, Welfare, and Recreation) for soldiers to take a break and watch movies, get on the internet and use the phones (for 10-15 minutes at a time). The thing I am mostly excited about is my room. It's got a red theme to it... A red and white rug for the door, a red and black wood rug for the floor, a red SUU blanket and a huge body pillow that is, of course, red! It's so comfortable! I've got posters hanging up, my "It's All Good" t-shirt nailed to the wall, too, and I made a quote wall where I write all my favorite quotes and scriptures on it. Who'd have ever thought I would have become more decorative at war than I was at college!*

After a few months of living there, and with the help of some other soldiers' carpentry skills, my room was perfect. As you walked into my room, there was a desk with a set of shelves going up in the far left corner. I filled those with books and other personal items. A window was right above the desk on the far wall. Some posters and pictures hung on either side of the window.

My bed was about three feet off the ground on the far right wall, so I could store things underneath. Then on the last wall just to the right of the door were some more shelves and where I put my plastic drawers. I had this genius thought of writing my favorite quotes on my walls as

I pointed out in my "journal entry." Why not? These walls were wood so I figured this would be an inspirational and motivational addition to my room. My "quote walls" actually became a great strength to me as I had two side walls covered, as well as my ceiling, giving a good reminder to have faith and optimism.

Port-o-Potties were my bathroom for the next year. It was kind of weird getting up in the middle of the night trying to find your way there and not trip over the rocks. We were warned before we arrived that it was really dark at nighttime. There were no streetlights to light things up because, obviously, that would be like a "hit me" sign to the enemy. Head lamps became a popular item to have for nightfall.

Showers were a few hundred yards away. Every morning I loaded up my backpack with the necessary items. It was usually after PT that I made it over. The shower buildings were made out of sheets of metal and were two stories high. The showers were on the top level while the water tanks were below. About half the time we had hot water, which was more often than I expected. There was one building for the females where I showered, and five for the males in the area. There were about three different locations for showers set up for the soldiers, each soldier just going to the closest one.

The Aid Station became my home away from home. When we first arrived at Bagram, the 10th Mountain Infantry Division (ID) out of New York was in control. The 25th ID (soon called Task Force Wings) out of Hawaii was going to be replacing them and that was who our unit, the 211th Aviation, was attached to.

The actual "change of command" didn't take place for another couple of months, as our unit was one of the first to replace the Apache unit of 10th Mountain ID. Working with the 10th Mountain Medics was wonderful. They were very laid back and we got along great. I could tell within the first few weeks of being there how much my medical skills improved by just diving in and learning on the spot. I felt the year was going to fly by and I was excited with how things were running— then the 25th ID showed up.

A lot of people have asked since returning from Afghanistan what the hardest part of the deployment was for me. Most of them expected an answer of rocket attacks, being under fire, saving soldiers, convoy missions, or something along those lines. Granted, some of those were tough to deal with, but that is the part of the soldier life that I love and crave. The toughest part for me was actually dealing with Regular Army (people who did this every day) and especially those in the 25th ID.

I have never seen a more unhappy group of people in my life. A smile seemed to be a foreign thing to them. It seemed many took pride in their rank and really took advantage of anyone who was below them as well. Don't get me wrong. Rank is a respect that is earned and most do earn that respect. But I love to see a leader who respects those under their command . . . a humble, motivational leader so-to-speak. This has been a rare thing in my Army career. I've seen these types of leaders, and they make me want to work a lot harder for them and give them my utmost respect. I just wish I saw it more in the military. They also seemed to really look down on us being National Guard, like we were unworthy to be called soldiers.

Journal entry on May 16, 2004: *Well, I have been here almost a month now. Crazy, it actually has gone by pretty fast. I have been looking forward to this next coming year but this last week changed my perspective just a little. The 25th ID, who we are attached to, have all shown up and they make me truly not want to be a part of the Army. The medics that came have been difficult to get accustomed to. They brought four medics and one Flight Surgeon.*

Things at the Aid Station took a sharp turn for the worse and I soon wondered how I was going to survive the rest of the deployment. Rule after rule was created and I felt like I was back to being treated like a "low-life private" at Basic Training. The new NCO-IC (basically our new boss) at the Aid Station changed everything that we had already in place. I believe it was his approach that set me off from the start. All the medics in Task Force Pirate (what our unit called ourselves in Bagram) felt this deployment just lost its spark and drive to continue on. The Aid Station used to be a place to hang out, but now, the second you were off duty you wanted to get out of there. For weeks we just "sucked it up and drove on" as we really had no choice with the mandatory schedule we were on. Confronting him with ideas just got us in trouble (and I got in trouble a lot).

After a couple of months of working with the others, I guess there was too much "clashing" and misunderstanding happening between some of the medics. So we were put on orders to be a part of Task Force Wings (25th) instead of being a part of our own Task Force Pirate. That didn't really work out like we had hoped. It was like we were Regular Army now, not National Guard. Our chain of command was totally different. Our unit basically had nothing more to do with us. In a way, it felt like we were being given up for adoption by our Commander. Instead of having PT on our own (which I loved) we had PT everyday with the Regular Army folks. I thought this might work to my advantage with how hard I worked during PT, and I shortly earned some of their respect.

I soon realized that the 25th was influencing me with their pessimism and I recognized that this was the opposite of the norm. I decided to fight back. If anyone should be influencing anybody, it should be for the better. I decided to smile my way through it and look for the excitement in my work. I also decided to make it a point to say "hi" to everyone that I had met already. I found that I had to be very careful about that one though, because men can take a simple smile and hello the wrong way. So I made sure to stick with people I trusted.

What also helped me get through the negativity was having an outlet for my frustrations, including projects I will mention later in the book. Life did end up going a lot smoother as we all learned how to work together, at least to where it was pleasant around the Aid Station. We got used to the new schedule. I think what made it seem horrible before was how it was presented. It was a "work in progress" and things ended up going well. This deployment sure taught me a lot (and tested me), preparing me for things ahead. You can truly learn from everything. I proudly earned the nickname "Smiles" as I fought hard to turn a bad situation into good and found I was now influencing the others.

Duties at the Aid Station

Everyday we were working in the Aid Station. We had certain hours called "sick call" where soldiers would come if they were sick or injured. It was mainly run like a Family Clinic, being there for soldier support. We gave a lot of IVs and meds because it seemed the flu and cold symptoms spread fast in these conditions. Another problem we would see a lot dealt with the ears. Ears are critical when it comes to flying, and a lot of soldiers were taken off flight status because of the problems that would occur in the desert. Most were simply impacted with wax, but many did end up with ruptured ear drums. We soon became experts on how to treat these symptoms.

During the other hours, we were on call for emergencies. Every now and then, soldiers would come in with emergencies that we would take care of right away. It was wonderful working under a Flight Surgeon (Doc Smyrski) and PA (Doc McKay). The protocol would always start out with us assessing each soldier and then presenting it to the Doc. He would then tell us what we needed to do while he met with the soldier. We learned a lot on the spot and soon were able to do a lot of the assessments on our own and just tell the Doc what we thought was happening and how we planned to fix it. It was wonderful medical practice. Each week, the medics would rotate who was on nights. The crazy stuff always seemed to happen when I went on night shift for a week.

Journal entry on August 8, 2004: *I think I am cursed! Something seems to always happen when I am on night shift. I pulled nights all this last week. My first night on, our NCO-IC (the rough one to work with) at the Aid Station had a petit-mal seizure and fell onto the floor in his hooch. I heard he has had them ever since his aircraft that he was flying in (a Chinook) got shot down when we was last deployed here around two years ago. No wonder he knew so much about being a medic. I don't know all the details of what happened when he was flying. All I know is that it crash-landed and he had a seizure when it happened and has had them ever since. He doesn't even take PT tests anymore.*

Well, anyway, he had to get sent to Longstuhl, Germany to receive further testing (CT scan, since the hospital's scan here broke) and it turns out that he is not coming back. Our "boss" went back on to Hawaii to be monitored on anti-seizure medication. So that all took place in the first couple of nights.

The third night I got a warning from an Officer that we could have four pilots coming in that are part of a "class C" crash. I had no idea what all that really meant and wasn't allowed to know, but I just followed the orders of the Doc, getting everything ready for a lot of blood work and urine tests. It turns out the damage wasn't as bad as they thought, so it got called off.

My fourth night, a pilot came running in saying, "We need a medic quick! Someone just passed out on the rocks." I ran over with a litter and had the pilot radio the Doc. We carried the soldier back and took care of her.

My sixth night, Hammy came in with a bloody brown t-shirt held against his face and blood all down his pants and shirt. I thought he was trying out a moulage kit and pulling a prank on me, but he came right in and said, "Call the Doc now!"

It turned out there was a loose sheet of metal flapping around by his hooch and so he was trying to move it around to secure it. A gust of wind came and blew the sheet metal at Hammy and lacerated his forehead and cheek (kind of like Scar's scar on "The Lion King"). It just barely missed his eye. He got lucky. We had MAJ McKay (our PA) do the stitches since they were on the face. He ended up getting around 25 stitches (very close together because, again, they were on the face).

My seventh night, I was awakened early by someone saying that a guy fell on the floor who wasn't feeling so good. It didn't end up being anything big. He was coherent when I arrived with a litter. I assessed the scene and found no injury was incurred. So I am glad to be done with nights now. It will also be nice to get back to a regular schedule.

The hospital

Entering into the camp of the hospital was like entering a scene of the TV show *MASH*. The hospital was set up in tents, each ward connected by a hallway. They had an Emergency Room, Intensive Care Unit, Medical/Surgical unit, and three Operating Rooms. The aid station helped me practice documenting and doing some patient care but the hospital got me more experience with the patients and trauma, which I loved.

About 95 percent of the patients that we took care of were the locals of Afghanistan. I only did about three rotations (each being a week) at the hospital during my deployment, but I sure wish I'd had more. I learned so much while working with the nurses there, such as scrubbing in on some surgeries looking for bullets in gun shot wounds, assisting in amputations, working with Anesthesiologists, giving meds with IVs, and doing assessments. I felt like a sponge trying to soak in all that I could. I also got to work a few days with the FLA team, which is basically the military's ambulance team.

While I was doing a rotation with the FLA team, we got a call that a Medevac was coming in with just one "local national" that happened in on a mine explosion. He had chunks of skin missing from his fingers, elbows, and knees. His face was full of shrapnel wounds, and his airway was compromised from the wound injuries and some swelling.

They used a laryngoscope and put an ET tube in. It was cool. I saw the Doc give a subclavian vein IV central line. It seemed pretty difficult to do. We then got a call that a patient was coming in on the flight line. It turns out it was a little girl around four years old who had a high femur fracture. She was really holding strong and hardly crying at all, although when we put her in the FLA, she started crying and looked pretty scared. Wanting to comfort her, I started singing different children's songs to her. She didn't make a sound! It's amazing how music can be such a universal language.

We then got a call to pick up a burn patient at the gate. When we got there, he was already bandaged up and had an IV running in him. He ended up having circumferential 2nd degree burns on both hands and frontal/temporal parts of the face. Nothing was interfering with the airway so I put silvadene burn cream all over the burns. What a day!

My first rocket attack

I had only been asleep one night for about two hours when I heard the girls in my hut saying we needed to get out into the bunkers with our flak vest and Kevlar. I heard over the "big voice" system: "Red Alert, red alert, this is not a test, we are receiving indirect fire, get into your bunkers, red alert, red alert . . ."

I wasn't scared in the least, but I was wondering what might happen. All my gear was up at the Aid Station, and I couldn't make it up there so I just ran into the bunker like I was. I took a picture of us in the bunker. I didn't have my gear, but I had my camera. I made a mental note to never have that happen again.

There are bunkers all over the post. Your assigned bunker is usually within 50 yards or even 20 feet of where you are. We all just sat in the bunker hearing the voice system repeat the alarm. We heard a few rockets hit way off in the distance. The Taliban are a pretty bad aim. We were probably sitting in there for more than an hour, giving our numbers for accountability. We then got an "Amber Alert" which means high stage alert. We all got out because a 1SG said it was clear. We then learned, the hard way, we were not supposed to do that. Only the sweep teams are supposed to go out at that time and clear the areas. Kotter and I, though, headed up to the aid station to check in there. Most of the other medics were at the bunker there.

My first flight in country

I was able to get on my first flight on a Chinook! But not just any Chinook, it was the one that was going to go pick up Toby Keith. Yep, that's right, the country singer. I wish I was a huge fan, but he was a celebrity anyway, and I volunteered to be the medic on the mission. During the flight, I got to hang out at the back of the aircraft, harnessed in, of course, and dangle my feet off the end. We told the pilots to make it worth our while, so they did some sharp turns to the point where I was almost lying vertical.

Another female soldier rode with me and we had a riot. She asked to film me with her camera while we were sitting on the edge, so I did, but after filming for a bit the pilots did this gravity effect (like the feeling you get in an elevator, but multiplied by 50). I screamed like I was on my deathbed and it just happened to get on tape. The other soldier showed a few people. I got teased here and there, but I didn't mind at all. Hey, if it makes people laugh and in a better mood, I'm all for it.

I tried to get sent out to an FOB (Forward Operating Base) called Salerno. It's optional for us to go out to the FOB's and I told myself that I was never going to go. Then I thought of the kind of medical experience I would get out there. The medics see anywhere from 70 to 100 patients a day. I convinced myself to go, and within two hours of making that decision, I was scheduled on the flight. I guess when I make up my mind about things, I don't stop until I make it happen.

I also wanted to do it despite my family's strong feelings against it. I had told them how dangerous FOBs can be and they felt if it was optional to serve there, I shouldn't volunteer to go. The command ended up taking me off the flight because the threat level raised, and Salerno had just been hit by a rocket attack and four soldiers were injured. They were still receiving fire around the base (it's right by the borders of Pakistan), and I didn't ever end up being stationed there.

Journal entry on October 4, 2004: *The last two weeks have been pretty crazy! Monday, September 22nd, MAJ McKay was in Salerno wanting two medics to come down there to help him with four locals with GSW's (Gun Shot Wounds). Four of us ended up going (mainly because it was something different and we thought it would be exciting). Well, the patients ended up being completely stable, so we didn't have to do hardly a thing. But as we were waiting for clearance to take off, we were asked to take some soldiers back with us. We of course consented because we had enough room in our Chinook.*

But I was completely taken off guard when I saw that these soldiers were "Special Forces" KIA (killed in action). There were three coffins lined up in the middle with the U.S. flag draped over them. It threw me for a loop and I was heartbroken at the sight of that. When we landed, some SF guys were there to take the coffins. We saluted them as they carried them off. It sure didn't seem like enough. It was a sobering experience.

The next two nights we were rocketed again. The 1st night it landed in the airfield. Then the second night, as we were in a briefing, we heard a big BOOM and the building shook along with it. We all bolted outside and saw that it hit inside the compound, just a couple hundred feet from us. I headed straight for the aid station and got on all my gear. A few other medics and I headed to the area where it hit. We heard two were injured. I ran back to grab the Ambulance. One had some shrapnel wounds in his leg. It all opened our eyes a bit… the Taliban are getting better at aiming.

We also were told that a soldier in our unit was killed. I was the medic on scene. He happened to live in the hooch next to mine. That was a hard one to take for our unit. The soldier had a lot of close friends that he has worked with for years. You really become family when you are in the military and for some, it is all they have. The medics were all back up at the aid station trying to comfort those that were really close to him and help them out. I slept in another hooch that night as I kept a close eye on a few female soldiers who were close friends with the soldier that was killed. One kept on saying it was her fault when it wasn't anybody's fault and we were worried what she might do. It was hard to still play the medic/psychiatrist when I felt I needed help as well. I got scared a few times sleeping in an unfamiliar room. It was just so dark and the images replayed in my mind.

On one mission a plane went down and crashed into a mountain. There were three civilians that worked for Black Water Aviation and three soldiers from a Cavalry unit. We tried two attempts to go up there and get them at such a high altitude but were unsuccessful. The other medics got to fly on those ones but finally our third attempt (which I was on) we were able to get them. COL Smyrski, Kotter, and I went on this one for medical support, along with a Special Forces search and rescue team with tons of equipment. They dropped Kotter and I along with a few others off at Bamyan (another city), while the search and rescue team and COL Smyrski went to recover the bodies. The whole mission ended up happening quick. They were back within two hours. I never actually saw the bodies, just the bags they were in.

Sabo (another female in my hooch) and I were asked to sing the National Anthem at the Memorial Service in Shindand (where the Cavalry unit was stationed). We flew out on Thursday but couldn't land because of bad weather, so they postponed the services 24 hours. We flew out again on Friday. The service itself was really touching. It is an honor that they asked us to do that but still one of the hardest things I will ever do...

Roll Call

I was asked to sing at certain ceremonies in Bagram, which was flattering and an honor (they only knew I could sing because I was always singing in the Aid Station). But when my friend, Sabo, and I were asked to sing the National Anthem at a Memorial Service, our anthem took on a whole new meaning. I would like to describe to you a little of what takes place in a military Memorial Service:

Sabo and I would begin with the National Anthem. We would also sing the third verse of the Anthem because we felt it had a powerful message, especially at a time such as this:

"And conquer we must, when our cause it is just. And this be our motto, in God is our Trust!"

An invocation would be given and then a few soldiers who were close to the one who had been killed would stand and share some good memories. The First Sergeant would then get up. He would start calling out soldiers' names that were members of the same squad of the soldier that was just killed. One by one each soldier would stand up in the audience in random places.

Finally, the First Sergeant would get to the deceased soldier's name. There was no answer. He would say it again . . . no answer. The First Sergeant would say it for the third time and you would see some of the toughest soldiers in there hanging their heads in silence. It was tough to realize that someone we were serving next to a couple of days before was now no longer with us, and that at any day it could happen to one of us. The silence was so thick you could almost bear it no longer. Then it was broken by the sound of a trumpet playing "Taps." I don't think I will be able to listen to that song again without remembering those who I have served with.

The Enduring Faith Chapel

We actually had the opportunity to go to church in Afghanistan! They had services for every denomination. Mine only lasted two hours there, even though at home it was regularly three hours. They assigned me to be "the greeter" handing out the programs and shaking every soldier's hand that walked through the door. It was the highlight of my week when I was able to go to the meetings. There were probably 100 people there each Sunday. Singing the hymns during the meeting was my favorite part. It was like singing with a men's choir every time, since there were rarely more than three women there. Sometimes my voice would become hoarse by the end because I was singing as loud as I could to make sure a female voice was heard. I had to represent!

The Bazaar

They had a bazaar every week on Friday just outside the camp gate. The people were selling rugs, fur coats, leather jackets, wooden antique chests, vases, gems, jewelry, watches, antiques, and mainly DVDs! Weapons (guns, knives and swords) were a popular item among the soldiers as a lot of them were antiques. (Who really knew if they were authentic or not?) I bought a lot of wooden decorations, a favorite in my family, and I would send them home. I tried not to buy too many things there. I did, however, get hooked on the TV series "24" and after watching two seasons, I wrote an email back to my friends and family:

Subject: TFA
"Twenty Four" Anonymous
"Hello. My name is Jill Stevens."
"Hello Jill," replies the audience.
"And, well, I have to confess that I broke down and watched the first episode of the television series "24" (gasps from the audience). Yes, yes, I know! And now two seasons later, I have come to the realization that I have wasted 48 hours of my life. I have come to face reality that I have fallen to the dark side. But I plead now, to those of you who have been more productive with your time, to stay your course. Do not give in to such an edge of your seat, jaw hanging, heart pumping, wide eyed, suspenseful thriller. DO NOT succumb to the dark side (looks of questionable terror from the audience). I know that some of you may not understand, but take my word for it. There is more to life than finding out if Jack Bauer comes out in the end, saving the world from another terrorist. You might be thinking to yourself, oh, the good guys always win in the end. Yes, that is true in the television wonderland, but how it is done is the weapon used to suck the viewer in. Whatever you do, do not ask that question to yourself. If ever you find yourself in that situation, turn off your television immediately and back away slowly. Do not turn it back on for at least two weeks."
"What about Oprah or Dr. Phil?" someone interrupts.
"I'm sorry, but the temptation is too great if the TV is on at all. It must be off. To those of you who have fallen, as I have, my deepest sympathies go out to you. Come forward now before the fourth season starts and you will have wasted 96 hours of your life . . . come back to the light! (Weeping and sniffs from the audience.) Thank you."
"Jill, I think you made a breakthrough . . . you are an inspiration to us all!"
P.S. Can you tell that *Findng Nemo* is one of my favorite movies?

The Egyptian Army

There were many different nationalities that served on the base, but the ones we ran into the most, and grew to love, were the Egyptians. They had a hospital set up to take care of the Afghanistan people. Many came through at certain hours of the day because the Egyptians had a gate that opened to the local community.

When CW5 Layne Pace (an officer who made a lot of things happen—you will hear a lot more about him) found out about this, he cleared it with the Egyptians to visit twice a week and give humanitarian aid to the people, which usually consisted of supplies sent to us from families and friends or perhaps even schools.

My first time at the gate, I was a little taken aback at how aggressive the locals were. There were no manners with them. Pace, others and I had to watch them carefully (1) for our safety and (2) for fairness that no one person got more than their share. We found that we had to be aggressive right back and start setting some rules like setting up a line and teaching them to wait their turn until we handed them something. Rules, of course, were only meant to be broken. It was a work in progress. This was my first interaction with the local people.

I wasn't able to make it every week because of my duty as a medic but joined the others when I could. Keeping up this tradition, we started to build a really close relationship with the Egyptian Army. We would go back to their camp more often, just to visit with them. There weren't that many Egyptians there. Maybe 100 at the most and five of those were females. The females were the nurses to take care of the locals that needed further medical attention.

When I visited there a couple times a week with Pace, I looked forward to seeing the nurses, watching their style of medical care and interacting with them more and more. After a few months, we soon became dear friends and would get together often for dinner at the American Chow Hall (one of about three that you could eat at).

I even had a "Girls Night Out" with the Egyptian nurses. They took me into their hut that they lived in, it looking quite similar to ours, but decorated and designed much differently. We did all the typical things during a Girls Night, but speaking in completely different languages and not understanding a word each other was really saying as we showed each other our favorite weapons, etc.

That's normal, right? My favorite part of the night, and I believe theirs too, was when they had me put on what I thought looked like an oversized night gown with a sash at the waist. They put purple lipstick on me and a headband.

The ensemble was not complete until they taught me the "Egyptian Yell." If only we could have a sound button put into this book. The yell sounds like what we would do as our Indian call—high-pitched using the tongue to shake the sound. I've heard these girls use it before. They use this yell in times of excitement. I have never met a more generous people.

The Korean Army

The Koreans also had a camp on Bagram as well as a hospital where I actually became a patient. It all started with one of my good female friends in the 25th who was actually Korean. She would visit the camp all of the time, eating at their chow hall and such. She invited me a few times and I became acquainted with a lot of the Koreans. I also met a lot of the doctors and medical staff.

They showed me around and one of the doctors mainly focused on acupuncture. I was intrigued and started asking a lot of questions. I was grateful he could speak English very well (I really need to learn the other languages . . . maybe one day).

Well, I told him about a knee problem I was having and he said acupuncture would definitely help with that. So I soon found myself as a patient in their hospital. I would go about once a week for five weeks. The doctor stuck about four needles in each knee. Then after a while he would hook up these cords to each needle. It kind of looked like he was hooking up jumper cables to my knees. This electrical current would shoot through my knees. It was a weird feeling. In the end, I'm not sure if I had better knees due to acupuncture or because of all the things I was doctoring them up with, but I did end up with some great friends in the Korean Army.

Running through a minefield

Running remained a great hobby of mine while deployed (which is partly why my knees were bothering me) and a great outlet for dealing with any frustrations I might have had. In a way, running became a new target to keep focused on, especially when someone brought to my attention that they were going to have the first ever marathon in Afghanistan. Okay, okay . . . you don't have to twist my arm. This would soon become my fifth marathon.

Being an avid runner, one of the first questions I asked when landing in Afghanistan was, "Where am I even allowed to run?" When I asked some of the departing medics that question, they said, "We made a six-mile route around the perimeter of the base during our tour of duty here."

"Sweet!" I replied. "Thanks for doing that. I'll try it out tomorrow."

"Just watch where you step, though, because it is through a minefield," added one of the medics. Everyone in the Aid Station instantly stopped what they were doing and looked up at him.

"You're kidding, right?" I asked hesitantly, realizing that he probably wasn't.

"No, but if you stick to running in the center of the path, you should be okay. There have been some close calls with some soldiers running on the side of the path, and it didn't work out too well for them."

I didn't really know how to respond to that, but I took their advice and decided to give the route a try. The route was a rocky, dirt road (much like the whole country) with a line of barbed wire on each side and little red signs every now and then that read, "MINES." It was a bit of a culture shock for me.

Someone gave me some information at the end of October 2004 that they were going to have the first-ever marathon in Afghanistan. That left me six weeks to train, and I felt I could do it. Folks, do not try this at home.

The inaugural marathon in Afghanistan took place in Tarin Kout (FOB Ripley). Why that base was ever chosen, I have no idea. This marathon was sponsored by the "Honolulu Marathon" because almost all of the 25th Infantry Division was deployed to Afghanistan and are based out of Hawaii. Some of the soldiers had run that marathon when at home, so they wanted to continue the tradition in Afghanistan. A few of them got to work on it and pulled it off.

I went out to try my first long run. The only way to fit it into my schedule was to get up around 0330, to start by 0400. Being in a combat zone, you don't necessarily have a lot of lights around to brighten up the place. You shouldn't ever give the enemies any help in picking you out. So there I was, running through a minefield, pitch black, squinting my eyes to see where I was going so I didn't end up off the rocky path into the minefield just five feet to my sides. And on my first long run, it was foggy! I soon found that desert fog was very thick because of the dust and dirt. I actually got lost a few times on the route and had to start walking slowly in circles to find the right path.

My battle buddies sometimes asked why I was putting myself through such torture, because my training was going so rough. There were times when I would come back with blood running down my leg because I face-planted it while I was running. (This seems to be a common theme in my life.) I kept at it, though, because it is not my style to quit.

The weekend of the race came and the runners were to meet up the day before at 0730. There were 75 of us coming from Bagram and Kabul that were waiting at the "terminal" to get on the flight out. Well, after a few hours of waiting, it was announced that it rained in Tarin Kout two days earlier and the runway was still too slick to land on with a C-130 so "no one is going."

We were all speechless and didn't really know what to think. We had been training a few months for this (okay, maybe just a few weeks for some). A few people started suggesting that we could get a race together quickly here in Bagram and run it the next day. We hung out for a little bit and found out that there was another possibility to get there. Finally about 1330, we boarded a C-130 that took us to Kandahar where we stayed in "transient tents." Take into account that the race was the following morning, and we weren't even there yet.

We were told to be out at the flight line the next morning at 0300.

I think the soldiers thought if we froze to death out there then we wouldn't be stupid enough to run a marathon. It was freezing and we stood out there shivering for more than two hours. This whole time while traveling we were wearing our body armor, helmet, carrying our weapon with 270 rounds of ammo, and our luggage. Talk about trying to rest up before a marathon!

We finally got on Chinooks that flew us to Tarin Kout. We got there three hours before the race started. When we got off the Chinooks, we started getting briefed right away about the course and the agenda for the next three hours. We got our race packets, turned in our weapons, and finally dropped off our gear at our tents after about a mile of walking with it all around the base. We quickly ran to the chow hall to get some food in us, ran back to the tents to change into running clothes, and then took off to the starting line. I got there 45 minutes before the race started. I felt like I had already run my marathon. What a rush!

I was kind of nervous for the race because I didn't have the mental preparation of what the course was, like I usually do. It turned out that the rain a few days before was a blessing, though, because it compacted all the "moon dust" and part of the course was gravel. It was perfect to run on.

The actual terrain had a few up and down humps (what goes up must come down) and then one really "good" hill. So that means we had five really good hills, since the route was 5.24 miles long and we had to run around it five times to complete the 26.2 miles. My favorite part of the course was on the top of the hill because the view was spectacular. You could see for miles and what a sight it was.

I felt pretty strong the first three laps, but then I felt the "burn" and fatigue kick in. The fifth lap, well . . . I was so tempted to yell out to the security guards, "Target practice right here. Please just end the misery." I ended up walking up the hill that fifth time.

I almost quit. The course was the roughest I've done, (probably because it was through a minefield). I didn't know how I was going to finish. I tried to tell myself, "I have done this before, and I can do this now" but the mental battle wasn't working its magic.

Then the full impact of what I was actually doing hit me! Here I was, a woman, running in a country where women are degraded and demoralized. Feelings of anger, frustration, and guilt came over me as I thought about how these women are treated. Then, feelings of pride came over me. I was proud to be an American woman and even more proud to be an American soldier helping to fight for these women and their worth.

A sudden drive came over me that helped carry me through to the finish. With every step, the thought of those beautiful women pushed me to go harder and not give up. I did it for them. These women taught me courage, as they continued on even though they are disrespected by everyone around them. They believed in themselves enough to carry them through the hardships.

I ended up finishing in 3:45:19. I couldn't believe I ended up being the first female to cross (granted, there weren't that many females . . . I believe 30 or so) and then seventh overall out of the 187 runners! I was done! I actually finished a marathon in Afghanistan.

We had an awards ceremony during dinner that night and I got a yellow water bottle for my first place prize. I'm glad it was yellow so I pretend it's really a "gold medal." I thought it was pretty funny.

What was even funnier was that I made it on the front page of the Deseret News in Utah: "There goes SPC Jill Stevens sprinting to the finish line . . ." but it was actually a picture of another girl! It was hilarious! I'm sure a lot of people in Utah that knew me were surprised at how much I had changed in Afghanistan.

Running for a cause became a great target for me to focus on while serving in this combat zone, but there were a few other targets that I concentrated on while I was there that really helped me make the best of my situation.

Before heading out on one of my many convoys during training at Fort Carson.

Here I am 4-wheeling in a Humvee with night vision goggles. This rocks!

I had my hair in these tight braids to keep my hair out of my eyes. It was very convenient for me but I guess it was against the rules and I found this out the hard way. I wish I was politely corrected but I was not and was told to remove them immediately. Well, this is what my hair did... this would be a good look to sport around. Maybe I could be the Army's new secret weapon. "If looks could kill . . ."

All of the Task Force wings, medics, and docs.

Getting decorative at war with my room. That shirt stayed up the whole deployment besides the time I ran the marathon in it. It's all good.

This was my favorite sign. I so badly wanted to take this home. It kind of has a double meaning. I'll let you figure that one out.

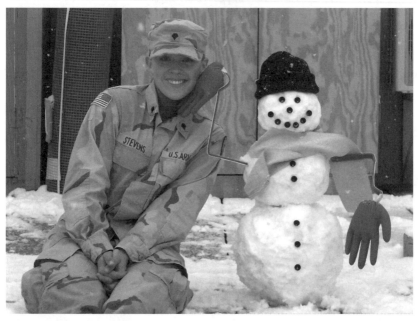

Having fun during the cold winter months decorating a snow man out of medical supplies.

I felt so important when I got to wear this headset on all of the flights.
I would key into the pilots about every two minutes . . .
"Pilots, this is Medic one-niner, just checkin' if you guys are okay."
"Stevens, nothing has changed in the last two minutes!"
"Come on, guys! Just play along!"

122

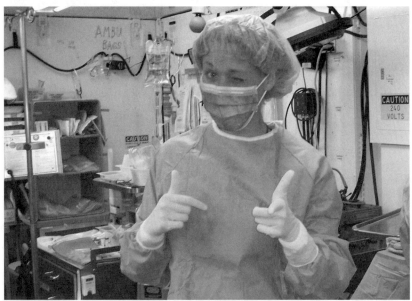

"Scrubbin' in" as a nurse in a few surgeries at the U.S. Army Hospital.

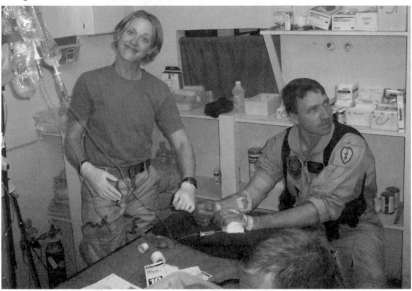

Another wonderful day at the aid station. We were getting really good at IVs with dehydrated soldiers coming in.

During my Girls Night Out with the Egyptian nurses when they dressed me up and taught me their yell.

The Egyptian nurses became my dear friends.

124

Feelin' pumped to run the Afghanistan Marathon after very little rest.

I'm about to reach for some water. I was trying to keep positive through the pain.

A few other women and I getting ready to board the C-130 after the marathon.

CHAPTER 8

JILLYBEAN
THE BAKING QUEEN

I wasn't the best at any particular target practice really, but I do know that having a goal, or target, is essential in all aspects of life. It was no different for me when I was called up to serve in Afghanistan. It could have been a terrible 17 months away from home, a rotten interruption in my education, a worrisome time for my family and even a scary situation for me as a soldier helping to fight the war on terrorism. But instead I tried to set some goals about what I wanted to accomplish and then worked to keep my target in view, to make the best of my situation. I found this by doing something I absolutely love!

I love to bake and soldiers just love to eat! So it was a win-win situation. We had electricity over there, so I had this genius thought, "Mom, send me a bread machine!" And with technology these days, these bread machines actually have a "cake mode" on them to bake cakes. I was in my element.

So, whenever I heard a soldier was having a bad day (which was often, being in a combat zone) or maybe their birthday was coming up, I would try to bake them a fresh, homemade loaf of bread or a cake. After a few months of this I earned the nickname "Jillybean the Baking Queen."

Baking had always been a huge stress reliever for me. One reason was because I usually got to eat the product afterward. But I also figured that if I loved this so much, others probably do as well. I found joy in making someone's day, which truly made mine.

I would often have friends and family send me certain bread mixes and necessary utensils. I also got my hands on a toaster oven which was a wonderful addition to my kitchen. I had mini-loaf pans sent so I could make more individualized cakes. My chef's hat was also sent to me and this truly completed the ensemble.

Birthdays

My commander's office (called the HHC CP) became my hangout place and a second kitchen for me to work in. For one, they had food and snacks that we could eat; two, they had a phone with NO TIME LIMIT; and three, "Skipper" (CPT Akre) and Top (1SG Skousen) were pretty hilarious! I got over there at least twice a day. I would grab a handful of Tootsie Rolls (which I was addicted to) to help dose me up for the day.

October 29th was Top's birthday. A few others and I were trying to get something together for Top's birthday coming up. A lot of people helped out to make his day a good but funny one. I showed up in the morning to make him scones for breakfast. That was sure fun. I just love coming up with something and actually having it work. Top and I baked a chocolate cake the night before in his bread machine. I came by a lot on his birthday to cook some brownies and spice cake for a party we were having that night. Quite a few people showed up, but we were able to feed most. It was a fun day.

Journal entry on February 28, 2005: *Happy Birthday to me! I can't believe I am 22 years old and I am entirely too blessed! My morning started with a PT test and the medics wished me a Happy Birthday. I did decent on my PT test (71 push-ups, 97 sit-ups and 13:32, 2-mile). I was just really excited that it was behind me . . . I put too much pressure on myself on the PT tests.*

Just after the PT test, I walked into our CP and totally face-plant it as I am walking in. I got a good laugh out of everyone so I started things off right that day. But it just got better . . .

After the evening sick-call was over, we were told that we had orders to be addressed by our Commander over in our CP. As I walked in though, all the lights were out but some Christmas lights. (I guess we never took them down.) The lights flipped on with a big "SURPRISE!" yelled by my close friends, who were really like my family out there. My 1st Sergeant made me 2 cakes actually, one carrot and one chocolate with frosting on each. Spelled out on the carrot cake was, "JILLY" with Jellie Bellies and on the chocolate, "BEAN." For a gift, they gave me "The Afghan Cookery" Recipe Book. I was so excited! But when I opened it up, everyone had signed in it. I was actually at a loss for words. That meant a lot to me. I knew there was a lot of thought that went in to that.

Holidays

I also decorated for most holidays to make our military base seem more like home. Some might think this task is impossible, but ah, where there is a will there is a way. My family likes to joke, where there is a Jill there is a way. With Halloween soon approaching us, I thought it would be great to have pumpkins around. There was really only one problem with that though—we lived in a desert and with that comes a lack of vegetation. Yet we had plenty of rocks!

I had this genius thought, "Mom, send me some paint!" So I painted these rocks to look like pumpkins. And just like you would do at home, I set these pumpkins (five of them) out in front of our Aid Station. I would have set them in front of my home, but I lived in an area where there wasn't a lot of traffic and, let's face it, being the Aid Station, we had plenty of traffic walking by.

I guess some soldiers really caught on to the Halloween spirit. As I walked up to the aid station later, I found my pumpkins hidden around the area. I had to go track them down and put them back. My soldier buddies decided to have some fun, and almost every day I went to work, I would find that my pumpkins had been moved around and placed in different situations. One day, I found the pumpkins in a circle playing a card game with the cards dealt out to each pumpkin. I loved it!

The culprits actually ended up making one of their own pumpkins. It was still a regular rock with just a face drawn on it. They called theirs the "King pumpkin" and so when I went into work another day, I found my pumpkins in a class formation with the King pumpkin "schooling" my pumpkins. I quickly switched that scenario because I thought that wasn't right. I couldn't wait to get to work everyday just to see what my pumpkins were going to be doing.

My favorite scenario, though, was when I showed up to find that one pumpkin was in the middle of a litter, while the 4 other pumpkins laid at each handle like they were carrying the litter with the "injured pumpkin." I'm kind of partial to medical things and that made a medic proud. It was hilarious! I left that one up for a few days. It sure made my month to see other soldiers get involved like that.

We had a Halloween get-together on October 30th at the Chapel Annex. People brought what costumes they came up with or small ones (hats, wigs, etc.) they had family send. I took a photo with all of my small costume accessories on and sent it to friends and family to have a contest to see if they could guess the right amount of costumes I was wearing. We watched *The Haunted Mansion* for the party with some snacks.

On actual Halloween, which was a Sunday, I wore my clown nose around. I got yelled at once, but I put it right back on when they weren't around. It was pretty fun to wear the clown nose while dodging high-ranking people who were caught up too much in the rules. I also wore it while passing out programs and greeting people as they came to church. It seemed to make people smile, which is what I try to do.

We also have a tradition in my family where we have a "Thankful Tree." We usually get a really small, leafless tree and each day during the month of November, we fill out one "paper leaf" with one thing that we are thankful for. So by Thanksgiving Day, you have yourself a Thankful Tree.

I wanted to continue this tradition in Afghanistan. Of course, I ran into that same problem we had with the pumpkins—a lack of vegetation. So I called my mom and said, "Send me some poster board and construction paper!" She really backed me up with a lot of my ideas and I couldn't have done it without her. I constructed this tree out of brown poster board. It took a lot of creativity as I used three different posters. Everyday I would carry around 20-30 paper leaves that I cut out. I would hit up the different soldiers in their working areas to fill out one leaf with one thing that they were thankful for. I once walked into an office and one soldier spoke out, "Great! Not you again! I'm not thankful for anything today! You can give my leaf to someone else."

Of course that didn't settle with me and I would try to kindly remind them of some ideas. "Come on, you're thankful for something. How about flushing toilets, warm showers . . ."

It probably wasn't too smart to be pushing the buttons of a soldier, but it was cool to see the light click on inside of them when they realized how much they should be thankful for. By the end of the month, the tree was overflowing with leaves.

Most of the leaves were filled with family members' names or kids that were born while the father was overseas. The tree actually stayed up the rest of our deployment. Soldiers would continue to walk by it, and the tree became more of a motivation and strength to us, reminding us of our many blessings.

"Over the Hump" party

I kind of felt like the "Activities Coordinator" for Bagram with all that I was doing. Once we hit about mid-October, we were on the downhill side to our year-long deployment. So a couple of days before the "day" I decided to throw an "Over the Hump" party. I got together a big Family Feud game. I made a survey and sent it around to 50 soldiers. I got about 23 back, which was better than I expected. I filled out the answers and categories on sheets of paper and pinned them on the wall. The categories I made were:

Hottest item at the PX: (in ranking order) chocolate, soda pop, chips, cookies, and light bulbs.

Worst places to be during a Rocket Attack: Port-o-Potties, showers, in bed, PX and talking to spouse at home.

Hottest wheels driving on Bagram: the "Gator," the "6-wheeler," the Blazer, Hemmitt (fueling truck), and Jingle trucks (what the locals drove).

A parched tongue's top choice for bottled water (that's all we could drink and brush our teeth with. We had a few different brands): Emirates, Nestle, Jeema, Tylos, Hayat.

Pick your favorite type of salute: "National Guard" wave, vertical, elbow (basically using your whole arm as you bring your hand to your head), and "fast motion."

Most quoted lines you hear from the locals: "Bahksheesh!" (gift), "Hey Misses/Mr.", "For you no problem", "Money change", and "My friend."

Worst things you could be wearing when running into the Command Sergeant Major: Brown shirt with PT shorts, civilian clothes, flip flops, no PT belt, and birthday suit.

Rules you hate to follow made by Division: No PT's in chow hall/PX/Church, no brown shirt with PT shorts, mandatory PT belt with PT uniform, no taking food from chow hall, and saluting in a combat zone.

The meals your taste buds seem to only taste at the chow hall: BBQ mystery meat over rice, baked chicken, meatballs, hotdogs, and mystery soup.

Hottest sought after items at the Bazaar: DVDs, junk, rugs, watches, swords/knives, and rifles.

What do you do to occupy your "down time": Playing computer/video games, reading, hanging out with friends, watching movies, and hiding so they won't find something to occupy your down time.

Best outdoor competition game: Volleyball, basketball, dodge ball, hiding from the Chaplain, and flight line drag racing.

I also started getting big muffins from the chow hall so we could have an eating contest. I snuck out 10 at one time. I was a little nervous about being caught but I lucked out. My First Sergeant decided to make a joke out of it and put up "Most Wanted" signs on a few buildings for the "Muffin Bandit" and had my picture blown up on it. It was pretty funny. I had another soldier make a slide show to sum up what we had done the past six months, and the party ended up being a big hit. What a relief!

Girls Night Out

I figured it was time for the few girls to have a "night out on the town." There were about 50 females in our Aviation Regiment to the 700 males. I made a flyer with these words on it: "*Let's get away from all of this overproduction of testosterone surrounding us. It's time for girl talk. Let's unite! A night to let it all hang out and run free; skin tight buns, neatly ironed uniforms, and bloused boots are not permitted. Come chill to get away from it all, to actually feel like a girl and not a soldier for a night. Hope you can come, it wouldn't be the same without ya!"*

The night ended up being a blast. This was the first time I can recall ever painting my nails and doing a facial. We watched some movies, turned up the music and danced the night away, making fools of ourselves—a true girls night.

NFS: Not For Stevens

I knew when deploying to Afghanistan that I would be associating with soldiers who might not be very religious and possibly didn't really have the highest standards for themselves. I was going to be with them for over a year and wanted to make sure I never deviated from the standards that I set for myself.

My colleagues didn't necessarily share that same point of view, but that doesn't mean they didn't look out for me. Remember Hammy? The one on the SWAT team? He just loved to tell stories and jokes about when he was chasing down the bad guys. He was always the hero, of course.

And every story that's told in the Army has got to start out with the words, "There I was . . ." you even have to say it with that southern drawl, otherwise, the story is just not going to be as good. So my friend says, "There I was . . ." and I knew we were in for another good cop story.

But then, as he got into it, Hammy paused and said, "Stevens, plug your ears," and so I did exactly that. It turns out that he was repeating words that were yelled by one of the criminals in his story that he knew I didn't like to say or hear. Well, from then on, we had a new rating at our Aid Station called NFS: Not For Stevens.

Whenever an off-color joke or story was going to be told or someone was going to say something inappropriate, they would warn me by saying, "Oh, this is NFS" and then I would leave the room or plug my ears. I loved it! I would walk into a room of people who were watching a movie and ask what they were watching and their reply would sometimes be, "Sorry, you can't watch it, it's NFS" or "Yeah, this one's good, it's FS" (For Stevens).

Actually the evening of Top's birthday there were about 40 of us gathered in the CP. Some other officers ended up making a funny memorandum to read out. They called out "Attention to Orders" and all of us in the room jumped up to the position of attention. The other officer gets ready to read the funny memorandum and starts off saying, "By the way, this memo is NFS."

Some people had confused looks on their faces, but most started laughing and I just waved to them. I said, "Oh, that's my cue. Let me know when you're done," and I waited outside on the steps while they read it and I heard them rolling with laughter. They came and got me about five minutes later and the party continued. Soldiers came up to me later that night and said, "You know, that memo was funny, but I sure wish I would have left with you."

I learned a valuable lesson that day: that even the smallest things make a difference to people. Someone IS always watching, and I'm glad that I have learned to be comfortable in being the "odd" one.

I believe taking on the role of "morale booster" helped the other soldiers, but it also helped me keep my own morale high while serving in this combat zone. My aim to bring joy and service to those around me wasn't limited to just the soldiers, but broadened to creating joy among the war-torn people of Afghanistan.

Experimenting with my favorite . . . No-Bake Cookies. This is too much fun!

This was the window to my room. I tried to go for the whole "Suzie Homemaker" or "Martha Stewart" look here.

Painting the rocks to look like pumpkins in my room.

My pumpins took on lives of their own, helping to transport injured pumpkins and even playing cards. It was fun to come to work each morning and see what my pumpkins were up to next.

Our "Thankful Tree"! I was really proud how it turned out.

A few weeks later, leaves filled the branches and became a great motivator for us.

CHAPTER 9

OUTSIDE THE WIRE

I was lucky to have the opportunity to go on a few missions among the people. I only wish I could have had more. But being in an Aviation unit, convoy missions, or anything else on the ground, aren't essentially your focus. Fortunately, besides the few instances of being among the locals on base through the Egyptian Army, I was able to get on some great missions "outside the wire."

Kandahar

While working in the Aid Station one day, Doc Smyrski came in and told all the medics to gather round immediately. He told us of some circumstances occurring in Kandahar. Missions were picking up and they were receiving more combat from the Taliban. So they needed more medical help. "Who wants to volunteer?" Doc asked.

Judd and I raised our hands. I was really excited to get out of Bagram. I needed a break from the camp for a while. We were to be gone for three weeks and needed to be packed and ready to go in 30 minutes. Whoa! Well, we got ready to go and then stood out at the Black Hawk for two hours while they tried to figure out a packing issue. Yep, it ended up being postponed until EARLY the next morning. So I had time to actually organize my packing.

Once in Kandahar, Judd and I settled in different tents that were the size of circus tents, it seemed, although the female section was just a small roped-off corner of one of the larger tents. We helped out at the aid station and then finally got our lucky break to get on a few great missions.

Journal entry on July 1, 2004: *Another month and a great month this has started out to be. Today was a good day! I got to go on my first mission outside the gate. It was a convoy of nine vehicles. About four were for security and the rest were medical people. I came along (I volunteered myself and Judd to come, I kinda broke a few rules getting on with them… oh well) to help with two other females helping the local women (cause only females are allowed to help females). We had a small room for them in one of the Afghan buildings in the village Haji Tuti. It was only around 8-10 miles from our post in Kandahar. When the women came in, they were allowed to take off their burkas to the point of showing their face.*

We had a female interpreter named Sarah with us who helped tremendously. We couldn't have done it without her. The women seemed so innocent, all so beautiful in their own way. As you look at them, you can tell that they have so much culture from others that are mixed in… a little Russian, etc. Some of them look very similar to the people I have seen in the States and yet they are here suffering, living in conditions like this. Not so much where they live, but how they live. A woman was put in prison for 14 days because she shook someone's hand. Others because they spoke when they weren't supposed to, or looked at someone (uncovering their face), etc.

I feel so sorry for these women. I want so badly to give them a better life, show them what they are worth and that they are Daughters of God, precious and loved. I was saddened at the thought that I had to turn some of the women down when they asked for medical help because we had to go. We were just doing basic care for fevers, colds, aches, and pains, cuts, skin care, etc. Some would come in with crying babies asking for something to help. We are definitely trying.

After a few weeks in Kandahar helping support the missions, it was time to head back "home." Yet what I saw in Kandahar and how I felt being among the people stayed with me. I wanted to be with them every day helping them the way we did. I found that I wasn't the only one who wanted to do all I could while I was there and help these people in a non-militant way. A few soldiers in my unit shared this same desire. It was already being done in many small ways, but I found one who wanted to do it on a larger scale, Layne Pace. He took the bull by the horns. Obstacles with Army regulations may have slowed him down a bit, but he always found a way to better the lives of the people. I couldn't help but join him.

There were many ways we found to perform humanitarian service once we knew who to talk to. It started small with local villages near the base but then grew to remote ones across the country. I became a part of the Humanitarian Committee there along with Pace and a few others. I was sort of the medical representative.

We actually involved some of the soldiers' families back in the U.S. to help us collect necessary items and ship them over. We were expecting lots of shipments to be made (medical and dental supplies, school supplies, clothes, shoes, candy, and hygiene items). I was so excited to be a part of it! Little did I know how much one village could impact my life.

Jegdalek

Pace learned about a village called Jegdalek (one that we decided to "adopt") that was really suffering from a lack of resources. We did a lot of humanitarian missions there and a few of those also included medical services. We met with the "Elders" (leaders) of the village to get acquainted with them, "make nice" with them, and let them know what we wanted to do during that visit and future visits to come. We had one interpreter with us named Shah to help us communicate. They were very accommodating and willing to work with us.

While on these humanitarian missions we would fill half of the Chinook with large pallets of products. We landed at the top of a hill in Jegdalek and after talking with the Elders for almost an hour trying to get everything clear, we would haul the boxes down the hill in a line involving the local men. We put them in a room in an unfinished building. The locals would be gathered in the hallway of the same building and a few at a time would be sent into the room to be given clothes, school supplies, shoes, etc. Basically anything would be helpful. This room was where I was usually stationed.

While on these missions, a lot of soldiers were simply there to do their soldier duty and perform the mission. I was too, don't get me wrong. Yet when I landed I was more like, "Let's play!" I wanted to learn all that I could there being among the people and learning about their culture.

The kids were who I spent the most time with. At first it was difficult to communicate with them. We spoke completely different languages and grew up in different parts of the world. I struggled with that. I would pray to find ways to connect with these kids. Finally I found a way.

As I was in the room handing out some of the supplies, I started to hear lots of yelling and screaming by both locals and soldiers. I peeked out of the room into the hallway and saw mass chaos... Fists in the air, kids screaming and getting trampled over, people kicking each other just trying to get to the front of the line. Our security guards were trying to keep it somewhat under control, which was taking a lot of work. All of a sudden, one of the soldiers yelled, "STEVENS! Get over here quick!"

I grabbed my aid bag, figuring someone must have been injured. I ran into the hallway asking who was injured and needed my help.

"No one's seriously hurt, yet," he said, "but we need your help in controlling the crowd."

I looked at him a little confused. "Okay, do you see the lack of muscle on me?" I asked. "There's a reason I'm not a security guard."

"Work your magic in some way," he replied. I guess they expected me to entertain the crazy crowd (I suppose being weird has its advantages). I turned to the crowd and my jaw just dropped as I looked at everybody pushing each other.

I started to point at them and yell "Kinai" which means sit down. It didn't work at all. I could barely hear myself. After staring for a bit, a thought came to mind and I just went with it—I made a funny face. I squished my face together and started pulling weird formations with my lips. Their reaction took me by surprise.

The men were mid-punch, mid-kick, and mid-headlock, but they just stopped and stared, looking at me. So I continued with the funny faces, pulling pig faces and such. There they were, jaws dropped, just staring back at me. I thought, "Okay, am I really that hideous?"

The monkey face seemed to get the biggest reactions and laughs.

I was really hoping they would make the faces back, but nope, they just continued to stare. It did the job, however, and I guess I was the new security guard for the Army that day.

Yet another embarrassing moment

After having been in Jegdalek for a few hours, I really had to go to the bathroom. I leaned over to Layne Pace and Shah (the interpreter) and whispered to them, asking where I could go. I didn't want to draw attention to myself because we were among the men of the village, conversing about many different subjects, mainly politics and war.

Shah got worried and said, "We need to find you a place now." He started asking all of the men where I could go to the bathroom (which is exactly what I didn't want to happen). All of them piped up and it looked like it was turning into an argument. Some of them started smiling and giggling.

Finally six of them escorted me, just so I could go to the bathroom. We hiked down to another building, their so-called pharmacy, where they had an exam room and a little room for a bathroom, which was really just a sectioned-off place with a hole in the ground. This experience was humiliating and hilarious all at the same time.

A Cinderella story

The little girls finally came to me after I was in the village for about two hours. Young girls were able to run around in public, but we guessed about the age of 14, they had to be in the homes and covered up. As we were there, I noticed a girl with a severe case of Congenital Esotropia (we just called it "Lazy Eye" at first). When we got back to Bagram, we realized that we could probably fix that for her. Within a couple of days and a lot of phone calls, we had it all worked out with the U.S. eye surgeon and the Egyptian eye surgeon on base. A flight was even scheduled to pick her up. The only catch was that no one in her village knew about our plans.

We arrived in Jegdalek and started talking to the Elders of the village again. It was difficult discussing the politics with them and determining who was actually in charge. The first couple of hours were spent discussing problems between us, our interpreters, and a lot of the local men. We still were at our landing zone and hadn't even made it down the hill to the actual village.

Some locals would try to sneak up as we were working out the problems. I tried to just pass the time and I saw the kids start to gather from their homes down below. A lot of the kids recognized me. I was so happy that they did. As they were staring at me, I waved from the top of the hill that we landed on and they got all excited. We had a lot of fun, but once the big discussion with the Elders was behind us, we found the little girl and her father. Once they found out we were taking them back to get her eyes fixed, they went home and got her changed into her "nicest" dress and combed her hair all pretty. Her name was Halima. Little did I know how much this girl would impact my life.

After I was finally able to go down to the village, the girls I met before during our first mission gathered around me quickly. I started shaking some of their hands and then thought I should teach them the "high five." They caught on quickly and looked like they were having a good time. I started making funny faces again and a little boy finally did it back! I encouraged it and all the others caught on. That was a proud day for me. At first they would just mimic the face I was making, but soon we made it into a competition about who could make the funniest face. It was great to find a way to connect with the kids.

The time came to head back to the base. Halima and her father joined us on the Chinook and they were with us for the next week. I was like her caregiver, but I liked to see my role more as her big sister for the week.

We treated her like a queen. The day after she arrived, we took her to what we nicknamed the "Bagram Day Spa" that we had on base that was run by Russian/Kyrgyzstan women to give them employment opportunities to earn a living. They didn't know very much English. They helped cut soldiers' hair and such things. We just went there to get Halima's hair washed, but she ended up leaving with her hair styled cute, a manicure and pedicure. Her face was expressionless throughout the whole thing. I'm sure it was a very different experience for her, but we got a bright smile out of her every once in awhile. We then went to pay, but the employees didn't accept the money because they thought it was so cute to have a little girl in there instead of another sweaty old soldier.

We took Halima and her father out to lunch at our chow hall. We got a lot of looks from the soldiers but it was great to see Halima and her father eat a decent meal. They sure loved the ice cream. We watched a movie (Pocahontas) at the Chapel Annex and gave them some popcorn for the true American experience. We then got an interpreter and interviewed the father, asking him certain questions. We videotaped the interview. I wasn't there because I had to be back at the Aid Station, but I heard he requested that I return to their village and meet his wife! That was a big deal! So far there had been no women present while we had been in Jedgalek, just little girls.

Journal entry on September 7, 2004: *Halima's surgery went well. Both the Egyptian and U.S. eye doctors operated on an eye. After two days of recovery, we took her the next day and I picked out a cute new pink dress and gave her a shower. My goodness she looked so adorable… a true Cinderella story! She is a very obedient girl. She just always let us do what we wanted with her. I think we built a strong, trusting relationship with her and her father that week. We watched Cinderella (of course!) later that day. I believe she liked it, even though she didn't understand any of it, because she busted into laughter whenever the mice were shown. It was such a great week! This has made my whole deployment worthwhile! I started calling her "my little Cinderella" from then on.*

We usually made it to Jegdalek about every two weeks or so. If only I would have known when I dropped Halima off that I wouldn't get to see her and "my girls" for another five months. Other missions were more important at the time and the weather was also very dangerous to fly in.

Soon after arriving one time, Layne Pace and I set off on another mission while the others handed out the usual supplies. We set out for Asahdulla's mother's house. Asahdulla was a boy with VSD (Ventricular Septal Defect) that could barely walk ten feet without fainting. I had never seen anyone so pale. It was a long process and a lot of sacrifice made by a lot of people to get him and his father back to the states for heart surgery. Loma Linda, California provided hospital accommodations, along with countless other people helping make the travel possible.

One hug forever remembered

When Asahdulla and Sirbaskhan (his father) were in California for the surgery, they asked Layne (he was able to go back for part of it) to give his wife pictures and money because she was left to care for five other children. We tried to be respectful of their cultural customs and I was honored to be the woman to present these gifts to his mother. One Elder of the village drove us in his truck on what used to be a road but was now a river (because of the weather), to the base of a mountain where they lived. We hiked up to the house after the half hour drive and met with the brother of Sirbaskhan. Shah was our interpreter again on this trip.

The home was made out of a hard mud and clay material. There was a front patio area on the right. As we walked into the home, it led into the bedroom. There was one cot against the far right wall with about 20 blankets piled on top of it. Five kids were huddled on the floor, staring at us as we walked in. I glanced at the walls and noticed that they were wet. The winter floods must have been leaking through already. It seems so many homes are lost there during the winter. We took a left into another room where there were some rugs and pillows on the ground. The uncle motioned for us to sit down while he left to grab some herbal tea and "foot bread" (like a pita bread). On the side of the house was a separate room used for cooking. There was a hole in the ground where the fire was built, while a metal sheet was placed over it to create the stove.

There was some small discussion while sitting on the floor among those present in the room. Finally Asahdulla's mother was brought in. This woman crouched low on the ground, so I knelt down beside her being very cautious as to not make her uncomfortable. I handed her the pictures of her son and husband, explaining them while Shah interpreted, telling her what had been going on with her family. She started to cry and expressed her deepest appreciation. She was so happy to hear this news! She then left to go to the other room. Women never stay in the presence of men (I hope that changes). We stayed and finished our herbal tea with the Elder, Sirbaskhan's brother and the wife's brother. They also brought out the foot bread. We sat and talked for awhile about the history of Afghanistan, the procedures of Asahdulla's surgery and so on.

We later were able to get pictures with the whole family, the mother with all of the kids. They were shy. What was very touching though was right before we left to drive back to the others, I got the "okay" to give the wife a hug. I had always hoped to one day have that opportunity—and I finally got the chance! I will never forget that.

My big debut in Afghanistan

We drove back to where our unit was handing out the supplies. I was so worried that the kids would forget me after five months of being away. When we got there, I put down my bags and headed over to where the crowds were gathered by the containers of supplies. All of the kids were so excited to see me, calling out my name, "Jill, Jill!"

It was like music to my ears . . . they remembered my name! They actually remembered who I was! It was wonderful to see some familiar faces and especially all "my girls." We started to play some games together. Competitions about who could make the funniest face would start. One girl in particular would always come up to me with the biggest eyes, her hands by her face in the "ready position," sneaking up to scare me. I would act like I didn't see her and then scare her right back. The game soon turned into a different game of "tag" . . . of course, I was always "it."

I would run around scaring them and tickling them. It was so cute to see their reaction and bond with them in such a way. They would scream my name to get me to look this way and that way. Then I would walk up to them slowly and then scare them . . . and the chase was on. Soon it backfired on me and they started chasing me. It was hilarious! Phew! They wore me out as I was running around in "full battle-rattle."

When I was playing tag with the kids, I saw one of "my girls" sitting down to rest. She got my attention by waving me over and then patted the ground right next to her, motioning for me to sit by her. How could I refuse such an invitation? She was one of my favorites. When she smiled, it made everything worth it to be there.

The girls seemed to love me sitting by them and soon it was like a collage of faces as the kids swarmed around me. They were getting loud as they were trying to get next to me, and so I joined in and started screaming, too. Then they stopped when I stopped. We had this whole scream thing going on. We had some good laughs together as I would count off "one" and then they would yell it back. "Two," then they repeated. Right after we both yelled "three," we would scream at the top of our lungs. They got really loud. We sat there together, repeating each other's words (I would slaughter their language and they always got a good laugh out of that one), making funny faces and such. Out of nowhere though, one of the girls started saying, "Bah bah black sheep, have you any wool?"

I whipped my head around toward her as I realized she was speaking English. She ended up reciting the whole thing to me. After she was done, I was dumbfounded that she knew that much in my language. I started to sing the nursery rhyme back to her, and I almost got the same reaction I did with the funny faces. Not only were the kids gathering around me but the adults started to come and listen to me sing. I continued on with simple nursery rhymes and songs like "You Are My Sunshine" and others. When I got to the words, " . . . how much I love you," in "You Are My Sunshine," all the older kids started saying, "Oooh," laughing and smirking as they sort of knew what that meant.

I started to laugh. At least they were actually listening. I was proud to share with these people something that has been such a huge part of my life. It was like I had my own personal concert in Afghanistan.

I saw my good friend Najeeb again, a young man I had met during the missions. He was very helpful in controlling the kids, since he knew a bit of English. He later gave me lots of ruby stones and asked for a gift in return. Everything that is on a soldier's body is usually owned by the government, but I tried to think of what else I could give him. I ended up giving him my "CTR" ring which stands for "Choose the Right." It is always a good reminder for me, but I wasn't really sure if he understood its meaning.

As I handed it to him I said, "Make good choices." I doubt that the message got through to him, but at least I tried. I hoped it would still be of great worth to him anyway.

The happiest moment of my life

After a few hours, I still hadn't seen Halima yet. A sick feeling hit me as I wondered if she was still alive. If you haven't seen someone for awhile in that country, you wonder if something maybe has happened to them and I prayed she was all right. It was getting time for us to leave because we can only stay in one place for a certain amount of time due to security and safety reasons. Right before I was about to head up to the landing zone, the kids around me started calling out, "Halima, Halima!"

I flipped around and called back, "Where is she?" I swear what happened next was straight out of a movie—the crowds parted, and here came Halima running straight toward me with arms wide open. We did one of those "swoop around" hugs and I swear I heard music in the background. I was near tears as we embraced. That was a definitive moment.

When Halima ran up to me and wrapped her arms around me, I knew every sacrifice I made to be in their country was worth it. Having that five-year old girl run up to me like we were sisters was precious. I realized this was why I was there—to make a difference in her life and have her make a difference in mine. This was and still is the happiest moment of my life.

Time to say goodbye

After a couple more missions, our time in Afghanistan came to a close. It was finally time to say goodbye. It hit me that I would perhaps never see these kids again! I got a little choked up but started thinking, "Soldiers don't cry . . . there's no crying in the Army!" That soon became impossible.

My girls gathered around me and I was trying to let them know that I was going back to America and would never see them again, but I could tell they didn't understand. One girl was just repeating what I said. I actually gave them all a hug and they gave one back. I needed that!

I started walking up the hill to the landing zone and would turn around every 10 feet or so and look back at them. There they were, "my girls" waving right back, blowing me kisses and showing the "I love you" sign with their hands . . . things I had taught them. I couldn't hold back the tears any longer. It brought me so much joy to see them do those things. I will forever miss them terribly!

I was saying goodbye to everyone really quickly. I gave my good friend Najeeb a hug. It was during the previous mission that I gave him my CTR ring, and he was wearing it on his necklace this time. He gave me a necklace to take to America to always remember him. He is a kind, genuine boy and I will never forget him.

We then loaded the aircraft. Layne Pace and I sat by each other in silence, not really wanting to believe that something we worked so hard for was now coming to an end. Yes, we were excited to get home and see our families but we were sad to leave our "new family" that we had become so close to the past year. Then Layne broke the silence and said, "Stevens, look . . ."

There they were, this war-torn people, waving an American flag in honor of what we had done for them! Those people, our new friends, were holding up our flag, a symbol of our freedom and now it symbolized theirs. There was not a dry eye on that Chinook as even the toughest soldiers shed a tear at that sight. It was an unforgettable moment.

Getting home

Journal Entry on March 25, 2005: *Well, this is my last night here in Bagram, Afghanistan! I will be home with my family soon. I'm getting so anxious! I'm so excited to get back to life: have movie parties with my little brother, cook with my mom, grocery shop, wear civilian clothes, walk to a bathroom and shower just five feet away, no more shower shoes, PT on my own, college life, classes, parties, cook my own healthy food . . . man, the list goes on.*

What I will miss: my battle buddies wanting to come to me about their problems ("Dr. Jill"), Hammy and his funny stories, wrestling matches at the aid station, my room/sanctuary, going on flights, smiles of the local people, "my girls", Najeeb, Halima, making my rounds to say "hi" at all the offices, baking for the soldiers, and "Jill HARDCORE Stevens" (a nickname I developed from a soldier who would yell it across the camp like it was a wrestling arena).

I thank God with a humble heart for the strength He has given me in living day to day out here with a smile. I have just spent the past few hours chatting with Hammy about many different things. He brought up a good point . . .

"The 100 year view: When you are old and looking back on your life, what are you going to remember? Are you really going to remember the times you got angry or irritated? Probably not, but you will remember experiences that made you grow and that were fun."

I can't believe it is coming to an end. This deployment has always been a huge task to finish ahead of me and now because of the help and prayers of my family and dearest friends, I am coming home. I could not have done it without them . . . especially my mother. She was always there for me and kept me going strong.

"The difficulty of life is a blessing" and "I have cause only to be grateful" for what God has given me.

As Paul says in the Bible, "I have fought a good fight, I have finished my course, I have kept the faith."

On the flight home, my emotions got the best of me and I started sobbing uncontrollably. It was a mix of everything. Part of me was scared to go back, though. I wondered what was life going to be like? I'd changed quite a bit. I was grateful for that long flight to mentally transition into getting my life back.

When I finally landed in Utah, I couldn't help but pick up my pace and make it to the crowds of families waiting for us at the Salt Lake International Airport. I peeked over the top of the escalators and with a big smile, I screamed as I saw my family. Tears of excitement were shed as we embraced. As we drove home and pulled into our neighborhood, the streets were lined with American flags and signs welcoming me home. That flag has definitely taken on a whole new meaning for me. What a sight . . . I was now home.

Finding new ways to communicate with the kids of Jegdalek . . . laughing was definitely one language we both spoke well and we had so much fun together.

Not only was I laughing so hard because, hey, I was riding a mule, but I thought I might have to administer Nitroglycerin to this old man who I thought was going to have a heart attack squealing with laughter. I almost fell off!

Becoming the new security guard for the Army making funny faces to control the crowd when the security guards called me over.

This is the day I first met Halima and noticed her eyes.

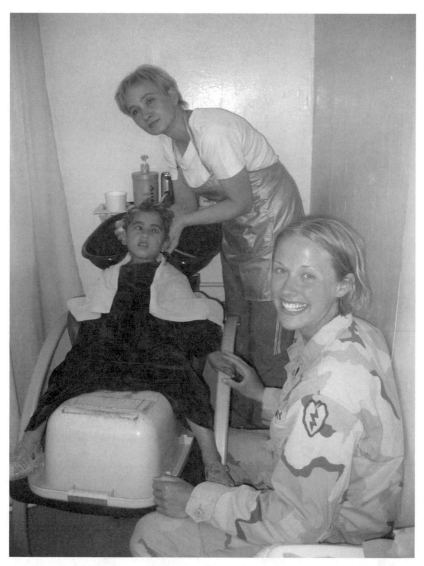

Pampering Halima at the "Day Spa" in Bagram. What a trooper!

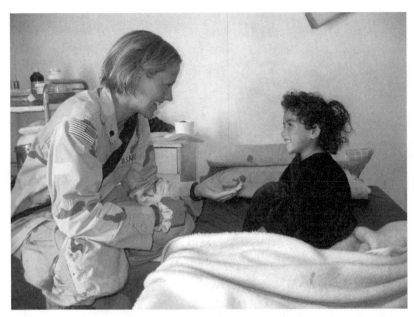

The day after Halima's eye surgery in the Egyptian Hospital.

My "Little Cinderella." I was standing behind Layne Pace when he took this photo. Halima was just standing there smiling. I raised my arms and said, "Halima!" and she did it back. It was like we gave each other an "air hug."

One of my "favorite girls" in Jegdalek that always came over to me with the wide eyes waiting for me to scare her. Her smile just melts your heart.

These are "my girls." I made each of them a bracelet to remember me by as I left Afghanistan.

On a medical mission in Jegdalek. This girl was very fascinated by the stethoscope. We tried to get the female interpreter to encourage her to grow up and be a nurse or doctor.

Playing tag with the children. Somehow I always ended up being "it."

Asahdulla's mother right after I was able to give her a hug. Notice she's not allowed to even look into the camera.

Najeeb and I after I gave him my ring and he gave me that necklace.

Layne Pace and I as we boarded the aircraft leaving Jegdalek for the last time.

My last sight of my new friends . . . an unforgettable moment.

After 17 long months . . . I was home!

CHAPTER 10

HOME AGAIN

When I got back from Afghanistan in April 2005, I got right back into the swing of things. Within three weeks of being home I had bought myself a new car, a cell phone, squared away insurance, found myself an apartment back in Cedar City and enrolled in school for the summer semesters.

While I was overseas, SUU had been approved to have their own nursing program, which was great news but also a little more work for me. I talked with members of the nursing faculty, as some were still around from a year and a half earlier. The requirements had changed with the new program and they said if I would take five classes during the summer, they would let me join the group that was starting that fall.

I got straight to work. I took CHEM 1110 (Elementary Chemistry) and the lab during the "May-mester" which lasts about three weeks, going to class every day, all day. You pretty much eat, breathe and sleep whatever class you take during that time.

The first and second summer semester consisted of CHEM 1120 (Elementary Organic Bio-Chemistry) along with the lab (it takes two semesters to complete), as well as an online course of Human Development through the Life Span. I had until August to complete that one, but I knocked it out in June because I started taking Pathophysiology in July.

It was a total of 16 credits that summer and I thought I was going to die, since nine credits were considered full-time in the summer. Running helped keep me sane as I ran my sixth marathon in July at the Deseret News Marathon in Salt Lake City. Some of my close friends and neighbors came to see me finish. They were watching the clock with my family, waiting to see me come around the corner.

"I see her!" Jo screamed.

My parents didn't expect me to finish so quickly, and my mom said, "I'm not sure that's her."

"No one else runs like that," Jo responded as she started to mimic my weird style. "That's totally her!"

Yes, I have a unique run, keeping my arms more out to the side like I'm charging someone. I think it developed from soldier training while running with gear on.

"Oh my goodness, it is her!" my mom screamed. "She's going to beat her record!" Everyone began cheering me on, and as I heard them, I was able to kick it harder. They gave me a lot of drive.

I couldn't believe I finished in 3:12:28! I must have really needed to let out some stress. I had changed up my training a little and added cycling classes (spinning) at Gold's Gym, which helped with intervals.

Once I showed the nursing department my completion grades, they were kind enough to let me join right into the nursing program because of my prior deployment situation. I enjoyed a two-week recovery from the summer semesters before I drowned myself in the challenges of nursing school.

Class of 2007

The first couple days of school are usually the easiest because you are just getting briefed about what to expect. If only that were the case in nursing school, as all hope was lost when we got our schedule. Our classes always took place over two days of the week, with each class lasting usually three hours. The rest of the week was spent doing clinicals either in the department's practice lab or in the hospital if the opportunity presented itself.

That was our life for the next two years. Days would shift around a bit as we would progress to a new semester, but our class and classroom never changed. The classroom soon felt like prison and we quickly nicknamed the Nursing Department the "Nursing Dungeon" because it was down in the basement with no windows. I couldn't have been more lucky, though, to have been put with this particular class. We were a very dynamic group and soon became like a family, due to how often we were together.

On our first day of class we were also given all of our assignments and projects that would be due throughout the semester. "Power point" soon became a curse word in our class as it seemed everything had to be done in a power-point format. I had never expected so many projects in nursing school. Even though they seemed like a pain at the time, I see how it got our minds thinking and preparing us for the real world. This program really taught me how to think on my feet.

Too many irons in the fire

Darn my ambitious self—I took things a little too far. Nursing school alone would overwhelm anyone, but getting involved is in my blood and I couldn't help myself. I became President of my Nursing Class but soon got involved in things outside of the department. I was a "Service Leader" at SUU and was in charge of different events on campus.

This was also the time that someone introduced me to pageants, and that really took up a lot of my time. I was still drilling one weekend a month with my unit as a medic. I also became a cycling instructor at Gold's Gym, teaching the 5 a.m. class three times a week, which really helped me prepare for my seventh marathon in St. George. I ended up beating my record I had just set in July, finishing this time in 3:08:33. I never thought that was possible. So far that is my personal record.

Those spinning classes really helped my interval training as I would really push myself and those in my class every time. I guess I built up a reputation. I once invited one of my nursing classmates to come to my spinning class and he said, "No way! Someone told me that the teacher who wears her hat backwards is ruthless!" (That's me.) I laughed hard at that one. At least people will know they will get a good workout when they come to my class.

I'd had a few speaking engagements since coming home from Afghanistan, but once I got into pageants, the requests increased. I was speaking all over the state after winning Miss SUU in 2006 during my second semester in nursing school. I also became a Commissioner on the Commission of Volunteers chaired by the Lieutenant General. I was doing a lot of work on Emergency Preparedness with the Commission and helping to kick-off the "Be Ready, Utah!" campaign.

Thank goodness our nursing program didn't go through the summer as I prepared for Miss Utah the first time around. After the competition, I had to go play soldier for my two-week training that happens every summer.

Come sail away

Before we broke for summer and the preparations for Miss Utah began, I had an opportunity arise the last week of school. In between classes one day, I ran into Brittany Hawkins, another Service Leader I worked with on campus. She asked if I knew anyone who was heading down to Las Vegas the next day, a Friday. I didn't, but I offered her my car and figured I could just ride my scooter around for the weekend.

"If I'm taking your car," she said, "then you're coming with me."

"Where are you going?"

Brittany then explained that she and her dad have been sailing on Hobie Cats for years, both professionally and as a hobby. They were on their way to a big competition for "Cinco de Mayo" down in Mexico that weekend. "Do you wanna come?" she asked.

My heart started pumping with excitement. "Boy do I ever! Let me make a few phone calls and I'll let you know in a couple of hours."

Well, after a few phone calls to reschedule meetings and a quick shopping trip, Brittany and I were on our way to Vegas. Talk about spontaneity!

On the way down to Puerto Pinasco, Mexico we found out that one of their sailing buddies needed "crew." When hobie sailing, there are only two people on board—the "skipper" and the "crew." They wondered if I wanted to join in. Brittany said I would catch on quickly and would love it. All I had to do was whatever the skipper told me. So I said, "Why not?"

So about 30 hours after even being invited on the trip, I was sailing in a two-day competition as someone's "crew" . . . and I did love it!

Timing was everything, and I watched (and listened) carefully for the skipper's instructions. I didn't want to let him down. The first day of sailing went well, and later that day we went to a local orphanage to hand out school supplies and clothes. It was unforgettable to have the opportunity to help these children out, while having an adventure.

The next day, it was back to sailing. Wow, being out on that ocean and rockin' in the waves was a great feeling. I really got into it, picking up on the game quickly and watching our competitors to see how we were holding up. I was at the "ready" position, waiting for any call my skipper would yell out. There were plenty of moments during the race where you truly got to enjoy the beauty of the ocean and let the wind just carry you through the water. I could definitely take this sport as a hobby.

The awards were given out the evening of the second day, and it turned out we took third place! What a memorable weekend! I was lucky to have such a skipper that knew how to time everything just right. That was my kind of spontaneous adventure.

Presidential Search Committee

SUU was in search of a new president at the time when President Bennion decided to retire. I was honored with the opportunity to represent the students on this committee, joining a few choice faculty and staff as well as prominent community members and Board of Regents. If only I had known what kind of process it was going to be! We had more than 80 applicants and these weren't just small application forms, but more like extensive books!

We had one week to go through them all and pick our favorites. Due to nursing school that fall semester, I had a two-day window to review them. I wanted to take this seriously since this was clearly a big position to fill. The committee got together to narrow it down to the top 16 applicants, all of which we were going to invite and interview over two certain days.

I ended up having to miss school for these interviews as they were all-day events. The interviews were quite fun actually. Meeting with professionals across the country was intriguing and I took a lot of notes just observing their answers to our questions. I was the one to always kick off the interviews. This one was my favorite question to ask:

"Every fall semester at SUU, we have a Welcome Assembly, welcoming in the incoming Freshmen. Our President usually speaks at this event. What would you say and what would be my first impression of you?"

I had a lot of fun acting like a professional myself. From the interviews we narrowed it down to five finalists, and then it was in the hands of the Board of Regents to pick the new president. The whole process was an honor to be a part of, and I feel SUU is in good hands with their new president, Michael T. Benson.

Marathon anyone?

I didn't run the Deseret News or St. George marathons in 2006 due to an injury in my hip flexor that was really annoying. As I got back into my last year of nursing school, a great friend of mine, Jed, told me about a marathon in Nevada called the Valley of Fire Marathon. He was going down with a group of people and it sparked my interest as I was craving a marathon. The only drawback was that it was the next Saturday. He said if I took it slow I should be fine. He made it sound like running 26.2 miles is no big deal. Jed was one of those insane runners who does the "ultra marathons" running the 50 and 100 mile races. I guess 26.2 miles wouldn't be a big deal to those runners. I thought about it long and hard . . . what the heck, let's be spontaneous and sign up!

They picked me up on their way down from Provo and we all rode down together. I only knew Jed but got acquainted with the others really fast and we were having a great time on the road trip. I did my usual thing that week before a marathon. I didn't know what to expect from the race except a lot of pain. I didn't feel I was ready, since my longest training run was only 13 miles.

We got to the hotel that night, and it was the epitome of "white trash" hotels. The toilet didn't work. The carpet and beds were old and stained. Holes in the wall . . . I just had to laugh!

Poor conditions aside, we got some good sleep that night (at least I did, since I can usually sleep anywhere) because the race didn't start until 8 a.m. We got to the shuttle stop and because of the long lines we didn't get up to the start until 8:10, so we started with the half-marathon runners. Jed and I stuck together the first half, just chatting away between breaths as we ran. Mentally, I was telling myself that I needed to take it slow and save anything I could for the end, being so unprepared.

But by mile 11, I decided I could step it up a notch and just go. I was feeling pretty good. The course was in the "Valley of Fire State Park" and there was nothing scenic about the place. It was 13.1 miles out, then back, with some good hills. I was feeling rather good, surprisingly, and I didn't understand it because I didn't really train. I think it was because I paced myself at the beginning and took it slower, saving so much for the last half. On the way back, I would pick my next target (the runner in front of me) and "take them out."

It helped keep me focused. I ended up finishing at 3:35:45 becoming the second female overall, first in my age group (20-29) and ninth overall. Let's face it though, there weren't that many runners. The guys I went with called me a "sandbagger" which I guess is the term for those who don't train, or say they don't and then kick everyone's trash. I still couldn't believe what I had just done, though. It was very random and I needed that!

I'm not an Olympian

This soon became a hobby to just spontaneously do marathons when presented with an opportunity. A good friend of mine who used to be a scout for running talent was still heavily involved in the running world. He told me that he had landed me an opportunity to run in the Phoenix Rock 'n Roll Marathon in Arizona in January 2007. Okay, okay, I'll do it! You don't have to ask me twice to get an all-expenses-paid trip to run a marathon. It was the next weekend and I figured I'd done this spontaneous thing before. It should work again if I listened to my body.

That weekend would be one I will never forget! I was put in as an "elite athlete" because of my finish in Afghanistan's marathon. Here I was, hanging out the whole weekend with world-class athletes—Olympians and athletes from Wales, Italy, Romania, Belarus, Ukraine, Kenya, and Ethiopia! Then there was me, this blonde girl from America who would be finishing at least a whole hour behind them!

I just had to laugh, especially since I wore this red jacket that had a Canadian Maple Leaf on it, making everyone think I was an Olympian from Canada. (This jacket sure seemed to put me in predicaments, as you will read later.)

I had some funny conversations with the other athletes. As I would talk to the other runners in simple English, the conversation would lead to our best times. I couldn't really lie. Granted, I was proud of my record so far, but when you are put in a group of athletes such as this, their faces said it all. I smiled as they tried to tell me my time was good.

I felt like royalty, though. The "Elite Racing" team really takes care of the elite athletes. I got to stay at the Buttes Marriott in Tempe, Arizona, where I was allowed access to the "presidential suite" with free meals, snacks, massages, you name it. At the expo, I was interviewed on Fox Sports News! It was incredible! I loved mingling with the other runners, though. They were so generous and fun to talk to. I wish I could speak their languages . . . maybe one day.

Getting to the starting line was very smooth. We arrived at a building by the starting line to warm up at and be out of the cold (it was about 25-30 degrees) and then 10 minutes before the race we walked to the starting line. Again, here I am, with no marathon training for this event, walking to the starting line with all the "really fast" athletes with escorts so we can be in the front.

I found a running buddy, Nicole, from the area, at the beginning of the race. She was shooting for a three-hour marathon and it was her first one. For some reason, I decided to stick with her because she was fun to be with and hey, maybe I could feel "really good" and race well.

We started off at a seven-minute mile pace. A girl came up to join us named Jen, from Chicago, because she liked our pace and wanted to do a sub 3:10. I thought, "Sweet, two girls to help keep me going."

Well, Nicole started taking off about mile 8 and then Jen took off about mile 14. I was all alone, getting passed by everybody. Usually it's the other way around, because I usually start in the back of the pack in my marathons so I can have the positive vibe of passing people. Mistakenly being one of the elite runners put me in the front of the pack and I was really trying to think positively about this situation as people passed me the whole time. I was starting to feel it in my legs about mile 19 and then especially mile 22! The lesson I learned was that I need to pace myself more at the beginning, and that I definitely need to train for these events so my legs can last a little longer. I still finished in a decent time of 3:17. That weekend was surreal and I was glad for the opportunity to experience what the "elite athletes" do for just a small moment.

Wrapping up at SUU

My last few months at SUU were hectic with the final research projects in nursing school and all that I had gotten my hands into. I gave up the title of "Miss SUU" and then won "Miss Davis County" the following weekend. All of a sudden, things took a turn for the worse. Maybe I had stretched myself a little too thin at this point.

Was nursing the right path? I put more of my focus on finishing up nursing school and graduating, because with just six weeks left of school, I actually wasn't going to graduate . . .

My classmates and I were told that we had a big comprehensive nursing test coming up in March, and that if we didn't pass it we wouldn't be graduating. When I was told this, I felt I had been studying for this test for the last two years of nursing school. I told myself, "I should be fine because my dream is to be a nurse and God knows this so he'll make it happen. I'll be fine."

The test day came and my brain was exhausted with all of the critical thinking we had to do. As I finished the last question, I said a quick prayer that I would please pass.

I FAILED!

"No," I thought. "This can't be happening." I walked out of that room in a daze, not really wanting to believe that I didn't pass. As I walked to my car, I was trying to hold back the emotions but my thoughts were making that very difficult.

"I'm not good enough to be a nurse... I'm a failure... After all these years of hard work I can't even graduate right now..." Have I been pursuing the wrong dream?

I couldn't take it anymore and the tears just flowed. I was listening to some random songs on my iPod in my car very quietly but then I heard the words of one song start off with: "I ache. I cry. My spirit's fading, I'm buried alive..." ("Wow, this is totally describing me right now," I thought.)

"I fail. I fall. Just when I fear I'm losing it all. I've reached the edge of what I know." (Now I started crying uncontrollably.) "He reaches out and I let go . . ." Here is the whole song:

I Know He Lives
By Tyler Castleton and Staci Peters

I ache. I cry. My spirit's fading, I'm buried alive.
I fail. I fall. Just when I fear I'm losing it all.
I've reached the edge of what I know.
He reaches out and I let go.

He is my light, He is my strength.
He is the anchor of the hope that I can truly change
He magnifies what I can give
With every step and every breath I'll worship him
He is the only way and I know He lives.

I wish. I dream. I hope for things that I can't see
I try. I pray. Finding my way through this test of faith
And when my best is not enough
He reaches down and lifts me up

He is my light, He is my strength.
He is the anchor of the hope that I can truly change
He magnifies what I can give
With every step and every breath I'll worship him
He is the only way and I know He lives.

Every broken heart, every fear I face
When I'm in my own Gethsemane, He know that place
Every lonely hour, every tear that falls
Every weakness and temptation, He has felt it all

He is my light, He is my strength.
He is the anchor of the hope that I can truly change
He magnifies what I can give
With every step and every breath I'll worship him
He is the only way and I know He lives.

I don't think it was a coincidence that I happened upon this song was at that moment. The message of this song has become very meaningful to me, and since really listening to it that day, I was able to acquire the minus track and I've sung it numerous times in different speaking engagements. It expresses very clearly what I felt at that moment—and in other moments since—when things haven't worked out the way I'd hoped, but it also clearly expresses my testimony of the Savior and that He knows everything we are experiencing and is there to help us through our tough times.

In this until the very end

The few of us who failed that test were given one more chance on the day before graduation. Talk about pressure. I could have given up, thinking all hope was lost, but that is, again, not my style. I had to give it this last shot. Those who failed really bonded together and decided to seize this opportunity to learn from each other, looking over what we missed and really studying those areas together. Discussing it with one another really helped us dig deep and better understand some of the content.

I can't dance around the fact that I was really nervous for the test. We all were. The morning came and we all walked into the computer lab more quiet than usual, some of us a little pale. We logged on and waited for instructions from our professor. When he said for us to go ahead and click the start button, we all screamed . . . literally!

"Aaah!" . . . "Oh my gosh!" . . . "Mommy!" . . . "Save us!" We were having fun playing up this peak moment in our lives.

The test was going a lot smoother this time. I had done all I could do to prepare for it. I had a lot of family and friends praying for me, and I tried to keep positive and alert during the test. I was a little hesitant in pressing the "next" button to find out my score when I finished the last question. I just stared at it, not really wanting to know.

Click.

I felt this huge relief wash over me as I saw that I had passed. I walked out of that classroom on Cloud Nine, feeling like I could conquer the world. I called everyone that knew about my situation, since my family was waiting to see if they were coming to a graduation or not. It was a great celebration that weekend, but I was curled over in pain for most of it. I believe I created an ulcer in my stomach due to how much stress I put myself through the last couple of months. (Hmm, or is that years?)

Graduation was still exciting and all too surreal. I was just in awe that I had survived the last two years since being back from Afghanistan. I was, of course, excited to be done but also sad because I felt SUU was where it all began for me. The university really provided me the opportunities to make a difference, and even showed me new possibilities and dreams that I never thought were possible. I seized every one that I could. I was grateful I was leaving SUU with my head held high, knowing I had made the best of it. Go T-Birds!

My dear friends Suzie, Misty, and Joleen cheering me on at the finish line of the Deseret Morning News Marathon. Seeing them there gave me a surge of energy.

My new ride I got that summer to get me around town. My favorite thing to do was to ride in one of my costumes just randomly on the busy streets.

Brittany and I in Mexico in front of one of the Hobie Cats.

I could get used to this sailing thing.

Nursing class of 2007.

My brothers, Brad and Tyler, along with my dad David at SUU graduation.

Chapter 11

Me In a Pageant?

While attending SUU in October 2005, DEl Beatty, the school's Director of Student Involvement, approached me. (Yes, that's really how his first name is spelled.) He told me I would have a good chance at becoming Miss SUU!

"Ha!" I just laughed at him. "Sorry, I wear running shoes and combat boots. I don't do heels."

Well, DEl never let it go and helped explain to me that "beauty queens" don't just prance around in heels and look pretty (that is all I thought they did) but that they get out there and make a difference, passing bills and moving people to action.

A light bulb clicked on for me and I soon became intrigued . . . if only I knew what I was getting myself into. Yikes, I never knew how hard it was to be a girl! There were a few times that I almost backed out, but luckily I had a few encouraging friends to keep me at it.

Finding a talent for the Miss SUU Pageant was also a huge obstacle to overcome. (I soon found that everything was when it came to trying to be a girl.) I was planning on singing for the longest time, but I just could never find a song that seemed to fit me. Then my cousin Sheri mentioned that I should consider a monologue. So about three weeks before the competition, I changed my talent. Something that was "me" was making a fool of myself on stage and making people laugh.

So I decided to find a talent that was comical and entertaining. I found a hilarious monologue from the play "It Had to Be You" written

176

by Renee Taylor and Joseph Bologna. Although I'm comfortable making people laugh, doing so in a formal setting on a stage is generally not within my comfort zone. I knew it was the Lord that gave me the strength and confidence to do it. And if it wasn't for the help of Kari Ann Young and her acting abilities, I wouldn't have performed as well as I did.

In preparation for the pageant, there were workshops every Tuesday night to go over different pointers of modeling, interview ideas, etc. Let me tell you, I sure needed a lot of work on the modeling and walking part, especially when it came to walking around in high heels. As DEl once put it, "Jill, it looks like you're ready to go to a basketball game!" Well, I was!

It was somewhat stressful leading up to the competition on February 3-4, 2006 with all the work that it required—deciding on a platform, finding and then perfecting my talent, finding a modest evening gown and cocktail dress, and fixing a swimsuit to not only be modest but to fit well with my body type. I set a goal from the beginning to show elegance in a different way—a modest way. It's who I am and how I was raised. I felt I needed to be true to that. That went for the swimsuit competition as well. Sure, it might have made the wardrobe portion a bit more difficult, because modesty isn't always the style, but there was no question about what type of clothing I was going to wear.

My Platform

Finding a platform was one of the hardest things for me. At first it was "Making a difference." Okay, how great and boring is that at the same time?

Then it was "Promoting fitness in children" . . . love it still, but not passionate about it. One day, while stretching after a workout in the gym, I swear, the heavens opened, there was music in the background, and it hit me what I am so passionate about! "Emergency Preparedness." I feel America needs to be ready for anything, so I called it "Ready When Disaster Strikes."

Kinda catchy, huh? It comes from my soldier side. As an army medic, there was no way to predict what injuries might occur during combat, and so I had to be prepared for any emergency situation. My aid bag was packed full of items necessary to keep a soldier alive, no matter the condition. But it wasn't always that way. We learned from our mistakes. Every month, we would have mock disasters (unless a real one occurred) and learned what we could do better next time. We soon had it down and became ready for anything, still practicing, of course, and keeping up on our training.

Serving a year as a soldier in Afghanistan taught me to be prepared not only for combat, but for any unexpected aspect of life. Now that I have been back home for awhile, I have realized that, however, a new enemy has emerged on our own soil—the enemy of an unexpected disaster. We are all living in a combat zone! Mother Nature and bio-warfare seem to be hogging the spotlight lately and doing more damage than all other terrorist attacks combined. Are we prepared for this kind of battle? Just as soldiers must be ready when a military threat emerges, families must also be prepared in the case of a major emergency in your own backyard!

At first I was so focused on getting everyone "grab-n-go bags" but then over time my focus changed when I learned more about the program CERT (community emergency response team) and especially Teen SERT (school emergency response team).

I am what some like to call . . . ambitious, determined, an "in your face" kind of girl when I find something that I believe in and needs to get done. I got my name out there so much that ever since winning the title of Miss SUU I found myself as a new commissioner (representing the youth) on the Commission of Volunteers chaired by the Lt. Governor, a Citizen Corps Council representative, SERT president for SUU, and just recently was appointed as the new State Director of Teen SERT. Yikes!

One Shot One Kill

I started to feel sick about the competition coming up so soon, and I really stressed out. This was such a whole new world for me—the pageant world. I did all I could to prepare, and then I just looked at it as something to have fun with, because this could be my only pageant.

It was so much fun getting to know the other girls. We all actually became really good friends, which sometimes is pretty rare. I taught the girls a new slogan that I picked up on and learned in the army: "One Shot One Kill"—which to a soldier means to not waste your ammo. But to a pageant contestant, or anyone else for that matter, it means to not waste your "one shot" on stage in life to shine, and to make every moment count.

A lot of the girls and others caught on and we had a lot of fun walking by each other with our "finger guns" whispering "one shot one kill." I even made a sign to put on the stage door during Miss SUU so we could be reminded of what to do right before we get on that stage. The contestants made a soldier proud.

On Friday the 3rd I performed my talent and modeled my evening wear. It was so much fun! I nailed my talent. The crowd seemed to love it! And evening wear went great as well! At the end of the first night, they announced four awards, and I received two of them. I got the runner-up to the "Quality of Life" award, which is based on an essay about your platform. And then I earned the "Miss Congeniality" award (spirit award).

All of the contestants vote for their choice for Miss Congeniality, and they said I won "hands down"! I was honored. I thought it would fit the part in true Sandra Bullock style if I "tripped" on my way up to receive the award. Well . . . I did just that! It was a hoot. The people who really knew me figured out that it was staged. A couple of girls helped me up and the emcee was really playing it up, which was great, because it got the crowd laughing more and I was just egging it on as well. The crowd seemed to be having fun, which is what I'm all about.

On Saturday, I did the casual wear, on-stage interview and modeling portions of the competition. I felt so comfortable on stage and had so much fun just being myself. I had come a long way in the modeling part, not that there still wasn't room for improvement, but I had lost a little of my previous boyish swagger.

At the end of the night, we all came out in our evening wear so they could announce the top 5. The emcee said, "Let's give her some help walking forward . . ." and he called my name!

I was so excited to make top 5 because that was my goal and I figured, "Holy cow, I just made 4th runner up, how cool is that!"

Then she was named: "Sweet! I'm 3rd runner up. No way!"

Then the 3rd runner up was announced: "My gosh, I made top 3!"

Then the 2nd runner up was made known and it just hit me that I might have a chance at winning this thing. Well, let's just say, I was a little taken aback that I had made it that far and was pulling some confused faces, turning around and saying to the girls behind me, "What am I doing up here? What is going on?"

It was down to me and one other and it finally hit me what was just about to happen. "…Everyone say hello to the next Miss SUU 2006, Jill Stevens!" I couldn't believe it! I guess I missed the workshop on how you're supposed to respond when you win a pageant. I lost all my poise and started cheering and pumping my fist up and down like I was at a basketball game.

"What am I supposed to do now?" I asked.

The former Miss Nevada, a judge, told me, "Wave!" Desiree Ball (Miss SUU 2005) was trying to pull me back to put on my crown. My reaction was probably overdone, but I don't care, it was me! The night was a whirlwind! Most of my nursing class was there to support me. They made me so proud. After sharing the excitement with the crowd, my family and I were taken over to the hotel to meet with the judges.

Preparing for Miss Utah

If only every girl interested in pageant competition could have someone like DEl Beatty around! After winning Miss SUU, he gave me a list of things that I must do for the Miss Utah competition, but emphasized he was there to guide me along. Having the paperwork to fill out for Miss Utah on top of my Nursing School class work was overwhelming to manage.

We met together often to fill out the necessary items and once again came across the obstacle of "What should I do for my talent?" We both knew my monologue was not going to be competitive enough, and "settling" was not my style. The Miss Utah Pageant is the largest pageant in America (larger than Miss America), averaging around 58 contestants vying for the title of Miss Utah. There were 63 contestants to begin with in 2006 but as the months went by, a few dropped out and there were 57 girls at final count.

I wanted to be competitive. When I get into something, I don't do it half-heartedly, but I give it my all. I consider myself my biggest competition and if that takes me to the top, that's wonderful. We were searching every possibility and talking to many others for ideas. I knew I wanted to stay with comedy of some kind.

After a lot of brainstorming, DEl recalled a character vocal he heard a few years back that was performed at Miss Utah. He looked through his collection of VHS tapes (okay, so maybe more than a few years) and found the year. We watched it together in his office and I knew right then that I had found my talent piece. It was a song from the musical *Once Upon a Mattress* called "Shy."

This character, Winnifred, was made famous by Carol Burnett. As I learned more about the character and the meaning of the song, it seemed to fit me and my life. Princess Winnifred is not like the usual princess. She likes to roll around in the mud and is not the most prim and proper. She hears that a nearby kingdom is looking for a princess to marry the prince. She shows up after just swimming the moat, realizing she must convince the people that she is "shy and demure" just like any other princess, even though it may not seem like it.

The irony wasn't lost on me. Here I am, this soldier, who likes to roll around in the mud and isn't the most prim and proper, showing up in a pageant after just serving in a combat zone, trying to convince the people that I can be a beauty queen! I guess I'm just a little too "shy."

"Mock away"

We also needed new headshots for the paperwork. Smiling in front of a camera and feeling natural hasn't always been easy unless I am pulling a funny face. Funny faces don't come across too well in the pageant world. We had the former Miss SUU help me with make-up that day and scheduled a hairstyle at the local salon to help look my "best" and especially like a "beauty queen." It felt so awkward standing in front of the camera for awhile. DEl was being encouraging, trying to bring out my personality but, I'm sorry, glamour shots were not going to bring out "me" in the picture.

I started laughing as he was offering different suggestions that weren't working for me. Then he finally said, "Just try mocking them and fake like you know it." So I did. The photographer took the picture and instantly DEl yelled, "That's it! Mock away, Miss SUU! Mock away."

The photo session then became really fun, but I was laughing hysterically inside at what I was actually doing. DEl would chime in singing, "There she is . . . Miss America." He definitely knows how to give people around him a boost.

We headed up north for the big "Spring Workshop" where all the paper work was due and I met all of the other contestants (a.k.a. the competition). It was a lot of fun but also VERY long. Part of me wanted to try and find an excuse and leave, but the big "lottery" was at the end. The lottery establishes which contestant number you are and what you will be doing each night of the competition. There are three groups of girls (Mu, Alpha, Sigma) and they rotate each night through the phases of competition.

One night is usually focused on modeling (swimsuit and evening wear), one is your talent, and then one is just "on-stage interview." There is some strategy involved based on how you want the judges to see you. For some, talent is their strength, so they might choose to do that on the first night and will therefore want to be in the corresponding group. Some might like to end with the best phase of competition and will want to be placed in that group.

As each girl is picked, they put their name and talent into the space they want. Talents are listed so girls can strategically place themselves away from those of their same talent. If you are a piano player, you don't really want to put yourself by another piano player so you can try and stand out even more against another talent. Every name is put into a bowl and as you are drawn, you get to pick where you want to be. So obviously, you want to be drawn at the beginning to have your first choice.

DEl warned me that it was the "Miss SUU curse" to get drawn last. And sure enough, we were one of the last three out of 57. There was one space left in each group. I knew which group I wanted already (since I had been sitting there long enough) but when I took the final spot in that group there were some "Ooohs" in the audience. I guess people thought it was bold to put myself behind one of the strongest competitors.

DEl had told me about some of the contestants who had competed in the past and were coming back. He warned me that they were good and were going to be very tough competition. Usually you don't want to place yourself by the stronger competitors because you might pale in comparison. I guess part of me wanted to show them how well I could shine, so I deliberately put myself by one of my strongest competitors to show, "Ain't no one going to break my stride. Ain't no one going to hold me down." I wanted to give them some tough competition.

Once the paperwork for Miss Utah was done, a huge weight was lifted off my shoulders and I was able to focus a little more on my nursing studies. I still met with DEl daily in his office (it became a habit just walking straight there whenever I showed up on campus) to go over interviewing tips or scheduling modeling workshops to learn how to walk in high heels. We were driving together on most weekends to meet with different people to get advice and tips for the upcoming competition in July.

DEl thought it would be great to meet with Sharlene Wells Hawkes, a former Miss America who also happens to be from Utah, to perhaps get a few pointers from her and words of encouragement. One of my judges at Miss SUU actually worked for her so we at least had an "in." We scheduled to have lunch with her in her office and figured that we were lucky, because she is extremely busy. We were expecting maybe a quick 20 minutes with her, but it soon turned into an hour and a half! We seemed to hit it off really well and had a lot in common.

"I just judged Miss America this year and you could have been in the top 5 easy," she told me. "You are going to be Miss America. We need you."

She even invited me to come over to her house that evening so I could meet her family. I couldn't believe it! When DEl and I climbed into the car, we just started laughing in disbelief at how well the meeting went. Sharlene was on board with helping me prepare for Miss Utah and who could have asked for more!

Training for a new "sport"

Working out came easy for me because it was such a habit and I loved it so much. But soon my workouts needed to be revised as

Sharlene was suggesting that I was a little "too muscular" for pageants. I couldn't argue with her—I'm a soldier, a cyclist, and a marathoner, and I need to have muscle to do what I do. I told her I would give it a try because, again, it was my nature to give it all I've got.

It was hard to change my workouts. This included not running and giving up my job as a cycling instructor at the local gym. My workouts consisted more of swimming and the elliptical cross-trainer to try and help my muscles elongate more. Now, I am a person that usually embraces change, but when you mess with my fitness passion, I have a hard time. It was weird that I had to actually work out less for this kind of sport. It was hard to adapt and especially lose an income of $150 a month from my cycling classes. To a single college student, that was a small fortune.

It was weird how my whole life was changing to prepare for this pageant. My radio station was now tuned to NPR (National Public Radio) to keep up on current issues. I would try to pick up conversations with my classmates, roommates and friends to hash out "Hot Topics" and dig deep into the issues to help me form my opinions.

I have never really studied and developed an opinion on big topics like "Abortion, Gay Rights, Gun Control, No Child Left Behind, Homelessness, Presidential Candidates, Immigration, etc." Am I Republican or Democrat? I had to really figure things out and know these issues so I could discuss these topics with the best of them (i.e. the judges).

Speaking engagements also started to accelerate and my social life was quickly coming to a close as my time was now devoted to either school, working out, meetings, practice, or speaking. It felt right, though, and I know I needed to do this for some reason.

I realized that before I could really dive into forming my opinion on all these big issues, I really needed to know myself and what was important to me. What makes me get up every morning? What are things that make me tick, or really tick me off? What are things that I really couldn't live without? I met with a former Miss Utah who helped open my eyes to knowing "who Jill Stevens is." When I was able to answer these questions, these became my "core values."

My Core Values Binder

As I discovered my core values, I put them together in a binder, giving each value its own page and anything that encompassed that value in a section after it.

Happiness: I cannot live without smiles and laughter. Happiness is so important to me and I decorated this page with yellow paper, making a big smiley face. I put words on it that made me smile. It was to remind me that smiling is one of the greatest features on someone and I needed to make sure I was smiling through it all.

Family: Yep, I do love my family regardless of the many times we have pushed each other's buttons. My family is my greatest support and I wouldn't be here if it wasn't for their encouragement through all of my weird adventures. I decorated this page with pictures and fun memories of things that we love to do together.

Faith: This, in a way, is why I get up every morning. A great woman named Marjorie Hinckley said, "When you see what great things are being done in the Gospel, it's thrilling to get up every morning." My faith gives a sense of purpose to everything that I do. I decorated this page with a Lighthouse and the words, "Let the light of Christ Shine forth for all to see," a phrase from my baptism song. I also printed out all of the words to this song and "My Tapestry" to put into this section. My faith truly defines me and I knew if I was supposed to win, the Lord would be there to help me shine.

Freedom/Service: Can anyone truly live without this value? Freedom is a gift from God and we are so blessed to live in this nation. Serving to help maintain those freedoms is something that I cannot live without. Being a Soldier is a huge part of who I am.

Zest for life/Health: Some say that I live for each new adventure I undertake and I would have to agree. I love learning all I can and trying new things. That is why I am in the military, why I have run marathons, and why I was now in the pageant world. I have a zest for new challenges and that has a lot to do with my health.

Knowledge/Education: Our mind is a powerful thing and it has unlimited storage. Granted, our recall might be a little slow and we might need triggers now and then, but education is a gift. There is so much to learn out there and the great thing about it is that most of it is at our fingertips because of technology.

Probably one of the biggest obstacles I faced while preparing for Miss Utah was finding an evening gown that I loved and that fit my style. There was never any question as to whether I was going to wear sleeveless gowns or not. I had made my decision at a young age that I was going to wear modest clothes. I figured if I wanted the Lord's help in this new combat zone, than I needed to be armored correctly.

After many shopping trips, DEl and I came to the conclusion that we were going to need one made by hand. We looked at some different patterns, found a local seamstress that seemed fit for such a job and got on the ball. Many hours went into making this dress as DEl and I had to place on every rhinestone by hand. We found that it was a good time to also practice interview tips and talk about any necessary items for the upcoming "game day."

"All American Girl"

The pageant had finally arrived and DEl was a huge help in making lists of all the needed supplies to pack in case there were any emergencies. I felt ready and it felt so right to be doing this. In my mind, the theme of the pageant seemed so perfect . . . "All American Girl."

"Wow, maybe this is really supposed to happen," I thought. It seemed so fitting as a soldier.

As the rehearsals got going throughout the week, I had a lot of energy and was having a lot of fun. But that seemed to deplete quickly as it became more apparent that I was having a hard time being around a lot of estrogen, especially for long periods of time. So many girls would go to the events together and I was more in the mindset that if I happened to run into someone on the way, then that was great, but I wasn't going to wait for anyone. Darn my independent self!

I would simply strike up a conversation with whoever was near but most of the time I was on my own, again, just watching the girls and being amused.

As the competition got started, I found it weird that after months of preparation, it really only came down to a few seconds on stage showing who you are. I remember walking off and thinking, "That was it? After 45 seconds on stage, modeling swimsuit and evening wear, I have now knocked out 35 percent of my score!"

It just didn't seem enough for all that I put into it. I felt the impression I made with the judges was truly in the Lord's hands. One shot, one kill right? I knew I had to make every second count, and I guess I did in evening wear. I was a little stunned to hear that I'd won evening wear on my preliminary night.

The final night had finally come. I felt good about my performances throughout the week and that I had a good chance at making the top 10. Well, I happened to be announced as a finalist and of course, threw my fist into the air... yep, I guess some things still never change.

What a rush! The night went by so fast. I was named top 5 and was ecstatic that I made it that far. I was trying to mentally prepare myself that winning Miss Utah might not happen even though it seemed like it would be perfect in my mind. I felt at peace, though, as they brought out the top 5 to get ready to announce the Royalty. The 4th and 3rd runners-up were announced, and then I heard, "Our 2nd runner-up, Miss SUU, Jill Stevens." I waved and smiled while walking off to my place on stage.

"Wow," I thought, "that was it. It was done. I guess it wasn't supposed to happen." I was a little sad because I knew so many believed in me and actually helped me to believe that I could do it. But now it was done. What were my family and friends going to say? What was Sharlene going to think? I felt I had disappointed so many people.

Sharlene met me on stage after the crowning event just finished. She said, "Jill, I am so proud of you," and gave me a hug.

I started to cry and said, "I am so sorry that I didn't make it."

"No, don't you be sorry. You controlled that stage out there and had commanding presence. You brought the audience in. Don't be sorry. You truly did it and we are so proud!"

I went straight to the dressing room to gather my things. I couldn't face my family and friends yet. I was exhausted and wasn't trying to hurry. I finally made my way up to the lobby and there was a huge crowd still there that cheered as I walked in. I couldn't help but smile and I realized that I was loved no matter what.

I was second runner up, which I should be stoked for, but I guess I really wanted to win and felt I could do so much for the organization. Over the next couple of days, I had feelings of relief but also anger. I felt, "Could the judges not see what I could have done for the organization?"

I just came to face the fact that the pageant world wasn't ready for someone like me. Sharlene gave me a call the Monday after it was over and said she went up to the judges after the final night ended and said, "What happened, I was kinda rooting for Jill to win."

"Oh, we just love Jill!" And half of the judges said they ranked me first and don't know what happened, either.

The other half said, "We see her not only being Miss Utah, but Miss America one day. We just want her to come back next year."

Sharlene piped in, "I believe she's not coming back."

Those judges felt sick! "No, she has one more year!" they said. They even got out their binders to look up my birthday just to make sure. The judges that ranked me first were "reaming" the others a "new one."

After hearing that, I have to admit, it made me feel better but all the more ticked at the same time, knowing that somehow politics got involved. Sharlene paused and then continued, "Jill, I think you need to compete again."

"What? I can't go through that again."

The thought of being in the pageant world for yet another year made me nauseous. That's not what I really wanted to do. I did my best and it was obviously not in the Lord's plan for me to win. I wanted to get on with my life.

Sharlene also mentioned on the side that the judges were offended by my slogan, "One shot, one kill." (What?) She said that it sounded not only offensive with the "kill" word, but also arrogant in going after the Miss Utah title. (You've got to be kidding me!) After I let her words soak in, it actually did make sense and I could see why they would think that. I was still bummed, though, because really the message behind the motto is meaningful. I guess I was on the search for a new motto in life, but one that defined me in the same way. Sharlene texted me one day as she was with some military personnel. The text read, "Jill, what about Lock and Load?"

"Oh my gosh," I thought. "That's perfect. It even goes with my platform!" It basically felt the same as "One shot, one kill" but without the possibility of offense.

In the Army we have a phrase we use in combat—Lock 'n Load! It means to be ready for anything and not waste your ammo, make every shot count. I've kind of taken this meaning to heart in all aspects of my life but have never really had a name for it. Now I have something to call my "drive and ambition" in life I guess . . . my new motto. I realized that it's important for anyone living in this country, though—to make every shot count and don't waste this one shot at life to shine. Lock 'n Load!

National Sweethearts

I got a call a few weeks after the pageant, inviting me to the "National Sweethearts" pageant in the small town of Hoopeston, Illinois as part of their National Sweet Corn Festival. It's a pageant for all of the 1st runners-up across the nation—a mini Miss America, so to speak—because those girls were so close to winning the state title and competing for Miss America. Well, wait a second! I was 2nd runner-up. It turns out that the 1st runner-up had won 1st runner-up before and had already competed. She didn't want to go again, so she opened the invitation to the next one in line—me.

After doing some research, it sounded like a fun, laidback opportunity that I would never get again... why not? It was to take place over Labor Day weekend and I was going to be missing two days of nursing classes. My teachers approved and everything seemed to be working out.

There were no obligations with winning the title of "National Sweetheart" so I decided to tell myself to have fun with this. There were 34 of the states represented and we all arrived a couple of days before the competition started. We were actually known by our states, like "Miss Utah" instead of 1st runner-up (because that was a given). Seeing these beautiful women from across the nation was kind of intimidating. Usually in situations like this I become more of the "group clown" to make things more enjoyable for the girls, and that's within my comfort zone.

Hoopeston was a perfect depiction of a small American town just full of heart and charm. There was nothing but cornfields and for the few days before we competed they had us touring the local factories and visiting the local shops. They wanted us to wear the state sashes wherever we went and we might as well have been big time celebrities as we met with the different Rotaries and service clubs.

Of course, people always wanted to know what my talent was, and after a few times I announced in front of the crowds that my talent would be to hula-hoop the sash. Going to these different events was a blast with the contestants as we learned most of America's PAM non-stick spray is made in this town. My favorite was the bean factory though. I took charge and decided to have a lot of fun with this one. I taught all of the girls the "Bean Salute" (which is kind of fitting because that is my nickname... now don't get any ideas, it's because of my true nickname, Jillybean). I would get the girls to do this as I would open the door for them to the different Bean factory rooms. Afterward, we gathered in the "taste testing" room and got to sample the many different kinds of beans (I had no idea there were that many). I stopped the girls before they dug in...

"Ladies, ladies," with a horrible mix of an accent, "Bean tasting is an art. There are certain steps which you must take to enjoy the delectable..." (dramatic pause) "...scrumptious fiber of every bean. First you must take the bean. Now go ahead, everyone grab your bean..." (Girls just started laughing, but I was excited they were participating.) "...wave it in front of your nose. Smell that. Your senses should awaken." (I was trying to hold back the laughter.) "Place it in your mouth but do NOT chew. You must suck on it and then mush it with your tongue." I soon lost it and couldn't keep a straight face anymore.

We sure had a lot of fun together. The rehearsals were a kick. I felt we were in a movie. Our choreographer looked straight out of the 1980s with big hair, hot pink lipstick, tight spandex/leotard . . . "Now girls, I need you to focus. These steps are difficult but I am sure you will be able to get them in the next couple of days . . ." And it was the "step-touch."

"You've got to be kidding me," I thought. "Wasn't this the dance move I had perfected in my kindergarten class?" How had I made it running through a minefield all the way to running through a cornfield? I will never truly know, but I loved my life nonetheless, and I was loving Hoopeston!

I heard through the grapevine that they had the "Sweet corn 5K." I, of course, became intrigued. If only I'd known that I would create a big stir, I might have been more reluctant. I guess out of the 50+ year history of National Sweethearts, no contestant had ever run the 5K. I was shocked. I thought for sure there would have been other girls that would have wanted to try it.

Once I mentioned to my host family, Bob and Wilma, that I wanted to do this, we looked over the schedule of the different events they had us doing that morning. All I would be missing is the breakfast, and I would make it in time for the big hometown parade. I thought it was perfect, but I guess the pageant directors didn't see that. They didn't like any change in the schedule and everything had to go according to plan. Once I walked them through the tentative plan and the great publicity that would give them, they consented. Another contestant overheard us talking and wanted to run as well.

So Miss Michigan and I signed up for the race. We ran with our sashes and the crowds were cheering loud from the sidelines as we would run by. I would hear people comment, "Look! One of the contestants is actually running the race!" I just had to smile. I think I found a way to break the pageant stereotype. I ended up taking first in my age-group and Miss Michigan was not too far behind. We represented well and the town went crazy at the news.

We joined the rest of the girls at the parade. Each girl had their own convertible to ride in and was to wear a summer dress. I guess I wanted to show my type of "summer dress" and showed up in my desert fatigues. The parade was a lot of fun as I challenged some of the crowd to push-ups, waved and saluted different people. The crowd was very welcoming.

Overall, I could say I now have friends across the nation. I was really hoping to make the top 10, but I came home with the only two non-finalist awards: "Miss Congeniality" and the "Director's Choice" which is chosen by the directors of the pageant. So everyone liked me except the judges, I guess. I was just fine with that.

Being with these girls helped me realize how far I still needed to go to become a "lady." As I left the National Sweet Corn Capital of the World, I felt ready to be that lady and finally let go of my old habits. I said to myself, "Here I come pageant world. I'm going to give this one more go!"

How I showed up to my first workshop with my heels from Payless. I was slowly realizing what I was getting myself into.

My talent at Miss SUU performing my comical monologue . . . my first time ever acting.

Showing the woman I've become, but being true to my soldier side by modeling the camouflage skirt in a casual wear number for Miss SUU.

The 2nd runner-up was just announced and it hit me that I might actually have a chance at winning this thing. Then I was announced as the new Miss SUU. Let's just say I was a little surprised.

Grace and poise were not factored into my training regimen yet. I soon was handed the bouquet of flowers and green stuff was everywhere as I pumped my fist into the air.

Sharlene Wells Hawkes and I first met and had lunch in her office just a few weeks after winning Miss SUU.

Welcome to the National Sweetcorn Capital of the world! My mom and our good friends Bonnie and Makayla came out to cheer me on, along with DEl Beatty, who is taking the picture. It was a blast having them there.

My host "Ma and Pa" at the National Sweethearts Pageant, Bob and Wilma, from Hoopeston, Illinois.

CHAPTER 12

EMBRACING THE PAGEANT WORLD

My year as Miss SUU was coming to a close. It was actually kind of fun to host the pageant and be there to help the girls, instead of having the stress of competing. Many people asked if I was sad to give up "the crown." I really wasn't. I felt I made the most of my year and was ready to move on—I guess moving on to another pageant. Deep down I couldn't believe I was competing again. I didn't tell too many people. I was afraid to have that label of a "pageant girl" because I still didn't feel like one even though I had now competed in three (Miss SUU, Miss Utah, and National Sweethearts).

I found another local pageant, Miss Davis County (where my family lived) that was going to take place the very next weekend after I gave up Miss SUU. How perfect! They had a few mandatory workshops that I could not make it to because of weekend Army drills and the Miss SUU pageant. I made sure to get everything to them in advance so that they would know I wasn't kidding around. I showed up the night before to learn the production number and to get ready for competition.

I was crowned Miss Davis County the next night, but after talking to my new director, I wondered how I had won. It turns out that the judges didn't really seem to like me, at least a few of them. I got a couple pages of comments from my director and looked forward to reading them to see what they had to say. I thought that it was going to be positive because I just won, right? I couldn't have been more wrong.

After reading paragraphs and paragraphs of them putting down my wardrobe, I was somewhat sad, but I understood. I figured everyone is entitled to their opinion. I agreed my wardrobe wasn't the best, but it hurt when they started commenting on my character and who I was.

"Is she really for real? She's in the Army and is now doing pageants. It almost seems surreal. I'd like to believe it." Huh? "She seems over the top . . ." That was a theme among the judges. Me, over the top? Sure, I have a lot of energy and get very passionate about some things, but I didn't feel that should be held against me.

Reading these comments didn't give me the "boost" that I had hoped for. Their words were just tearing me up inside. After a few days I wondered if this was really the direction for me. Maybe the Lord didn't want me to compete again. Was I being tested right now? Maybe I didn't really want this anymore. I was getting tired of the pageant life and was anxious to get on with my own.

I was also dating someone at the time and we started to take a step forward in our relationship. Things were getting serious now and there was talk of marriage. But I had just won Miss Davis County and couldn't get married for a year. And what if I won Miss Utah? Or even Miss America?

I was getting really confused as to what direction I should take and starting praying intently and digging into the scriptures. The man I was dating was being very supportive, taking a neutral position as well so that I could make the decision on my own. I met with my church leader and he helped me talk through the pros and cons of each path. He gave me a quote that hit me hard and stuck with me a long while afterward. "Sometimes Satan distracts good people by having them do good things to keep them from doing the essential things . . ." such as eternal marriage.

I also had a talk with DEl Beatty because I felt he understood my situation the best by knowing what could happen in the pageant world for me, and by also being well-acquainted with the man I was dating. The whole conversation seemed to be centered around having an eternal perspective. The next Sunday, while sitting in church, I really had some strong feelings and had to write some of them down.

I wrote: "I feel like the Lord can use me as an instrument in His hands, by what He has taught me. Is it wrong to pursue this desire to serve? I know my purpose as a woman of God is to be a mother and raise a family in the gospel. Is this a sin to see if this is something the Lord needs me to do? It has felt so right to pursue but a good part of me wants to be done with that life, get married, and begin on that path."

After much fasting and prayer, I felt I had my answer . . . it was time to give up the crown. I drove up to northern Utah to meet with Sharlene and my pageant director to tell them. I was so nervous and felt sick about what I was just about to do. I felt that if I followed through with this and proved to the Lord that I would listen to His promptings, that I would then feel the peace. But it didn't really happen that way.

After I visited both of them at their homes I couldn't believe what I had just done. I had actually given up Miss Davis County, but why didn't I feel any peace? Wasn't I supposed to feel comfort after I showed the Lord that I was willing to take that leap of faith?

The next morning I went for one of my long runs. It gave me some great time to think. I thought this time would be good for me to hash out in my mind what I had just done, and receive the confirmation that it was right so I could feel peace about it. It was just the opposite. Running for me really sends some positive endorphins flowing throughout my body and I always have a lot better day when I go for a run.

So doing this run then, I felt like I perhaps just made a mistake. I was SO confused! I just didn't know what to do. As I headed back down to southern Utah, it hit me that maybe I wasn't feeling the peace because I hadn't actually called my first runner-up to take the title. I then got her phone number and called her the next day.

"How would you like to be Miss Davis County?" I said, thinking she would be stoked about the opportunity.

"Uh, I don't know," she said. "I really felt right about the outcome after that night. I'll have to think about it."

"What? Are you kidding me?" I thought. I gave her a couple of days to think it over and as the rest of the day went on I was praying that I would have courage to accept whatever happened. Then all of a sudden the next day my prayers turned more to pleading that she would refuse the title. I felt so sick now about what I had just done. I couldn't give this up! It was my last year to ever compete for Miss Utah because of my age, and I knew I would always wonder, "what if?" I felt I would have to follow through to make sure this was right. I suddenly felt I needed to call her because I could not wait any longer.

"Hey, it's Jill. I was actually thinking about what we had just talked about and . . ."

"I would love to be Miss Davis County!" she interrupted.

"Really?" I was at a loss for words. "Why?"

At first, I was trying to make it sound like she wouldn't really want to be Miss Davis County... "There are a lot of appearances, and the paperwork for Miss Utah is insane..." I said, trying to make the role sound less appealing. But she had actually had been to Miss Utah before with another title so she knew exactly what she was getting into. We chatted for the next 45 minutes and really listened to each other. We finally came to the conclusion to just go with the original plan with me being Miss Davis County.

After I got off the phone with her, I felt this overwhelming peace. This was right. So why did it feel right for that little bit to give up my title when in the end it wasn't right? I remembered a presentation I had attended a few years earlier where one of my church leaders shared a similar example he experienced while hunting one day with his son. As they were hiking back, they got lost and came to a fork in the road.

They decided to pray and both felt that they should take the right path. After a bit of hiking they came to a dead end, realizing they now should have been on the other path. Once they got to the other path and hiked a few miles more, they reached their car. On the drive home, his son asked with confusion, "Dad, why did we both feel it was right to go down the other path when in the end, it was wrong?"

After some serious thought, the man responded, "If we had chosen the other path we would have gotten about half way and felt that it wasn't the right one, whereas, starting on the wrong path first, we were able to realize that it was wrong with just a short bit of hiking. We started on that long path knowing we were on the right one and never questioned it."

The church leader summarized this idea that the Lord will sometimes prompt us to go one way just to know with certainty that the other was right. Now after a few weeks of terrible confusion, I knew that I was supposed to be Miss Davis County and compete this last time for Miss Utah.

It's crazy how when you know what you are getting into, having done it before, you feel much more at ease the second time around. Getting the paperwork done, headshots, going to the spring workshop, etc. was a lot easier that year and didn't seem nearly as stressful. At the spring workshop, they announced the new partnership of the Miss America Organization with Children's Miracle Network as their National Platform. Each contestant had to raise a certain amount of money for the Network and the kids they benefit. "Hmm, this is great," I thought. The wheels started turning and by the end of the workshop I sold the Miss Utah Director on my new idea . . .

The Queen Team

Getting into the pageant world, I really wanted to break the stereotypes of "typical" pageant girls that I was guilty of believing for so long. I wanted to show that there are brains behind the beauty and a great passion to make a difference. My mind was going crazy with ideas and I was getting so excited just thinking about combining both my passion for running and serving. Many of these pageant girls are hardcore athletes and work hard to keep in shape (and yes, there are those lucky ones to whom it comes naturally). As I thought about it, why not show America who we really are and what we really do by creating the "Queen Team" and running races to raise money for this new platform.

This was a win-win situation for both organizations, and for America. I could hardly contain my excitement and I just had to tell the director on our next break. She was sold on the idea as well. I was already passing around a list for the contestants to fill in their contact information so we could keep in touch and help each other out in the upcoming months before competition and figured this could come in handy to rally the girls for the Queen Team.

As I thought about it and talked more with the director after the workshop, we realized that the girls would probably be reluctant to join, knowing that one of their competitors started it. I decided that I could do all of the work, find a race, create the shirts, write all of the emails sending them off to the director so she could put her name on the bottom and make it look like it was from her.

She felt bad that I was doing all of the work and not getting the credit. Frankly, I didn't really care. I really felt this team could make a statement and really put the focus on the cause that we are running for—the children.

I sent off the first email to the director a few weeks after the workshop. It went something like this . . .

Being that we are from Utah, where the Children's Miracle Network was established, I think we should represent our state and show the Miss America Organization what we are made of. I think it would be great if the contestants work together along with the Children's Miracle Network to kick-off the "Queen Team," showing Utah that we are more than just beauty queens, but that we are titleholders running for a cause.

This is a team celebrating the crown we all wear but more specifically, the children. I would love for us all to get together and run a race for the kids. We will get everyone we can to run the race. There are many races in the months of May and June. We can run a few of them together. What a great way to stay motivated and in shape for the upcoming competition week the end of June.

This race will also give you a chance to get your donation money. I hope that all of you have already set up your accounts. You, as contestants, can go to different businesses to pledge a small amount of money per mile that you complete in a race or even a few races. It's up to you how far you want to go. The businesses can then log on to the Children's Miracle Network website under your name to donate the money.

Let's work together on this and show the Miss America Organization that we are committed. I am even getting together new designs for shirts that we can all wear. I can't wait to show you how they will turn out. This is exciting!

If you want to join the cause, the kick-off race is May 19 at Thanksgiving Point. It's a 5K, so I know we can all pull through this. I am currently working on getting the media involved. You won't want to miss this boat, ladies.

We had about 18 girls show up to the race. Not bad, but not great, either. You have to start somewhere!

Miss Utah dress

I was grateful when I graduated so I could focus a little more on Miss Utah prep and Queen Team details (the actual race and getting shirts made). After graduating nursing school I moved in with a family friend in St. George to start transitioning into the "real" life after college. Sure, I still had Miss Utah the end of June but in my mind, I had a 1/50 chance of winning (there were 50 contestants) and if I didn't win Miss Utah, I wanted to make sure I had something to look forward to and get started on my future.

I loved southern Utah and started looking into working at Dixie Regional Medical Center. They had a few different Residency Programs starting up the beginning of June. I could make it work. I could make up the class time before and after the competition.

Well, not exactly. It turns out that my "two-week annual training" with my guard unit came the first two weeks of June. I was going to miss too much. I talked it over with the Human Resource people and we thought it best that I pull out and wait to see what happens. So it wasn't too long before I had to move everything again up north to store in my parents' place. Good thing I'm a soldier and know how to pack. I camped out on an empty bunk for two weeks, working out before work and studying for my nursing license exam and Miss Utah stuff in the evenings.

I was figuring everything out for the competition, but then I came to the obstacle again . . . what do I do for evening wear? Someone recommended a seamstress that lived in Vegas. I was able to get in touch with her and started talking about possible designs. When I finally met her in person, I found out she was from Kyrgyzstan. I was so excited to hear that, but not nearly as excited as she was when I told her I had been there. She said not many people have heard of that country. We started sharing different stories and she told me a little about her family. She worked on the Army base as an interpreter because she speaks at least four languages. She actually interpreted for the LDS Church Services quite a bit. I was so excited to hear that, so when I went home,

I emailed her some of my pictures that I took while in Kyrgyzstan. We were around the same age and she was also trying to get into nursing school at UNLV, so we had a lot to talk about.

I quickly got in a few fittings before I left southern Utah and was able to get away once during my annual training. Once my two weeks were done with the military, I had one week until I checked in for Miss Utah… and still no evening gown.

I headed for Vegas to have the final fittings and my new friend worked hard into the night. I felt so bad that this ended up taking so much of her time. She was a perfectionist, which I was grateful for. I put on the dress for the final show and I was excited to see the masterpiece. It was a beautiful dress but it turned out far different than I had expected. A huge part of that was my fault as I believe the material I chose didn't work too well with the design. I found that I was trying to convince myself that this was "the" dress.

I drove back up to northern Utah and tried on the dress again. I came out to show my mom and just started crying before she even said anything. There was no way someone could compete in this and I felt sick with the competition just five days away. We thought that with a few "touch-ups" on the dress, it could probably turn out. I wasn't even home 30 minutes before I was on the road again, back down to Vegas. I was grateful for that 7-hour drive to really think things through and come up with back-up plans. I met up with the seamstress at about 2 a.m. and didn't leave until about 5:30 when it was finished. It looked so much better with the minor changes. I caught up on some sleep in St. George before I headed all of the way back.

Was I supposed to relax before competition?

It was now Wednesday and I had a couple of days to pack because, silly me, I joined a two-day race that started Friday and I was supposed to be checking in on Sunday. It was the Wasatch Back Relay where you have a 12-man team running 178 miles, with each runner running three different legs of the race—yep, that even means the middle of the night. This is adventure at its greatest! I joined up with this team a couple of weeks earlier because one of their female runners was injured and they asked if I was available . . . I'm a sucker for spontaneous challenges. This team was a competitive one too. They were planning to place as one of the top finishers. I was wondering why they got me to fill in the blank spot, because I knew there were faster females out there. They said if I kept a 7-minute mile pace (8 minutes on the hills) then that would keep them on target. Sure thing. That was just a walk in the park—to them. I was runner #7 on our team, split between two vans, so I was the first to go in our van (6 runners in a van). We met up Friday afternoon and I was scheduled to run around 8 p.m. We kept in touch with the runners in the other van to see if everyone was running on the pace that we had projected. Each leg of my race was about 4 miles (I had one of the easier slots). One at 8 p.m., the second at around 2 or 3 a.m. and my last at around 9 a.m. on Saturday.

The runners in my van were a joy to be with… and also really fast, I might add. We got to know each other quickly, spending that much time together driving from check point to check point, dropping off another runner and cheering them on as we drove by to meet them at the next one. We actually ended up placing in the top 3 of the combined gender teams and 7th overall, I believe.

Here we go again

When I got home it was time to get everything ready for the pageant check-in the next day and go to bed early. I feel that having so many things to do before the competition actually helped me not think about what was ahead of me. I really had no time to be nervous about it and I went in with the attitude, "Well, this is me, no doubt, and this is as good as it's going to get."

I showed up to the hotel, loading everything I needed in one trip (the soldier life prepared me well for this) as I walked by the many girls with their family members helping to carry everything in. I was so much more relaxed this year. I often wondered why I felt so overwhelmed throughout the week when I competed the previous year. I guess I had learned a lot about what it takes to "become a woman" and now it was becoming more natural. Throughout the week of rehearsals, I felt like the contestants' big sister because of how much older I was than most and because I now felt like a veteran (my soldier side coming out).

Preliminary nights seemed to be going well and I felt that I nailed my private interview and on-stage interview. So I had a good feeling about making top 10. The final night came around and I was still just as calm as ever. It was actually quite nice so that I could be there for the other girls that were really nervous. As they were calling the top 10, they got through 8 names and now all of a sudden I felt a knot forming in my stomach. I was called out as the ninth contestant, and then the competition began again to show the judges what I was capable of.

When it came to narrowing it down to the top 5, I was a little more nervous because the competition was so close and they had already announced four of the finalists. I was holding my breath and praying for strength to accept whatever the outcome… "Jill Stevens, Miss Davis County. There you have it Ladies and Gentlemen. Our top 5!" Phew!

We were then all given a question that more or less dealt with our experiences throughout the week. I was last, of course, and ready for it: "What was your most memorable moment this week?"

A smile came to my face as I pictured this, "Probably doing Turbo Jam, a kickboxing workout, with some of the hostesses to get our workout in the morning. It was a kick doing that together and they made it a lot of fun." Weird answer? Yes, but it was true.

Finally it was time for the awards for highest in each phase of competition. I wasn't really expecting any but hoping for one… the overall interview winner. To me, this was the "big one" and most credible. And really, if you won overall interview, you are probably winning the title because it has the biggest impact overall.

"And winner of overall interview is . . . Miss Davis County, Jill Stevens!"

I couldn't believe it. Could this really be happening? I just won interview! That was like winning the gold! And soon I actually heard the words, "Jill Stevens, our Miss Utah 2007! The stage is yours."

What? Could this be real? A soldier had just become Miss Utah? I was now Miss Utah? It was all surreal. I couldn't believe this new dream had taken place. This was a dream I never grew up thinking I would pursue, let alone have it come true.

I felt ready for this new "deployment" as Miss Utah because of where I was in my life. They say the life of Miss Utah is a busy one and I *thought* I was ready for it. Lock 'n load, right?

Other Miss Utah contestants and I helping to kick off the Queen Team at the race.

Becoming Princess Winnifred and performing my signature talent "Shy" that I am known for in the pageant world.

"Can you believe this?" My mom said to me just after I was crowned Miss Utah.

Hugging my "little miss" Amy (one of the girls that escort contestants during the pageant) after winning the Miss Utah title.

The Miss Utah 2007 Royalty. From left to right, Brittany Harper, Sarah Pettit, me, Ashley Boulter, and Kendyl Bell.

My brother, Mitch, goofing off and acting like he just was crowned the night I won Miss Utah.

CHAPTER 13

OUT OF TOUCH WITH REALITY

"I'm kinda nervous about this reality show coming up," said one of the state contestants, referring to the TV show "Miss America Reality Check" that we would participate in. It was October 2007, and many of the 52 contestants were at sea, participating in the Miss America Cruise. Her comment made us all stop what we were doing and look up to see the others' responses.

Soon every girl was expressing concerns about this new "combat zone" we were about to step into. I listened for a bit to hear what these girls were nervous about and then I seized this opportunity to get the girls excited about what we were about to do.

"Ladies, we are in control. They are filming us. If they want a show, let's give them a show that we want," I chimed in. That opened the door and the girls seemed to light up with new ideas.

"Why don't we bring different items for random filming ideas?" I asked.

"We could play some night games," one girl yelled out as we were still backstage during the performances of other contestants while on the cruise. Another girl joined in as they were finished performing.

"Perfect! Wait a second . . . ladies, I could totally get camouflage paint for each of the girls, give you all a make-up lesson and play some great night games," I led on.

That got the girls excited and talking and the ideas just kept on coming. Each girl volunteered to bring different items and I said that I would work on getting 52 camouflage kits for the girls. We all left the cruise feeling a little more at ease even though we had no idea what we were getting ourselves into.

Stepping into the unknown

I didn't know what to expect. How could I? The producers of the show gave us very little information concerning anything that we were doing over the 10 days of filming the Miss America Reality Check television show. I was really more curious than nervous. Being a soldier had really prepared me for the unexpected and to just go with the flow. Goodness, this was like a "Boot Camp for Women." I guess the reason I wasn't too nervous was because I felt there was nothing questionable about my character. I didn't really feel like I had to watch what I would say or do because really, I didn't do anything of the nature that I believe would hurt anyone or myself.

We all flew in on a Sunday. They bused us to a hotel to stay for the night until we kicked off the Reality Check the next day. We had a meeting at 10 a.m. to meet the producers, learn the important rules and to be divided into our "squads." I was on the Purple team and they said we had until tomorrow morning to figure out why we were put into these specific teams. Each team was assigned a specific camera crew to follow them and interview them. We learned quickly that interviews were called, "OTFs" (On The Fly) meaning that interviews were usually on the spot and right after an event that we should "express" our feelings about.

The main rules were that we couldn't go anywhere without our sashes (my name was now Utah); we had to be miked every morning by one of the crew members and could not take it off under any circumstance until we were going to sleep; and they wanted us in our evening gowns, packed up and ready to go by noon, only to really sit for another four hours in the lobby. The military theme of "hurry up and wait" was only just beginning. During these times, we got to know each of the contestants really well.

They bused us to an equestrian estate that was a couple of hours away. As we pulled up, we couldn't believe how beautiful it was—there was a long winding road with trees and equestrian stables, leading up to the mansion where we would be staying.

We were filmed getting on and off the bus . . . and on and off the bus, etc. Cameras had to "re-po" and film us at different angles. There were also sound problems with airplanes flying in the background.

"This is going to be awhile," I thought, and I decided to hang out in the back behind the girls. The girls caught on quickly to the new lingo and would start yelling out the terms for the producers. ("Re-po!")

We met our host, whose enthusiasm really gave us a boost during the filming. That night we also got to meet Stacy London and Clinton Kelly, the hosts of TLC's hit show *What Not to Wear*.

All the girls were screaming with excitement as they came out to greet us. Frankly, I couldn't have cared less… It was getting really cold outside in just our gowns. I was tired and needed food. I hung out in the back and took off the heels while Stacy and Clinton went through some of the girls' luggage. This was only the beginning.

We met our *advisors* for the Reality Check and learned what their role would be. It turned out that every two days or so of filming (which was only one episode when it aired) we had "tops and bottoms." Basically, the top 3 were the girls who most embraced the new image of Miss America and then the bottom 3 had a lot of work to do, according to the advisors. These advisors were from different areas of the "entertainment/celebrity" world and observed all that we were doing throughout the show.

We finally got dinner about 10 p.m. and then went to find our assigned sleeping quarters. They tried to group the girls by their colors as close as possible in each of the rooms.

That night's journal entry: *My feelings about being here: I feel good. I, for a good reason, am not worried about how I will be portrayed. Mainly because I am doing all that is in my power and the rest is not in my control. I feel the strength of the Lord and the comfort of the spirit. I am doing my best to portray a daughter of God.*

"My group is a big kick! Lea, Miss Georgia and Grace, Miss Tennessee, are hilarious . . . especially Lea. My goodness, she is creative and witty. We are staying in this estate. Not a cozy place, but nice. There are about a

dozen of us staying in the "Hero Room." It's a circular room and is a fun atmosphere because of the girls.

Tuesday

We woke up to bags placed at the end of our beds. As I walked down to breakfast, I saw all of the girls pulling out different outfits that were in these bags. There were a couple of shirts all signifying your team's color along with some black shorts and pants. Cool, I thought, these are going to be great workout clothes and could mean we are going to be doing something active today (finally). Then I saw all of the girls pulling out swimsuits. My heart sunk as I saw that they were all two-piece swimsuits. Well, there is one event, whatever it may be, that I won't be competing in. As I finally got back to go through my bag, lo and behold, I pulled out a one-piece swimsuit. Holy cow! How did this get here? We never placed orders for these.

It turned out that I was the only girl out of 52 contestants that somehow ended up with a one-piece swimsuit. I really had no idea how this happened but I was so grateful. After asking around, I found out that when the producers of the show were calling the Miss America Organization for swimsuit sizes, the CEO of Miss America threw in a quick, "Oh and make sure you have at least one 'one-piece swimsuit' because for some reason that is all Utah wears."

I laughed when he told me the story but thanked him for doing that. I was sure grateful for the former Miss Utahs who helped make that statement and make this possible for me.

We were finally told that we were to be doing an "active" event that day. Thanks for the details. Until then, the members of the purple squad had some great bonding time as we were trying to figure out our similarities and why we were put together. College degrees? Platforms? Talents? Age? And so on . . .

After much thought it turned out to be our age. Yep, we were the "senior citizens" of the group. We had a blast together as we then started to come up with team cheers. This is where I jumped in with some military ideas and what was so great was that they were liking my ideas and adding to them. We ended up writing a cadence. I called them to attention. "Group! Atten-hut!"

"PURPLE," they yelled.

"Forward, march! Your left . . ."

"To the left, to the left," they would chime in, mimicking a popular song at the time and doing a funky dip to their walk. I guess you could call it the "21ˢᵗ Century March."

"Right or left."

"To the left, to the left."

"I don't know what I've been told . . . the purple squad will win the gold . . . the purple squad is now on deck . . . get ready for a reality check! Sound off . . . (one, two) Sound off . . . (beat you!) Bring it on down now . . . Lock 'n Load!"

That was music to my ears and it made a soldier proud!

As we walked down to the nearby fields, we passed by some interesting objects. We passed by our state flags, as well, and *most* of our team started to identify where theirs was. All the girls lined up at the beginning and different teams started to call out their cheers. You might be wondering if we had to come up with cheers . . . no, we're just girls and its one thing we're good at. We, of course, had to come back with our cadence.

As we were getting instruction for the obstacle course, I started to think, "Oh boy, this is what I am supposed to be good at, being a soldier and all." So many of the purple squad was yelling, "Lead us on Utah... this is going to be a piece of cake for you." Being a soldier does not mean that you are the fastest. I find it funny when people think that when you are a soldier, you are good at any physically active event, whatever it may be.

The horn sounded and we were off. I tied my sash around my waist so it wouldn't be a bother hanging on my shoulder. Up and over the beams we went to go grab different puzzle pieces that ended up making the United States, and then it was through some more beams. Next was to put the puzzle together on assigned tables.

Well, I didn't know they were assigned and being in the front of my team, I led them astray to an empty table that I seized. After putting some of the pieces together another team came to kick us out. I just wanted to tell them to go ahead and build on the other table. I guess rules are rules, so we couldn't. We quickly had to relocate all of our puzzle pieces to another table to start over. Whoops! We ended up being the third team through the puzzle and figured we could catch up finding our flags. Every squad member ran straight to their flag and it looked like we could take the lead . . . except that one girl was still looking. I went back to help, as did the rest of our team, and I couldn't believe how similar all the state flags looked. I only know how to recognize my own but if you didn't know exactly what was on your particular flag, it's a difficult thing with 30 flags left staring you in the face. More and more teams passed us. We finally found it and took 5th place! The "seniors" finally made it in the end.

That night we had a dinner and were told we were to have a special guest. That got all of the girls in a buzz about *who* it could be. Big stars and celebrities were being named and to our disappointment... it was "Controversy." Huh? You've got to be kidding? How lame is that? Each table was given three different issues to *discuss*. Ours were: the war in Iraq (oh boy, I thought), sex before marriage, and illegal immigration.

Some of the girls immediately said, "Utah, I can't wait to hear your opinion on this!"

I responded, "Oh, I definitely have an opinion all right, but let's hear from everyone and then I will wrap it up."

Most of the comments were general but very supportive of the war and what we were doing. One of the advisors ended up joining our table during our "discussion" to listen in. After each girl was done, they all turned to me. I had to laugh. I was flattered that they cared that much for my opinion.

I'm really torn about the war in Iraq (and Afghanistan). I personally know the difference we have made and are making over there. But I also know a lot of my battle buddies are getting injured and making the ultimate sacrifice. We can't stay there forever and there isn't one specific event that we are waiting to be able to say, "Oh, now we can come home." What I do know is that whenever we leave, my role as "National Guard" will really live up to its name and we will need to be prepared to fight the war on our own soil.

It was necessary to go over there, I believe, to show that we do not stand for terrorism and that we are here to help establish some control in those countries. Yes, there are centuries of hatred in this people's blood, and that will probably never change, but hopefully we can teach them how to handle it in a different way. A government is not formed overnight. Goodness, our country should know that. I believe the real difference will be seen as the children grow . . . seeing at such a young age how their world can be better.

We moved on to our next issue of "sex before marriage." I was surprised to see how conservative most of the girls were, but relieved at the same time. I just decided to listen in on this one. For some it was an emotional and personal subject as the effects of premarital sex in their family have taken its toll. After awhile, the advisor finally interrupted, "I find it hard to believe that all of you here at this table are still virgins."

I was shocked and it looked like it took most of the table by surprise. It was silent, but some girls started commenting, "This is who we are and we have standards. We are not what some make us out to be."

"I'm not buying that," the advisor said. "I still find it hard to believe that you are all virgins."

I was ready to make a comment or two, and right as I made noise, one of the crew members pulled the advisor out, along with the other advisors that listened in on other tables. We guessed they were going to discuss who the "tops and bottoms" were so far.

We were all given the chance to change into a "dressy/casual" outfit and then head out to the field, the official filming site of the "tops and bottoms." It was freezing! This was more cold than I had planned for. The only jacket I had brought was my red running jacket with a Canadian leaf logo on it.

After explaining the layout, the host called down six girls and I was actually one of them. As I stepped down to the front, I guess the logo on my jacket was a huge problem and caused quite the stir as the crew looked for red tape to cover it up.

I turned around to all of the girls and said, "Was this not Miss Canada?" The girls really got a kick out of that one and some started to sing, "Oh Canada!" It was hilarious.

They pulled each girl forward to announce if they were in the top or bottom 3, and then listen to the advisors tell you why and what they think of you. As it was my turn to step forward, I said, "I'm used to dogdin' bullets, so give me your best shot." That got a big laugh out of everyone and was told I was in the "top 3."

"Utah, you are one cool cat," said one of the advisors. "What were you thinking, though, as you got ready to come out tonight?"

I could tell she was hinting about my unusual outfit. "Well, I do have a nice outfit on under this jacket, but it's freezing and this is the only jacket I brought. You've got to just roll with the punches."

"Oh," was all she had to say. You would think that being in the top 3 they would have more positive things to say about you, but one advisor, especially, focused on how he needs to see "more" from me and that I need to embrace the glamour.

Hmm . . . you need to see more?

Wednesday

Every morning we usually had a "brief" with our host that would give us clues as to what our next event might be. These briefs usually didn't take place until somewhere around 11 a.m. On camera, they would say, "You've got 20 minutes to be out there and ready" but in actuality it was about three hours later. I have a whole new outlook toward and respect for reality shows. There is a lot of work put in by the camera crew and a LOT of waiting around.

We were told that we needed to be in our swimsuits that they told us to bring on our packing list, and that we "could" be getting wet. Well, as we were waiting around, the purple team and I got to talking about last night's "tops and bottoms."

Georgia then got this great idea: "Utah, you know what would be so funny is if you show up today with *more* on. But not just more, but over-the-top more to kind of poke fun at what they were saying."

"That's brilliant! We could really go over-the-top with the hair and make-up to show that I am doing *more*."

We got right to work. Georgia was hilarious about the whole thing. As she was helping me with my hair she would comment sarcastically, "Jill you should totally do this to your hair for competition," as she would wink to the cameras. She cracked me up.

I had a few other girls help me with the make-up and when I saw the final look, I busted up with laughter. I felt like Bozo the Clown. As

I would walk around the house with my new look, some of the other contestants actually commented that it actually looked pretty good. "You're kidding," I thought.

We headed out to a pool that we had no idea was there and lined up according to our squads (everything was done with your team). Each event/game that we did was to test us on something that is used in the Miss America competition.

Today was going to be our "smarts." The game was called, "Are you Smarter than a Miss USA girl?" which stemmed from the infamous Miss Teen South Carolina and her answer about "U.S. Americans not having maps . . ."

A girl from each team would step up to the table and be given her question. Most of the questions dealt with our nation and the history of it. Every now and then they would throw in some random ones. We would write our answers on a piece of chalkboard and if we got it right, we would move to the back of our line. If we got it wrong, we had to jump in the pool, swim across and we were out of the game. Sometimes if the girl knew there was no way she was going to get the answer, she would write, "maps" on the board. It was funny. A lot of the girls would wait for each other and dive in together, while some would do a cool dive.

Of course, our team was the one standing closest to the advisors and when we walked in, they noticed right away my big hair, earrings and lots of make-up. As I tried to overhear what they were saying, it sounded like they actually liked it! What? Georgia and I looked at each other in confusion and then just had to smile.

I stayed in for a few rounds and then hung my head in shame as I realized the question I just missed. They listed some characters and asked what TV show they were from. The first one I heard was, "Fonzi," and I immediately thought of an old family sitcom. I couldn't think of the name and a random title finally came to mind, so I went with it. I wrote, "Hawaii 5-0." Some of the other girls had "Happy Days" and I realized that is the one I was trying to remember. But then, a contestant on the last team said, "Hello, it's Fozzie of The Muppets!" I could not believe I led myself astray and missed that. I put down the board and just ran to the end of the pool to do a big cannonball. I was done.

The pink team won and deserved to with the random questions that they were getting. Afterward we found out that since our make-up and hair were now a mess, they were going to give us all makeovers from top consultants that they brought in. There was a catch, though. As you were individually assessed, the make-up and hair artists would tell you what they recommended . . . it was all or nothing. You couldn't just take the makeup/makeover without taking the hair changes, and vice-versa. As it was finally our turn to meet the artists, they each had our headshots that we turned in to the Miss America organization (so they could really see what we looked like apart from just coming out of a pool).

It was being recommended that some girls make drastic changes (hair color change, cutting 12 inches off, and so on) while others' changes weren't really going to be that noticeable. I stepped up to the plate, and the hairstylist said that I should I go shorter or longer because my hair was an awkward length. I thought to myself, "Well, I'm always up for a challenge and usually have short hair. Let's see what you give me. I'm in!"

It was a few hours before they got to me (no surprise) and the haircut was by one of the consultants' team members. The purple squad helped me find a cute style in a magazine that I actually really wanted to try and it seemed like it could work. I showed the hairstylist and she got to cutting. And boy, did she cut. I couldn't believe the length of hair I was seeing coming off. How short was she planning on cutting my hair?

I was getting a little nervous because I could tell it wasn't going to turn out anything like the picture. She had a mirror nearby but I told her I didn't want to look until the end, even after my make-up was done. Finally, they were done with me and I had my chance to see it.

"AAHHH! OH MY GOSH! Wow, that's different," I said. "This could take some getting used to." Well, I swung at a chance to try something new and I believe I struck out with this one. Oh well.

After our makeovers, we were given the opportunity to take some new headshots to show off our new look. I got up there and started smiling. The photographer started snapping the pictures and said, "Show me some more." So I turned to the side.

"Give me some attitude." Uh . . . attitude? Well, I was trying to change it up all that I could and he obviously was wanting something different. "Come on. Show me some of those sexy poses," he said. "You've got to think you are the sexiest thing out there."

I just started laughing. "I'm sorry. This is all I know. Tell me what poses you are thinking of."

"Just let it come naturally. Go with the flow."

"I am. But this is all I know. I didn't grow up modeling."

"You obviously know how to model if you have gotten this far in the pageant world," he said.

"I'm sorry, this is all I've got."

"All right! Come back later when you have talked to some of the other girls and they can teach you how to model."

Well, I think I'm probably the first girl to get kicked out of her own photo shoot. That's a record I don't mind holding.

Thursday

Mornings were usually uneventful and calm. The camera crews were busy rushing around setting up for whatever we had going that day, which was always a surprise to us. Each day seemed to drag on longer with more sitting around. Today they brought in a modeling consultant to help us learn how to strut our stuff. I could just predict what they were going to do with me. They wanted us in the swimsuits that they gave us. So all of the girls had two pieces and I was the only one with a one-piece. A lot of the girls actually expressed that they would rather be wearing the one-piece because the two-pieces didn't fit that well.

There were three runways set up in front of the house. I've never heard of or seen the "modeling expert" that they brought in. He had two other girls with him to help show the new style of modeling that they wanted to bring to Miss America. The organization wanted to get away from the "robotic Barbie style" walk that is unnatural, and move to more of the fun, individual style.

We broke into three groups and switched after a little while so we could work with each consultant. After seeing some of the girls walk, I started to think that there was no way that I could walk like that. I wanted to at least try though. Soon it was my turn and I knew I wasn't doing that well. I had to laugh, though, as one of the ladies said when I walked back, "The best way I can describe your walk is that you sort of have this stiff military walk about you."

All of the contestants that were in earshot laughed as they knew that this lady had no idea that I was in the military. I didn't get much out of the lesson except that I knew I had a lot of work to do after seeing those girls work the runway.

Our next event was fun and really short. This competition was to show off what we learned on the runway . . . in a weird way. Each team had their own teeter-totter to walk across, holding a container with colored liquid that represented their team color. The first to fill a bucket on the other end was the winner.

It was fun and also very nerve-wracking at the same time, because you wanted to hurry but you had to balance and also be careful with the teeter-totter getting slippery from the liquid that was spilled along the way. We had to wear these helmets for safety reasons and it just increased the challenge of hurrying.

The producers would pause us every now and then so they could wipe off the teeter-totters to keep it clean. During one "freeze" they noticed that one of the contestants, as she was in the middle of dumping a glass, had her helmet on backward. It was hilarious and looked so funny! The purple squad lost yet again. They always said there was some prize for winning each event but it seemed nothing really came of it. Really, the event was fun but over quickly.

Now it was time to get ready for "tops and bottoms."

"Utah," the host called out as one of the six.

"Oh boy," I muttered under my breath. I wasn't surprised and I felt I had a pretty good idea of what "3" I was going to be in. When it was my turn to step forward, sure enough, I was in the bottom 3. But why I was there took me completely by surprise.

"Utah, what you did a couple of days ago really offended us," said one of the advisors. My jaw dropped from the shock of what I was hearing. "We are here trying to help, and we take our jobs seriously, while it seems you are just mocking us."

"Don't get us wrong, Utah," another advisor interrupted. "We have a sense of humor but that really cut deep when we thought you were being serious, trying to improve, and we find out that you are making fun of our advice."

"Wow, I'm truly sorry!" I said. "That was not what I intended. Please forgive me. I'm the type of person that tries to make the best of any situation that is thrown at me. It's what I'm trained to do as a soldier. I lived in a combat zone in Afghanistan. This is a different type of combat zone that we are facing as I am learning to dodge the bullets of the judgments being shot at us by making the best of my situation and having fun. Truly, I am so sorry that I offended you. That is the last thing I would ever want to do."

They nodded their heads and I stepped back. I felt sick and downhearted. As we were walking back, Georgia came up to me and said, "That was all my fault. You should not have been up there alone taking that from those judges. It was my idea and I was the one that encouraged you. It's me that should be in the bottom 3."

"Georgia, I think I would have done this regardless. It was me. I had fun. I don't regret doing it. In actuality, I am glad we did it. I know I would have looked back thinking I should have. Granted, I feel horrible about offending them, but I've done all that I could now. We are just trying to have fun with this reality show."

Friday

Goodness, did this offense take a toll on me! I felt like someone just blew out this flame inside me. I woke up feeling sad and not really motivated to do much. And to top it off, during breakfast, Wisconsin came up to me and said, "It meant a lot what you said last night because I was really offended at what you did the other day. Here, I was trying to help you put on make-up and you were just making fun of it all. It made me sad. But I know what you said last night came from the heart and it was good to know that you really didn't mean that."

"I am so sorry that you even felt that way for a second! I should have explained myself better when I was asking for your help. I am truly sorry. I sure didn't mean that."

"I know and it's okay." I gave her a hug and we went our ways but I needed to be alone. Crying doesn't happen very often for me. Sometimes I've wondered if I had a dry tear duct or something as I would see others get emotional over something and I wouldn't. Things touch and affect me, but I really don't show my emotion through crying. Unless it's a time when I don't live up to others' expectations of me—I hate that feeling. I do hold the highest expectations for myself and I let myself down all the time. But when I let others down and perhaps offend them, I'm crushed! This instance here really seemed to burst my bubble and I decided to back off from the "lime light" a bit.

The day seemed to get better as we sat around and mingled with the girls. That night they didn't have much planned for us and so the producers decided to have a casual night around the campfires having s'mores, cookies and hot chocolate. As I was talking to some of the girls, we got to thinking that we should play some night games tonight since they didn't have anything planned for us. I thought this was a perfect time to bring out the camouflage paint!

That night would have made any soldier proud. I handed out the camouflage kits to each girl and they seemed so excited. I couldn't believe it. I was a little reluctant because I didn't want the girls to think that I was just trying to find different ways to get in the spotlight. I was actually getting tired of it.

We had a "make-up lesson" in the make-up room and it was a kick. The girls were really getting into it, and they seemed to transform from Dr. Jekyll to Mr. Hyde. They put their sashes around their head "Rambo" style and their personalities totally changed. It was wonderful. For the next couple of hours we played "Killer" which is like "Mafia." Man, it got intense! It was SO funny to see all of the girls' different personalities come out. It was a whole lot of screaming, yelling, laughing, arguing, "killing", etc. Miss Iowa, was the real star of the night, though. She is the one that really knew the game and played the "narrator."

She played it like an auctioneer and really got into the story telling to make it sound as real as possible. She pulled me aside to get "military" terms to use in the story and title the characters, such as Military Police, Enemy, Doc (that's the same), etc. And the "killings" dealt with bombs, IEDs, shootings, etc. It was the most fun I've had in a long time with girls. It brought me back to the college days with my roommates. The girls were really getting into it and I couldn't have been happier to be there among my "new friends."

Through all of the downtime during the week, we were really able to get to know each other well. A lot of the girls would come into our room because it was the only way to get to other rooms, and so they would stop and visit every now and then. I was shocked one time to see California come in, climb up on the beds and just plop herself right between Arkansas and Tennessee.

I thought to myself, "She did that without asking? I could never have the courage to be like that around girls and think that they even wanted me there. And Arkansas and Tennessee didn't even say anything. Is there something I just don't know about being a girl? There must be some type of 'girl bond' that I must have missed growing up . . . the closeness and the friendship that I never really knew."

Saturday

Journal entry: *Saturday, was a good and partly emotional day. I've already been sort of down ever since I offended the advisors on Thursday with my "mockery". My patience is starting to wear thin though and my emotions are flowing more. It must be from all of the estrogen around me. Today I was getting a little annoyed with so many girls talking, giggling, singing, and doing "girly" things. My style is more of just shutting up when I am supposed to. But here you have so many girls that have grown up with the best friends, girl chats, etc. and when they get together, they bond and dish out the "silliness." Okay, I am obviously being a little pessimistic right now. These girls are so fun and crack me up (Miss Virginia, Miss Georgia, Miss Tennessee, etc). And this is the closest I feel I have been to girls in a long time.*

We got into our evening gowns and had a special consultant come with some advice on what would best suit our figure. We were going through the opening and introduction with our host and Randolf, the guest consultant. Then Randolf said he was going to pull a girl out to personally advise her. He pointed to me because I was the easiest access and I think they planned to pull whatever girl landed there.

At that point he was cut off because of some sound issues (airplane in the background) and the girls around me were excitedly saying, "Utah, you were picked!" But I felt sick about it. I got so nervous and thought to myself, "Oh no, how do I do this tactfully and not offend this guest?" My concern was that the only gowns he had brought were all sleeveless. I just said a quick prayer and asked for guidance.

While I was doing this, though, Kristen (Montana) and Jenny (New Mexico) pulled the host aside and said that Utah only wears gowns with sleeves and asked if the guest had any. They checked and he didn't, so they let the guest know to call up another girl. I didn't know this until afterward, and I just felt a huge relief when my name wasn't called. Jenny came up to me a few minutes later explaining that she told them. She apologized because she suddenly felt bad that she spoke for me and might have messed up my opportunity to work with a top fashion guru. She started to get emotional and that triggered me because I was emotional already, and I told her how grateful I was to her that she did that for me. She was an answer to my prayer.

For some reason, as my team was getting "consulted," I was really emotional. Maybe I was tired of being in the spotlight, maybe tired of the pressure of my standards constantly being tested, who knows . . . but I felt weak. The consultant's suggestion for me was to go sleeveless and show off my shoulders and collarbones. I didn't feel like getting into a lengthy discussion at that moment and just said, "Thank you".

We had our next challenge after that. We had one hour to make an evening gown with this black turtle neck dress that they gave us. I was relieved to see that they gave us that much of a dress to work with. They did provide some accessories and tools to use and they expected us to apply the suggestions of the consultants and make it our own as well.

There is a reason I don't do crafty things—I get frustrated way too easily at my lack of creative skill. I had fun, though, and felt that I made myself shine through. I made a "makeshift" collar with half sleeves and a knee-length dress. I felt good in it. It was so cool to see all of the creativity that the girls put into those dresses! We got to show off our dresses on the runway that evening out on the field. It was FREEZING and really windy!

I got some great pointers from Miss Virginia and Miss DC on how to "strut my stuff" out there. I was laughing so hard as they were showing me different styles. I don't think modeling is for me, period. I decided to just let it loose out there and just act like a model. I don't have to be a model but I can at least act and mimic them for the time being. Tops and bottoms were that night and thank goodness I was safe in the middle with the other 46 girls not named. The judges did comment on my look and how I was grasping this "change." Huh.

I had an OTF ("On the Fly" . . . basically just commentary about what's going on) right after that. Our team's director had some really good questions and I had a great opportunity to explain why I am modest: "This was how I was raised, my religious beliefs, it's what I am comfortable with. Plus, I wanted to be true not only to who I am, but to God and show that by the way I dress." I felt so excited at how I got that across. I really hoped it would get into the final show after all of the editing.

Now that the show has come and gone, I was really sad that my OTF about modesty didn't make it in, nor did the camouflage night. It just goes to show that the producers wanted drama and would try to create it anywhere. Sometimes the girls would get pushed with questions just so they could get certain sentences on film and then later, piece it together to make it into something it wasn't. It got really annoying and soon girls were really trying to be careful about what they said so that it wouldn't get interpreted in a different way.

Sunday

Since all of the previous events focused on a phase of competition for Miss America (interview, modeling, poise, etc) in a twisted way, there was really only one phase left . . . talent. We didn't really know how they were going to go about this. A lot of the girls started brainstorming together . . .

"Maybe they are bringing in different artists to work with each type, like a dancer, a singer, an instrumentalist."

"Do you think they are going to have us each do our talent?" ("There's no way," someone chimed in.)

"What if they get the dancers to sing and the singers to dance? Each girl has to do a different talent." (That got the girls laughing and thinking that would be fun.)

The ideas kept coming, but we were nowhere close.

"Ladies, I hope you have been warming up your vocals and brushing up on your history because we are going to test how well you remember our nation's famous anthems," said our host. Some of the girls' jaws dropped (mainly the dancers of the group) as they just found out they had to sing on camera.

One girl from each team went at a time and the music would start to play while the host would point his baton at a contestant, signaling her to sing. The first few contestants were singing beautifully and remembering all of the words. The National Anthem was the first song. "Whose broad stripes and bright stars," belts one of the contestants, a dancer, completely off key. We all couldn't help but giggle.

The girls thought they were done after the first verse but the host still continued, as well as the music. We had to know *all* the verses of the songs? All of the girls that stood in the back watching were now looking at each other in shock. Some of the girls continued on while others were eliminated.

As a new group of girls got up, they would either continue where the other group left off or start a new song. Some of the other songs were, "Yankee Doodle", "My Country Tis of Thee", "America, the Beautiful", and so on. Then we would just rotate through the songs again.

So we got to pick up some of the words from the other girls that knew them while they were up there singing. Finally, but hesitantly, I was in the next group, and I was just praying that I would sing on key. "My Country 'Tis of Thee" was our song and I croaked my first note. Sure, I can blame it on not being warmed up but really, I'm just not that good. The song was also in a high key and so I started over in a lower one. We went on to the second verse and I was done for.

"Can I do push-ups and still stay in?" I pleaded, trying to hold on for the purple team because we were actually tied with the lead.

"Sure," the host said. So I dropped and did 10.

"Like that's going to save you . . . you're gone," laughed the host.

I can't say that I didn't try. The game was soon over and there wasn't much else to that day.

Monday

The day of the big finale arrived when they would pick a top 10 and then award the three winners who most resemble the new direction of the Miss America pageant. They brought in some big fashion designers to work with each team at the beginning of the day. The designers worked with the girls in picking out a new outfit to wear on the "red carpet" that night right before the finale.

Our team's designer was great to work with and really tried to find an outfit that worked with our personality. She pulled us aside individually, while the cameras, of course, were filming, to find out what kind of styles we usually like. I simply explained that I like things with half-sleeves and that go to my knees without really using the word "modest" and offending her style.

We found a couple to work with. The first one looked hideous on me and I took it off immediately before I gave someone nightmares. The second one I loved! It was a bright royal blue, with half sleeves, a popped collar, and length down to the knees—how much more perfect can this get?

The only problem with it was that the slit for the neckline extended down to the bottom of my rib cage. That was easy to fix with a little bit of double sided tape that I borrowed from the camera crew.

I was actually impressed with the "red carpet" event that night. It was in the front of the house. We came down the stairs in groups of 3 (to help speed things up) onto the red carpet. There were lots of lights, some flashing in the background to make it look like lots of people were there taking photos… there was really just one, and we had places to pose on the red carpet. It was a roped-off, square section with our "screaming fans" on the other side. Really, it was just all of the extra crew members that didn't need to be used to help film this. It made me smile but I was really impressed how they pulled it off and made it look so good.

I really wanted to have fun with this. I walked down with my group and then we each took the red carpet individually spacing out. Ya know, to give us our time with our "fans." I had lots of fun with them. Each of the advisors were on the carpet ready to ask the certain girls that were assigned to them a question. I met up with mine and she hit me with her questions, "How do you think you relate to Americans today?"

"By being who I am. I believe that being a soldier, runner, student, volunteer, and nurse, that I can relate to most Americans. We live in such a diverse nation and I feel my life helps represent that diversity."

"If you could change anything about yourself to help relate to Americans better, what would it be?"

I paused for a moment. "What would I change?" I thought. Then I just went with my answer, "I wouldn't change anything. This is who I am and I'm proud of the woman I've become. I think that helps me relate to others . . . by being myself."

"Thank you."

"Thanks." For some reason I just can never say, "You're welcome."

We lined up at the end to get ready for the big finale and announcement of the winners. I didn't really feel one way or the other about whether I would be up there or not. I hadn't been in the best predicaments with those advisors this week, but maybe they see what I can do for this organization, because I am so different . . . and isn't that what they are looking for? As the top 10 were announced, I wasn't one of them. Georgia turned to me in shock, "I can't believe you are not up there!"

"Ah, I'm not too surprised. I really feel I offended them big time." They started to announce the top 3 winners who get the "amazing prize package" that had been talked about all week. Before the last one was announced, Georgia leaned over and whispered, "They are totally going to pull off a surprise and announce Miss Utah is our final winner!"

I just laughed. A lot of the other contestants came up to me afterward that night and said they thought I was going to be up there. I really wasn't too surprised. I think I'm too different for the change they are looking for and I don't portray the glamorous side enough. Sure the "amazing prize package" would have been nice, but I was relieved when it was done because it meant that it was soon time to leave this "combat zone," and I was ready.

Tuesday

You could tell a lot of the girls were relieved that this was coming to a close as well. We had our "wrap-up" interviews that day to get our feelings about the overall experience and cover certain questions they still had. It took about 30 minutes to an hour for each girl, so it was on-going and girls didn't finish until that evening. Mine was easy as we recapped feelings of the week. They also had a few questions about why

I feel I should be Miss America, why I am the best candidate and so on. I sometimes struggle answering those. It sounds so boastful when you list things off like that. I do my best, but it is sure uncomfortable.

The rest of the day was left to packing up and getting our cell phones returned to us! It was funny to see 52 girls jabberin' on their cell phones the rest of the day. We were warned to not say anything about what took place until after the show aired in six weeks.

Before we even came to the reality show, we had to make a DVD answering 30 random questions, and we didn't know what they were going to do with it. We were told on this night that they were going to use some of the film on the "Miss America: Reality Check" website so America could get to know the contestants. They announced that there was a winner for the most creative segment.

We were told, "If you girls want a good laugh, you have got to watch Miss Utah's DVD. She is the winner."

I just had to laugh to myself when I heard that. I'm glad they were entertained. I couldn't have made that DVD without my neighbor, Mike, and his ingenious ideas.

Wednesday

Girls were getting up at odd hours of the morning. The first bus was taking a group to the airport at 3:30 a.m. I wasn't going until 5:30. Cell phone jingles started going off for some of the alarms at 2 a.m. I tried to fall back asleep, and then I heard Georgia pop up after that first jingle went off. She said, "Is Tinkerbell here?"

I could not hold back the laughter, "Georgia, you crack me up!" She's witty even in her sleep.

Overall, it was a good 10 days—a good chance to get to know the girls before the big competition. We could go in as friends, cheering each other on, instead of competitors.

I left thinking, though, that I would be lucky if I made "top 51" at Miss America. These girls were incredible and I couldn't believe I was among them.

Chapter 14

Miss America

"Bring it on!" I thought. I felt ready. I had been studying, practicing, and preparing the best I knew how. Then just two weeks before I had to leave for competition, my competition wardrobe was not coming together like I had hoped.

It was a long, hard, emotional couple of weeks, having just one piece of my competition wardrobe (the swimsuit I got at the Reality Show). It wasn't a good sign. Thanks to a few of people who stepped in, I felt miracles happened.

Preparing for Miss America

After coming back from the reality show, I put my game face on, knowing now who I was up against. I still had a lot of speaking engagements to do through December and part of January. I just tried to put forth a little effort each day and it was crazy how things were falling into place. One of my friends was very savvy in the political world and well, there is a reason I avoid it, because I don't understand it. He offered to meet with me every week leading up to the competition to discuss hot topics such as the presidential debate, the war in Iraq, immigration and other big issues at the time. He really helped me dig in deep and discover my own political values and that helped me establish an opinion on big issues. I was learning a lot about the different political terms and was soon finding this world interesting.

My mom happened to mention that someone in our neighborhood was a dance instructor and owned a dance studio. My mom brought it up one day while talking with her, and asked if she would be okay with letting me practice my talent and modeling there and if there were times available throughout the day. It turned out that she didn't even have classes until about 3 to 8 p.m. everyday and would love to help me out. I was so excited to hear this news, I couldn't believe it.

I started practicing there about three times a week starting mid-December and was also meeting with a modeling coach, Tewa, to help find a style that worked for me. Tewa really taught me some simple techniques that helped me get rid of some of my "stiff military walk" but still stay true to who I was. She was a lot of fun to work with and was also very patient with me. Things just really seemed to be falling into place... except when it came to wardrobe.

Come December, I still only had one competition wardrobe complete: the Reality Check swimsuit. I would have chosen a different suit, if there was an option. It turns out that there is a "swimsuit sponsor" each year at Miss America and every girl has to wear that brand. This year, they gave us eight suits to choose from and only two of them were one-piece, if you could call it that. Sure, they connected in some way, but these one-pieces were almost as revealing as the two-pieces. I was a little worried about how I was going to approach the Miss America Organization.

I tried to do it in a fun, business-like manner to explain my standards and asked if I could wear the Reality Show suit since it was in their guidelines. I got a "go" and was excited to leave that behind and move on. My director as Miss Utah lined up some designers to make my talent and evening gown. I was a little nervous about that idea because I didn't know them and, well, hadn't really done business with them before (having done this for a little while now, I guess I was developing a business-woman side of my personality). My director assured me that she had and really trusted them so I had to trust her. We confirmed in October they were making the dresses, and figured out "general" designs in November, telling them both what I wanted and praying that they had the same vision. It turned out one of the designers did . . . and one was completely off.

My time was really running out and it was now just two weeks before I was to leave for the pageant. I finally got the dresses in the mail and was praying to have an open mind. The talent dress couldn't have been more perfect. It was a beautiful teal/aquamarine, elegant princess-style dress. I was glad to see it had "bell sleeves" to help with my acting. As for the evening gown, words cannot express . . . but I will do my best. At first sight, I turned pale and just held my breath in hopes that it was one of those dresses that miraculously changes when it is on.

It really just got worse. It was this black knit sweater that fit like a circus tent on me with a rhinestone collar. I still had hope that maybe if we just took it in so it fit, it could still work. I went to a seamstress, Raychellene Talbot, that I knew in Spanish Fork, Utah that had previously fixed some of my business suits. I tried it on for her and when I saw her facial expression, it said it all. I started to laugh and cry at the same time—laughing at how ridiculous it was, and crying because I was only two weeks away from heading to the biggest competition of my life. I told Raychellene what had I explained to the designers.

"I want something that is a sheen black that is able to stretch and fit snug around my body, while long and flowing from the thighs down. It has long sleeves and a type of turtle neck in a way that I would love to jewel the heck out of. It's very simple but in my mind it is so elegant."

"The design you want is a simple pattern. I know I can do it." And this one I trusted. It was New Year's Eve and we needed to be done by January 12th, the night of my send-off party. Before I headed to a family party that night, she called me with great news that she found some material that she believed was what I was looking for.

I was so excited to hear some good news. I was a little worried, though, that my dress was taking her from her holiday and celebrating with her family. She reassured me that she needed to go to the fabric store anyway and was planning on being with family that night. She said that she should be ready for a fitting in two days. Things were looking bright.

My director and I ordered some cocktail dresses to have for interview suit options (on-stage and private interviews). I was relieved to find that they both fit beautifully after Raychellene took them in a bit. I felt like I was shopping everyday, getting accessories and outfits for each of the appearances. Shopping is not one of my favorite things unless it has to do with food. I love grocery shopping! There is just something relaxing about having that cart in hand and filling it up with fun things to bake. I'm getting all giddy just thinking about it! Okay, off of my tangent and back to the pageant . . .

After a few fittings with Raychellene, I put the dress on for the final fitting. I started to cry, but this time was because of how beautiful it looked. What she did far exceeded my dreams. Now, after two years of trouble with evening gowns, I am now wearing my dream dress, and I couldn't wait to show America.

Human Art

During this time of getting my wardrobe all together, meeting with my "political advisor," practicing modeling and talent, and fulfilling numerous speaking engagements, I discovered "myself." Well, at least the tools to help let "me" shine more.

One of my mom's friends in the Mormon Tabernacle Choir mentioned that she had a cousin who had done years of research in discovering a person's unique design and color. Her cousin's company was called "Human Art." When my mom told me about this, I must admit it sounded cool and boring all at the same time. I got a number to call and thought it wouldn't hurt to meet with them. I mean goodness, how long could it really take to tell someone what colors work for you? So I gave them a call…

We scheduled a time to get together at the beginning of December and they wanted my address so they could send me the book that helped explain a little bit about what "Human Art" is. When I got the book, I was intrigued by what I was reading:

Human Art awakens us to who we really are. It is a measurement, an equation that finally makes sense of our divine nature and how we are made. It gives us back something that we came to this wonderful earth with, but of which we somehow lost sight. Human Art is a gift; it doesn't change who we are, it simply helps us recognize ourselves. It points out all the wonderful qualities and traits that we all uniquely possess, and in helping us to get to know ourselves better, it gives us a glimpse of what we can do with our lives. Consequently, it empowers us and gives us a direction for greatness in life that is totally individual. (Excerpt from *Human Art: Understanding Your Own Personal Design* by Brook and Rod Thornley, p. 9.)

Whoa . . . how does it do that? I started skimming through the rest of the book and looking at the pages. I saw different sections on "designs" and was just becoming all the more curious. I went to the meeting and met with the founder, Brook Thornley and her public relations team. I was expecting to get all of my answers. I did get my answers, but it in an unexpected way.

This meeting was really just to help schedule the many other meetings that were ahead. "You mean this is a process?" I thought. It turned out they wanted to film it to help show all of the different aspects of what Human Art can do, which I still didn't really understand.

From the very first moment I met Brook, she was just a delight. I looked forward to every meeting with her as we got to know each other more and more. She explained to me a quick overview of what I would be going through.

There are four designs: saturated, whitened, grayed and blackened. We all have these within us and around us, just a different percentage of each, making each individual unique. They consist of types of personalities, colors, moods, lines, patterns, sound, and movement. They truly are in everything. Brook has done 25 years of research to discover this.

Here's another quote from the book:

Trying to categorize and define different types of human beauty has been one of humankind's favorite pastimes. Each branch of this particular kind of science has touched on correct principles, but most have not delved deep enough into the sum total of who we are. The concept of Human Art is composed of design, art, and behavioral principles that are organized into a methodology. The principles are empirical, meaning you can observe them. You can trace them consistently throughout nature, animals and most importantly, human beings. (Human Art, p. 33.)

And my process soon began . . .

Discovering Jill Stevens

After just a few minutes with Brook, she knew my designs, at least my two prominent ones. I was very "blackened and saturated." Cool.

Now what does that mean? She then gave me a *very* basic rundown of each of the four designs.

Saturated: The central focus for a saturated person is competence and accuracy. They take charge. Their beauty is striking. We describe them as logical, authoritative, decisive, as well as a clear thinker. Their personality is competent, capable, disciplined, intimidating and sophisticated. We innately recognize these people and surroundings because, when exposed to them, we automatically stand a little straighter or sit up in our chairs. Even when describing these elements we become quiet. We have the same reaction when we walk into a black tie event: it demands our respect.

Whitened: The central focus for a whitened person is to have fun through understanding and connecting with others. Youthfulness and innocence are their inherent beauty. Their personality is like the sunshine coming into a room—they brighten things up. They are extroverted, lighthearted, spontaneous, high energy, and bubbly. We can't help but be happy and laugh when in the company of a whitened person.

Grayed: The central focus for a grayed person is to be appropriate. These people study the details and process all contingencies. They have the imprint that calms people. Their personality is seen as introverted, soft spoken, diplomatic, empathetic, graceful and proper. They prefer to observe rather than participate. The grayed design brings a refinement and a grace to the earth; whenever we see these elements we slow down and experience life.

Blackened: The central focus for a blackened person is to get the job done. These people are very task oriented and build much of what we see around us. They take problems head on and deal with them with the intent to solve them as quickly as possible. They believe in getting things done and moving on. Their personality is assertive, direct, confident, conservative, practical and efficient. The blackened design and traits are wonderful. These people just seem to know how to deal with life. They also possess a very natural attractiveness. (*Human Art,* pp. 33-47.)

I was blown away by the incredible depth of these designs and how you can see them in every aspect of life. Brook then broke it down specifically for me in a later session. My dominant one is blackened being at 40 percent. Next is saturated at 30 percent. Grayed at 25 percent and whitened at 5 percent. Being blackened and saturated didn't surprise me at all after I heard the brief descriptions. I was a little surprised though at how much grayed design I had and so little white. Brook explained that my "grayed is definitely there and even though whitened is only 5 percent, after getting to know you, when you are whitened, it is as if you are 100 percent whitened. It just happens 5 percent of the time." Interesting . . . I can actually think of those "whitened" times.

Our first couple of meetings dealt with making my "color wheel." There are literally thousands of colors but we only went through about 400 of them, as she held different colored strips up to my face while I sat there. You would think it would be boring just sitting there for hours while someone holds up a color to your face but really it was quite entertaining to watch Brook's reaction with each color.

I guess my face did something as she held up a color, and she would either throw it away or put in my "color wheel" pile. Every now and then, she would get all giddy and excited and leave that color off to the side. I later found out that these became my "personality colors" that depicted my mood and really helped me shine out. These colors would help me design any wardrobe, pick any outfit, design any house, etc. It was fascinating. We did this in two different sessions.

Brook wanted to know about my wardrobe, and well, as I noted before, it was in the works. I told her we had people working on different outfits of my competition, except for interview, and that we were still on the look-out for that. She said that they would like to take that project on and specifically design one that incorporated all of the designs according to my style. I brought in some pictures of interview suits to show her what I usually like in a suit and she got to work. Our next session after the color readings, Brook had the sketches laid out for my interview suit. I couldn't believe it! They had a seamstress on their team that got to work on it.

While the interview suit was being made, Brook and I were trying to coordinate our busy schedules as to when we could fit in all of the other training sessions. I couldn't believe all that they were doing for me and the fact that they were sponsoring it all. We scheduled the hair appointment next. She drew me up some sketches to show what she wanted to do to my hair. There were four different heads on the paper to show precisely how each design was going to be cut into my hair, pertaining to how dominant each one is. Wow, I was getting excited!

Brook worked on the color in my hair, while Tommy, one of her colleagues put the extensions in. It was extensive work. Tommy cracked me up as he got to an area, "There seems to be an area void of hair back here." I just started laughing!

"My hair went MIA on the reality show."

"Yeah, they chopped it up bad," Tommy said. It turned out we needed a lot of extensions to fix what they did on Reality Check. After a few hours, it was fun to walk out of that salon with a little bit longer hair than when I came in, when usually it's the other way around.

After make-up lessons, interview coaching, fittings for my interview suit, digging deep into my designs, a new hair style, new friends and many laughs—all in six weeks—I felt Human Art had given me the tools to realize my potential. I was truly locked and loaded, ready for competition.

Game Time

I had two different "Miss America send-off" parties, one each in northern and southern Utah. It was wonderful to see how many supported me through this wild, unexpected journey. A lot of family was there, as well as friends. It gave me such a boost to see them cheering me on. The send-offs were a great way to see if I had everything in place.

I showed everything that I was going to be doing at Miss America, so it was a good warm up for the big game ahead. The Sunday before I left (January 13, 2008), our neighbor, Hollie, came by to give me a book called "I Like Myself." She explained what this book had done for her and that her kids say their favorite line each day, "I like myself, I'm glad I'm being me, there is no one else I'd rather be."

After she left, my mom and I read it. We both got emotional at what a powerful, yet simple message that book delivered. We both started talking and had the same idea: every contestant needs to hear this, especially during one of the hardest weeks (emotionally) for most of these girls. We wondered how we could get this done in such a short amount of time. I was leaving on Wednesday to check in on Thursday and the competition started the next Monday.

As I went off to speak at a few last-minute engagements, my mom called me with wonderful news. She had decided to call Windridge Elementary School in our neighborhood to see if they could order the books. The secretary, Aloha, was a good friend of ours and my mom told her why we were looking for it. Our friend seemed excited and said, "I'll get on this and let you know by noon."

Within the hour she called my mom back with incredible news. "I have over $300 donated from friends and teachers that know Jill and really want to help out. I am expecting a lot more. I looked it up and found that we can order the books on-line."

My mom shared the exciting news with me. Again, the emotions came as we both could not believe this was all coming together so quickly. We placed the order to have 51 books shipped to my brother in Las Vegas. My mom got some ribbon to tie around each book. She helped me write a message that we printed out on stickers to place in the cover of each book for the contestants.

This is the message I wanted each girl to know:

You are beautiful both inside and out! I am so privileged to have been able to have my path cross with yours over the past few months. We live in a world of harsh judgments. We are judged by our behavior, by our looks, by our clothes, by our actions, by our words. Never let those judgments diminish the incredible value that comes from the inside—the value of knowing you are a daughter of God.

This is your week to shine, my friend . . .
"Cause nothing in this world you know
Can change what's deep inside, and so . . .
No matter if they stop and stare,
No person ever, anywhere
Can make me feel that what they see
Is all there really is to me."

All my love,
Miss Utah

After it was complete, I felt a huge release come over me. All the stress of the past few weeks with finding wardrobe and getting all the last minute things together really added to the tension and stress I carried. I hated that it was all about *me* and getting *me* ready. But once this project was made possible, to give someone something, especially something so meaningful to me, gave me this overwhelming peace. I was now ready.

On my trip down to Las Vegas, I felt unsettled. I felt like I should be able to take on the world with all of my preparation, but something was not quite right, and I didn't know what.

Comfortable heels anyone?

I was lucky to live close enough to drive, not having to worry about cramming everything into a couple of suitcases and leaving some things behind. My car was packed. I brought everything I could think of to make it as comfortable as possible. I packed my blender so I could have my protein shakes every morning (Isagenix was the diet I craved and loved), DVDs to work out to (Turbo Jam) in the mornings, and enough food to last throughout the week (about 30 protein bars, three boxes of Reduced Fat Wheat Thins, Kashi High Protein Cereal, eight chocolate protein drinks, etc).

I try to stick to my normal eating habits (which is "mass consumption") as much as possible when traveling. I have learned from experience that I seem to get sick when I get too far off my routine while traveling—and this was not a time to be getting sick.

From the moment I checked in, I could tell this was going to be a long week. We were assigned to certain hostesses and they had to be with us at ALL TIMES! I was lucky to actually get into a bathroom stall without them holding my hand. It was kind of annoying but understandable at the same time because of security reasons. Las Vegas was no place for these contestants to be wandering alone.

It was fun to see all of the girls again. I was rooming with Louisiana. I felt bad for her because I wasn't the type of girl that loved to stay up and chat about nonsense things and really express a lot about myself. It was great to see when she found contestants to bond with across the hall. I don't know why I'm not that way. Darn my independent self!

We had a few appearances each day throughout the 10 days that we were there: fundraising events, receptions, a gondola ride at the Venetian. Whenever we would just be standing there waiting to enter an event, I would seize this opportunity to take off the heels to prepare my feet for the long night ahead at whatever appearance awaited us. The balls of my feet were bruised by the end of the week.

Press interviews were held each day for certain girls as requested by their local news stations that came to cover the pageant. A lot of military press was there to cover my journey. I couldn't ask for a better support team. The military has backed me up through all this and it was nice to have family across the world. The saying is true: "When you're military, you're family!"

Rehearsals were long and at first, fun because the show started to fall into place. It got really old really fast, since the steps to learn were basically just walking from point A to point B. We went over the walking patterns for hours everyday for the 10 days straight. There isn't much to walking down stage. Of course, the practice was nice, I guess. It was really to keep us all busy and in one area. You would see some of the girls mingling with each other in small groups that they had already clicked with.

Most girls were on their own, practicing their talent, doing exercises (crunches, lunges, push-ups and yoga), on their computers studying for interview things and so on. Sometimes I would just be rolling with laughter as a few of us would be back stage before practicing the show. Miss DC would be teaching us "hip dance moves" and we were all trying to do them. Now, there is a reason I don't dance. My favorite reality TV show to watch is "So You Think You Can Dance" because sometimes I do, and it's embarrassing. Miss DC just cracked me up!

I would have to say that the best part about the rehearsals was the wittiness of the girls. They had me laughing so hard as they would come up with a different saying each time to announce who they were, such as: "Where we disregard the letter R, I'm Miss Massachusetts."

"Where the subway is a way of life, not just a food, I'm Miss New York."

"From the state that moved up their primaries and nobody cared, I'm Miss Wyoming."

"Where we have potatoes for breakfast, lunch and dinner, I'm Miss Idaho."

"Where your child is likely to have more teeth than you, I'm Miss Kentucky."

"Where you're more likely to hit a moose than a parked car, I'm Miss Maine."

"From the state where everyone knows their state flag, I'm Miss Pennsylvania." We all laughed at how she played off the reality show with that one.

"Where we place a huge emphasis on our geography, I'm Miss South Carolina." The whole place roared with that one, referring to the funny mistake Miss Teen South Carolina USA made a few months earlier.

"Where you can have a southern accent and a college degree, I'm Miss Georgia." She just cracks me up.

I loved these girls! I couldn't really think of anything very creative. The only funny things I could come up with were too much of an inside joke and would really only be funny to "Mormons." Thankfully my mom and her group of friends brain-stormed and helped me come up with a couple:

"Where a minivan is considered a luxury car." and "Home of the country's highest birthrate, as long as the Osmonds don't move!" (We love the Osmonds!)

Miss America preliminaries

I couldn't believe this was it! As Sunday approached, it was hard to believe that I had my private interview the next day. This was really the event it all came down to, even though the interview is only worth 25 percent of your overall score. It is where the judges really get to know your personality.

I really wanted to get the "I Like Myself" books to the girls on Sunday so that they got that message before the competition started. My brother delivered all of the books with my message stuck inside the cover and ribbons around them. They looked wonderful and I was so grateful for all the many people that made this possible. I coordinated with the "people in charge" to have the books in the girls' rooms when we returned from our appearance that night. When I saw some of the girls later that night and especially throughout the day on Monday, a lot of them expressed how much the gift meant to them. What was most touching to me was that a lot of them said, ". . . And I know you meant every word." That meant the world to me.

Interviews were scheduled throughout the day on Monday, starting at 8 a.m. I was contestant #14 and didn't have my interview until around 1:30 that afternoon. They broke us into different groups according to our times. I guess it was the luck of the draw as the contestants before us got to stay in their rooms and prepare while we, the next group in the line-up, had to still go to rehearsal that morning.

We were praying that they would allow us enough time to get ready for interview. We needed to be there at 12:30 completely ready. I was trying to plan the best way to prepare and be most "refreshed" and decided that I would take a shower when we were allowed to go back to our rooms to get ready for interview. I needed about an hour to get ready and figured that we would be allowed that, since other girls that morning were getting a couple of hours. We had a break during rehearsal at about 10 and I went to approach the hosts to see if we could get ready since they were going to be rehearsing with other contestants.

"No, I'm sorry. But I have here on the schedule to take you back to your rooms at 11:45," replied the hostess.

"You mean to tell me that you are only giving us 30 minutes to get ready for this interview?" I asked, trying to hold back my shock and anger at the same time.

"Rules are rules, and I can't do anything about it. That's what it says." If I have any pet peeve, it is when someone says, "I can't do anything about it" from the very start, without a hint of even trying.

I tried to approach the situation from a different angle. "I understand that you have strict times to keep a close watch on the girls and that means a lot to us that you are looking out for us. We appreciate that you have given us 30 minutes to get ready but 1) we're pageant girls. (I tried to throw in some humor to lighten the situation.) 2) Other contestants are getting 2-3 hours to get ready. 3) This is one of the biggest competitions some of us will ever do in our lifetime. 4) We are just sitting here at rehearsal because they are working with other girls, when we could be getting ready. Really, all we need is a hostess to escort us back to our rooms, and we have found you. Can you please do this for us?"

"I understand," the hostess said, "but the people in charge are very strict and have to keep to the schedule."

"Can you at least talk with them?" I asked. "I'll come with you."

So we walked over to the one who is in charge of the hostesses. She wouldn't even listen to me explain and was furious. The other hostess and I tried to talk her through it, but I decided to step out and let them talk it through while I figured out a back-up plan to getting ready in 30 minutes. I was flashing back to my "boot camp days" of getting ready in 10 minutes, no problem. There wasn't much to it. You just wash your hair and use the shampoo that rinses off to wash the rest of your body. Throw on a uniform and you're out the door with wet hair. I don't think that look would go over very well with the judges, however.

Time was ticking as they were trying to work out the details. I had given up hope when finally the hostess came back and said she could take us now. It was now 11:30 as they had taken the past hour to work this out. At least we had 40 minutes instead of 30 now. Every second counted. I was going through the game plan of how to do things most speedily and efficiently as we were walking to our rooms. Forty minutes later, after a shower (shaving my legs even) and getting the most "business like" I knew how, the hostess knocked on the door. I grabbed my military backpack (a.k.a. my purse) and was out the door. I did it! That was "Pageant Boot Camp" style.

I called my mom when I was down in the "holding room." She was always there for me to give me a boost. Before I left for Vegas, she gave me a bag of little things to open each day of the week. My first gift was a CD of her singing the two songs that have given me so much strength in my life: "My Tapestry" and "Let Your Light So Shine."

After her pep talk, I felt ready. I glanced a little at my "values book" to be reminded of who I want to portray, hopefully showing the judges that I can be Miss America. I knew I had done all that I could to prepare, but of course there are always those thoughts that creep in. "Could I have done more? Should I have studied this?" I realized I needed to clear those thoughts out and just have fun with this.

My interview

"They're ready for you," said the judges' chair. I felt good and ready. She escorted me in and announced, "Here is contestant number 14, Jill Stevens, Miss Utah." I smiled and walked in confidently. It was a large room. There was a glass podium in the center that I knew was for me. The long table of judges was ten feet in front of the podium. There were some spotlights and cameras on the side to record everything.

From my right to left sat the judges: James Arthur Ray (from the field of leadership development), Robin Meade (communications/interview field and CNN anchor), Kim Lyons (field of fitness-trainer from the hit show "Biggest Loser"), Jackie Joyner-Kersee (field of community service; Olympian), Jason La Padura (field of talent), Sarah Ivens (field of national press defining today's "IT girl"), and Trace Ayala (field of beauty and fashion).

James started off the interview by giving an example of how in business, if you focus attention on an issue, it seems to bring about more attention. He then asked, "Do you feel with so much of the news covering the war in Iraq, that it is actually bringing about more terrorists?"

"I can see how that can be true . . ." I said.

Robin, the head judge, interrupted by asking, "So do you think we should stop covering the war?"

"Absolutely not! It's what is going on in the world. I do wish more of the positive stories which I experienced firsthand were being told."

Kim then interrupted, "So do you feel if we focus on peace that would stop the terrorists?"

"Of course peace is a great thing to be focusing on, but that won't stop the war," I said. "Terrorists will still come and we have got to still stand up to them."

Wow! We started off on a heated topic. There were some other questions that related to the war but I do not remember specifics. Sarah chimed in with a few questions dealing with "religious profiling" and "Muslims." I remember focusing on "religious freedom" and that they are not all terrorists.

Kim joined in, "Why did you join the military?"

"Too easy." I thought.

"I've been a combat medic for seven years now . . ."

"Wow," she replied.

"I loved the medical experience I could get for my nursing career, paying for my education, and the chance to serve my country. I loved the challenge of it as well. That's how I live my life, rising to the next challenge and that's, in a way, how I got into pageants, because it can be challenging being a lady," I said, trying to bring my passion and some humor.

A few other questions were fired. I did a quick assessment and wondered why this interview was feeling different. It wasn't having the "spark" that I can usually bring. I would keep trying.

Someone asked about my platform and I remembered answering to some extent, "With all that is going on in our nation . . . terrorist attacks, shootings in schools and malls, we need to be prepared; have a plan (some of the judges nodded). You can make it fun by having a scavenger hunt with the family to involve the kids because most of what goes in your survival kit is already in your home."

Kim said, "Health and fitness seem to be a huge priority for you. Which comes first, taking care of yourself or others?"

"Definitely yourself, because that will only help you in taking care of others, by setting that example." Now I tried to personalize it. "I even brought a blender with me so I could have my protein shakes every morning." Robin started laughing.

"I hear ya," Kim said.

"Did you workout this morning?" James asked.

"Yes. I did Turbo Jam in my bathroom," I said, smiling.

"What makes you sad?" Kim asked.

"Not living up to others' expectations. I hate that feeling."

"Have you ever cried?" Robin interrupted.

"Yes. A lot of people find me intimidating and notice that I don't cry often, thinking, 'Soldiers don't cry. . . . There's no crying in the Army,'" I said as some of them laughed. "But I have cried a lot, even in the last couple of weeks."

"Do you think Hillary Clinton's outburst helped her win New Hampshire?" Robin asked.

"Yes, I think it did. It even got me feeling for her as I watched it."

"Do you think it was staged?" James asked.

"Ah . . . part of me, yes. I think it was good timing, but it's hard to tell."

"Do you feel a president should cry?" Robin asked.

"To win votes . . . no! But I feel a president should be able to express emotion."

"If you were a superhero, who would you be and why?" James chimed in for a complete change of subject.

"The first one that comes to mind is Elastigirl . . ."

"Who's that?" Sarah asked, and Kim answered, "From the movie *The Incredibles.*"

I continued, " . . . because I actually have a costume of her and run races in it to motivate kids to do fitness."

"Why?" James asked blankly.

"I love the attitude that Elastigirl has for life. Very optimistic, and she has a lot of humor, which I always try to have."

"Which presidential candidate are you going for?" James asked.

Before I could answer, someone behind me called out, "Time!"

"Oooh. and we are out of time," Robin said. "Dang, that would have been a good one," she muttered to James. "Is there anything else that you would like to add that we didn't cover?"

"Yes," I paused, ". . . I hope you see Miss America in me and what I can do for this organization. As a soldier, I feel I am prepared for this one-year deployment, and as a marathon runner, I know have the endurance to keep strong and positive. As a nurse . . ."

"Thank you, Miss Utah. We are out of time," interrupted Robin.

"Thank you," I said and walked out another door thinking, "That wrap-up couldn't have been 30 seconds. That was it?"

After all of those months preparing, my interview was over. How are they going to feel and can they see me as Miss America with that? I didn't really know what to feel. I was sad and bummed. I felt I could have done a lot better. But it wasn't like I could say, "I'll be sure to change that next time." There wouldn't be a "next time."

I didn't feel the interview went horribly, but I didn't feel it was fantastic either. Something was missing to me. I felt I did all I could with what I was dealt. Probably the questions I didn't handle the best were the ones about Hillary Clinton. I was a little "wishy-washy" on those. I told myself, "Oh well, it's done now. I sure wish I had done better, but it's in the Lord's hands, if He wants them to see something in me."

I talked with my mom and DEl afterward. I think they heard the disappointment in my voice and sent me encouraging texts throughout the day to give me a boost.

Opening night of preliminaries

All the girls were excited to get the show started. I had a pretty easy night for the Tuesday, opening night preliminary. All I had was an on-stage question which is worth only 5 percent of the overall score. I planned it this way because it was a pattern I was used to. Both years at Miss Utah, I had the same order of competition: on-stage, modeling (swim and evening wear), then talent. I liked knocking out the interview first and then moving on.

It was finally time to do the "parade of states" for an audience. A lot of the girls used some of their witty lines they came up with in practice and some played it safe. The night went by quicker than I expected. When girls weren't competing, we were in a white tent that was made for our dressing rooms outside. It was time to get ready for on-stage question. I was excited! I loved my outfit and we knew the questions dealt with our platforms. How hard could it be?

While I was waiting backstage and the other girls before me were going out one by one, I was chatting with the girls by me to make sure I was in a "conversational mode" to make the experience more natural and easy on stage. I went through about four points in my head to be prepared for any type of question. I felt ready. I walked out on stage and met up with Heather French-Henry, a former Miss America, who was the host that night.

"Hello Jill, your platform is emergency preparedness. How can families today be better prepared for tomorrow?"

I went head-on with my answer, "The CERT program. It stands for Community Emergency Response Team and really helps communities prepare for the unexpected." I should have kept my mouth shut after that, but no, I kept going. I think I went through all the points in my head instead of just using one. I said I "think" I did because really, none of it made sense to me and I can't remember exactly what I said. At least I stayed on subject, but it didn't go as well as I had hoped.

I met up with my friends and family afterward at "visitation" (it kind of sounds like we were in prison). We got about 20-30 minutes with them each night after the evening was over. I was excited to see them. I walked over to them as they cheered, "GO UTAH!" "YEAH, GI JILL!"

I felt better already. I finally found my mom and she could tell right away just by looking at me that something was wrong. "I bombed it, Mom," I said softly, while hugging her.

"Well, it wasn't your best, but you were really one of the top ones out there." I looked at her in confusion. "There weren't that many that did that well in your group." DEl Beatty overheard and joined, "Don't be so hard on yourself," as he gave me a big hug. My mind flashed back to Miss SUU and I had to smile. I couldn't believe I had just competed on the Miss America stage.

"Its only 5 percent, and it's behind you now," DEl added. I had to keep telling myself that. I have to admit, it was such a boost to see so many people there to cheer me on. It gave me a second wind to focus on the next event. I went back to my room feeling down because, so far, I didn't feel great about either of my interviews, but I was still keeping my chin up thinking, "I get to show off my evening gown tomorrow!"

Wednesday preliminary

I woke up that day in a somber mood, not feeling very motivated. I felt so confused. Why was I not feeling the comfort of the Lord? One of my friends that came to Miss America could tell that I was beating myself up and felt strongly to share something with me. He sent me a text saying to check my email because he really felt I should read it before I left for the day…

I know you are busy but I just wanted to share a quick thought with you. Hopefully this can help in some way. I do not mean it in any other way than to perhaps be a help and a comfort to you. I can't help but feel that because of some of the attention and publicity you've received that there's a piece of you that feels you might be letting people down if you do not win. I want you to know what matters most is that you do your best, be confident in yourself and trust in the Lord.

I know you probably have had a lot of feelings and emotions go through your head over the past few days, some of them perhaps of some doubt or questioning whether this is even right. You are an extremely strong spirit and the Lord knows that. He wants nothing more than for you to move forward with his plan for you in confidence. However, there is someone who does not want you to feel confident in yourself or any of the choices coming up, and that's Satan. I know you know this, but sometimes before the light is when we receive the biggest opposition from the adversary. It could come from anything from thoughts or feelings that it's just not right, you're just not up to it, or just plain discouragement.

Jill, Satan would love for you to be down on yourself in any way that might affect your ability to perform, concentrate, love, and serve those around you. He knows how hard you've worked for all of this and he knows how much good you will do regardless of whether you win or not.

I guess what I am trying to say is that you can have full confidence in your abilities because the Lord is with you. To him, you already are Miss America, but have the confidence in his promises that you can do this if you are called.

Imagine yourself as Miss America as you interview with the judges. Imagine yourself as Miss America as you greet people and thank them and walk on stage. See yourself connecting personally and emotionally with those you talk with or look at. Imagine yourself being this person in all you do this week and then let the Lord take care of the rest. The Lord empowers those that envision themselves and exercise faith even before the "miracle" has happened. Regardless of how the final judging turns out, you will know you performed and did everything with full confidence and light because the Lord is with you.

One of the things that makes you so remarkable is your ability to believe in the cause you represent. Perhaps that ability to believe is being tested a little bit right now, but have full faith to believe in yourself and in the Lord's help, because with the Lord all things really are possible. You are the most wonderful, qualified and perfect candidate for Miss America and I believe that with all my heart. Whether it is right or not is in the Lord's hands, but know that you truly are remarkable!

I am sorry to rattle all of this off now, but after I spoke with you I just felt you might be a little confused or discouraged right now and I wanted to see if I might be able to help in any way. You are in all of our prayers. I can't imagine the difficulty in answering questions under time constraint, but I know you are doing just great.

Keep your head up! Keep your smile fixed! Love and serve everyone around you and the Lord will take care of the rest.

Wow! That left me at a loss for words. It completely changed my perspective on the events of this week. I held my chin a little higher that day.

I felt modeling went well that night. My lip didn't quiver hardly at all. I have had a huge problem for some reason with my lip quivering on stage or during a photo shoot. It's been a problem for as long as I can remember. I even recall it happening during my school picture being taken in pre-school.

Going out in swimsuit, I finally faced the challenge of thinking "I'm sexy" just for a moment and then throw it out immediately afterward. It actually worked for me. I went out there and had fun. My last pose didn't go too well. I tried to do a back pose, but it was more like I was shaking my behind in front of the judges. It didn't work out, so I turned back around for the last pose and then headed off the stage.

But with evening wear, I felt like I owned it! I nailed it and couldn't have been more excited. I was a bit more upbeat and positive during visitations that night. It was time to put it all behind me and focus now on what I do best . . . making a fool of myself on stage for my talent.

Thursday preliminary

Journal entry for January 24, 2008: *The last preliminary is about to start. I am in "high spirits because its talent night for me. God has given me many talents and I want to show my gratitude by letting them shine out tonight!*

We just got back from a "Red Carpet Premiere" for the new Rambo movie. Thank goodness we weren't planning on watching it or Miss Idaho and I would have had a great game of Uno going on in the bathroom to pass by the time, due to its R-rating, and we both don't watch those.

On the way back, Wyoming said she knows who is going to win—Kirsten Haglund, Miss Michigan. I absolutely agree with her and we both said we would be proud to have her represent us. I have felt it from the beginning. She has it all. Right now I am just praying to make it to the top 8 to still have the opportunity to show America who I am. It will all work out how it should.

I was actually sad with how I performed tonight only because of one note, which to me is the most important note of the song… the first time I belt out "Shy!" My voice croaked on it a little bit. I was so upset while performing that I tried to really make sure I kept the "spark" up in the rest of the talent and not let that get to me. Overall, the acting and singing really did go well. It was just that one note that ate at me.

My mom greeted me with excitement tonight. She was surprised to see me down, because she thought, along with everyone else, that I nailed it and did a fabulous job. I am really being too hard on myself this week.

The final night

I knew there was nothing I could do about the outcome now. I was just praying the judges had vision and looked beyond the "game" we had to play on stage because if they were looking for the best model and most talented, then I was not their girl. But if they were looking for someone who could handle the job and take the organization somewhere, then I was their girl. I hoped they would see what I could do not only for the Miss America organization and the Military, but for America.

The show started for the last time and I walked out there blown away by how packed it was. Planet Hollywood was sold out that night. We all started waving to the audience, just as excited to see them. There was a large section of soldiers off to the left that the American Legion had sponsored tickets for. It was a great sight to see so many of my "military family" there to support me.

Signs filled the audience with the different states they were supporting—flashing signs, and big posters with certain contestants' pictures on them. I saw the "Utah" crowd with their signs spelling out "U-T-A-H" and "Go GI Jill." It was surreal. This was Miss America!

The energy was so alive in the auditorium as we went through the "parade of states." It was now time to announce the top 15 finalists. One by one they were named. Of course I was holding my breath as they would mention, "Our next finalist is from the purple group . . ." and it was another contestant. Soon all 15 were called. There was a mix of excitement and disappointment in the audience, depending on the contestant they were rooting for.

"Wait a minute ladies and gentlemen. We have one more finalist. You were given the chance to vote online and catapult one of these girls into the finals. America voted . . . Miss Utah!"

"AAHHH," Miss Wyoming and I screamed as we grabbed each other. As I headed down to the front of the stage, I pumped my fist in the air and shouted, "Yeah!" I guess there are some things you still can't change about a "tom boy." I thanked the audience, opening my arms to them and then looked straight into the camera to thank America for voting for me as their choice for Miss America.

The next few minutes were truly a blur. I quickly ran back with the other finalists to the dressing room to prepare for the swimsuit competition. We had two and a half minutes. I was last because of when I was announced, and I felt I modeled very well on stage (making up for "shaking my behind" in front of everyone on the preliminary nights). We came back out on stage in short robes over our swimsuits while they narrowed it down from 16 to 10 finalists. Talk about cutting out a big chunk based on just a 15-second strut on stage!

They had already called out four girls that would be eliminated— leaving two more to go. I was just praying that I would make it through one more round to show the world my evening gown.

"Our fifth finalist to be eliminated this evening, Miss Utah, Jill Stevens," the host said.

I wasn't really surprised, but of course I was still sad. The crowd booed as I waved goodbye, then Miss Wisconsin pulled me aside and said, "Utah, let's do the push-ups now!"

I replied, "Let's do it!"

We dropped down right there on stage. I had wanted to do some push-ups during a commercial break earlier in the show because I thought the crowd would love it, especially the soldiers. I thought it would be perfect, right after the "parade of states" to run up to the front, call the girls to "attention" and do about 10 push-ups for the crowd. Some of the girls were excited to do it as well, and they thought it was a great idea (Wisconsin being one of them). But the producer shot it down. He said we didn't rehearse it, so we shouldn't do it. "What do you have to rehearse about push-ups?" I thought.

Within a moment we were doing push-ups on live television—in swimsuits and heels, mind you–with *most* of the top 10 finalists also dropping down and doing push-ups. I couldn't have been more proud. I obviously must have had some influence on these girls for them to drop down with me like that. The crowd went wild and was on their feet. It was an awesome feeling and a great way to go out with "class." I felt like I took the gold that night. I knew I was true to myself until the very end.

As the rest of the show went on (the eliminated girls had to watch it on a set of bleachers on the side of the stage) we were a little upset about the harshness of the "reality" aspect of the show. Even the audience booed a few more times at how girls were eliminated.

I wish I could have at least competed in evening gown, because I loved it so much and wanted to make that statement. But I felt at peace and relieved with the outcome. I knew I didn't perform well enough to make "top 15." I tried to forget the feeling that I didn't live up to my potential the week it counted. It's like an Olympian having a "bad run" or getting injured during the Olympics—it's your one shot to prove yourself, and I didn't deliver.

When Miss Michigan Kirsten Haglund was named Miss America 2008, I couldn't have been more happy for her! She has the whole package. Not only is she beautiful and talented, but she's also witty, intelligent, and faith-driven. She represents us well.

We had an awards ceremony afterward where they recognized every contestant. It was wonderful to see so many supporters. So many came up and just wanted to congratulate me and take pictures because they "loved Utah." So sweet! I couldn't believe how many "liked" me.

We planned a big party afterward with whoever wanted to come, to either celebrate winning Miss America, or getting my life back. Obviously, we were celebrating a great journey, but it was one to now finally close the door on and start living a somewhat normal life. (I use "normal" in a broad sense.) Some close friends at SUU helped put the party together, and it was wonderful to see so many people happy for me, and that helped me as well.

A highlight was getting to see my battle buddies from my combat medic training)—"Moldie" (Kristen Moldenhauer), Hubbard, Pagac, Kilpatrick (now Jennifer Melin), and her twin sister. I got to see them from the audience during the show and they just made my night. It was a delight to see them after all these years. They flew from all different places to meet up and have a reunion, and it meant the world to me.

That night I crashed in my parents' hotel room. I don't think I moved an inch. I was out "cold" and slept well. On the way back home, I devoured so many sweets and almost ate a whole pizza.

I couldn't help but think, "It's all good."

The result of what they did to my hair on Miss America: Reality Check. This became my headshot for the Miss America Pageant.

Below, Brook Thornley and I discovering my "colors" with Human Art.

DEl Beatty and I celebrating at one of my "send-offs" before Miss America.

This was the back of a sweatshirt that my dear friend, Maddie Brian, made for me. It made me laugh and I felt it captured it all!

260

Having fun at one of the sponsored breakfasts by IHOP during the week of Miss America.

My on-stage interview at Miss America. Just picture intelligent sentences coming out of my mouth right now because in reality, that is not what happened at all. Ugh!

"Home of the country's highest birth rate as long as the Osmonds don't move . . . I'm Jill Stevens, Miss Utah!"

Wow, what a support team! I couldn't have done it without them. Hearing them cheer me on gave me such a boost. Above are my family and friends. Shown below are my wonderful battle buddies that I hadn't seen since Combat Medic Training. (Left to right: Melin, Moldenhauer, Pagac, Hubbard.) It was a happy reunion.

My reaction to winning America's Choice. Whoa!

This reaction takes me back to the time I won Miss SUU . . . some things never change. I just can't hold back my emotions.

Modeling swimwear at the Miss America Pageant in front of a packed house and millions of television viewers . . . crazy!

One of the proudest moments of my pageant career and probably in my life. I was true to myself to the very end, and having these girls drop down and do push-ups with me was an honor.

Hanging out with the contestants who have been booted out, trying to enjoy the show from the side of the stage. I felt relieved and was having fun.

At the Miss America "After Party" when they announce every girl into the room.

CHAPTER 15

EACH HAPPY ENDING IS A BRAND NEW BEGINNING

Once upon a time, a man by the name of DEl Beatty asked, "Hey, you should run for Miss SUU!" I can't remember a time I was more baffled on how to respond, so I just laughed. Little did I know how much this man and especially this organization would change my life. I stepped out of my comfort zone and discovered a new me—"Wow, maybe I do have some talent, and I guess a soldier can be beautiful." Little by little, I started to believe.

Now, more than two years later, I find myself traveling the nation as a motivational speaker and even singing at some of those events. WOW, who could have imagined? That's exactly what the Miss America Organization does, though. It helps us discover that the person we thought we were is no match for the one we really are, giving each girl her own Cinderella story.

My year deployment as Miss Utah

On the night that I was crowned Miss Utah, someone on the board said, "During the coming year there will be weeks where you will be so busy you will wonder how you're going handle it all. Then there will be weeks where you'll be bored and wonder what to fill your time with." But as the year came to a close, I had yet to hit a week where I felt "bored." Every day was filled with as little as one engagement, and as many as twelve in one day. (I once hit nine schools and three media interviews in one day. I learned my lesson from that one.) It probably had more to do with my personality, though. If I didn't have anything planned on a day, I would make sure that I did, and I soon found my day packed down to the second. Here are a few main highlights that stand out during the past unforgettable year.

Interviews

I've been interviewed by local newspapers before—and even by a few local TV stations—but national TV was a whole new ballgame for me. Just two days after winning Miss Utah, I answered my phone and CNN happened to be on the other line.

"Wow! Hi there," I reacted.

"We would like to interview you and talk about your story. Are you available in the next couple of days?" asked the cheerful CNN representative.

"I could do it tomorrow."

"We'll get it to work." We had a short interview over the phone so they knew where to guide the actual interview on TV. My family asked if I was nervous going on a national news program, and well, I actually wasn't. You're just talking to another human being (multiplied by a few million). "You just have to be yourself," I thought. I always felt pretty comfortable for my interviews and had a lot of fun.

Within that first week, I was interviewed on CNN twice, Fox News twice, as well as *The O'Reilly Factor*, and six different local TV stations. It didn't really slow down for another two months. The same pattern followed right after the Miss America pageant. I really enjoyed talking with people from around the nation and met some great people through the interviews.

I did get the question a lot, "Being in Pageants and the Army are on opposite ends of the spectrum and really have nothing in common. How did you end up doing both?"

"Well, actually, the organizations are quite similar," I would always reply.

"Really?" they would ask in a skeptical tone.

"The Army and Miss America Organization both promote getting an education and provide scholarships to do so. Both promote fitness and taking care of yourself. Both teach you how to be a leader and think on your feet. But above all, both give you a great opportunity to serve your country. Those are the organizations that I want to represent."

Magazine interviews started coming up. "This is so weird," I thought. They actually made me more nervous, though, as the writers seemed to take my story in any direction they wanted. Also, some photographers were never allowed to show the photos that were selected to go in articles. I was frustrated with this because with some of the magazines, I wondered what had possessed the editors to choose certain photos. I really wish I could have had a say in some of those as it was a bit embarrassing to me how they turned out when you know millions of people are viewing them. Ah well.

Marathons

Now, when I was first getting into pageants, I was advised that I should not run anymore because of the muscle I build up. Instead, I was encouraged to focus more on lengthening exercises like yoga and pilates. I tried, but I just got too bored and more marathon opportunities happened to land right in front of me . . . how could I resist?

The Deseret Morning News Marathon: One of our big holidays every year, specific to Utah, is Pioneer Day on July 24th, celebrating the Pioneers that came in 1847 and settled Utah. The Days of '47 Parade is the biggest in Utah. I felt that parade would be a great one to be a part of as I began my reign as Miss Utah. I really wanted to make the most of my year and reach out to people in my home state. I contacted the parade committee and got shot down. I guess they felt that my title "trumped" their Days of '47 royalty (not affiliated with Miss America). That wasn't enough to stop me so I discovered a better way to reach the people . . . why not run on the parade route?

One of the marathons that I've run for the past few years is the Deseret Morning News Marathon on July 24th. It just so happens to run on part of the parade route. About four weeks after winning Miss Utah, I needed to go for a run and just think about all that had just taken place. My run turned into an 18-miler and I thought, "Hmm,

I think I can do this, and what an even better way to show Utah who represents them? This would show I'm not the stereotypical beauty queen, but that I'm an athlete and work hard to stay fit."

Lo and behold, it worked! I made a jersey for me to run in that said, "Miss Utah, GI Jill" on the front with my slogan, "Lock 'n Load" on the back. I ended up finishing in 3:24:24.

The St. George Marathon: One of my judges at Miss Utah suggested I run the Marine Corps Marathon in DC. What an opportunity that would be as a soldier, beauty queen and of course, a marathon runner! I loved the idea. I started coordinating with the Public Relations Director and got everything squared away to run the marathon the end of October.

Well, as part of my training I needed to run about 22 miles just three weeks before the race, and I was getting burned out doing these long runs on my own. It just so happened that the St. George Marathon fell three weeks before the Marine Corps Marathon. How convenient! The race lottery had already been completed the previous May, so it was going to be tough to get in. About five days before the race, I made a few calls and wrote a few emails. I got in and flew down that Friday, the day before the race. Yet, because of some complications, we couldn't land in St. George.

We were supposed to be landing at about 5:30 p.m., but at 6 p.m. we were still hovering above St. George. The pilot got on the intercom, "Folks, it is too windy for us to land. We have tried to wait it out to see if it will die down, but with our current fuel supplies, we now have to turn back to Salt Lake City."

Everyone on the plane just looked at each other. A few of us were there to run the race but others had business meetings or were trying to get to family. On the way back, we ended up landing in Cedar City. The only problem was that the airport was closed. No flights were coming in or going out that day.

So there we were, stranded in an airplane in the middle of a non-functioning airport. The crew would not let us off or get our baggage because they needed the right equipment to do so. It was getting close to 7:30 now. The marathon expo closed at 9 p.m. and here I was stuck on an airplane, still a 45-minute drive away from St. George.

They finally contacted some airport personnel and they got there by about 7:45 p.m. Everyone was making arrangements how to get to their final destinations. A lot of the passengers had family there, and a man yelled out and said his brother had a truck that could fit four others and take us to St. George. I got on board.

There I was, riding in an old truck with complete strangers that soon became great friends. In the truck were a pair of brothers, an older couple who owned a restaurant, a man was from England, and myself, the soldier undercover. It was a riot! I made it to the expo just in time. I finished the race in 3:27:51.

The Marine Corps Marathon (MCM): I flew into Washington, D.C. a couple of days before the race, so with the extra time I had the privilege of visiting Walter Reed Army Medical Center. It brought back a lot of memories seeing soldiers in such conditions. We were just supposed to be there an hour but it turned into three, talking with each of the soldiers. What an incredible experience!

I met up with a program called TAPS (Tragedy Assistance Program for Survivors) which helps families who have lost loved ones in battle. I wanted to run for their cause and ended up speaking at their event the night before the race. I also actually ended up as the keynote speaker for the big MCM "Carb dinner" that same evening.

The morning of the race came, and I'd never seen so many runners in one place before! This was the biggest race I had ever participated in. I met up by the pace-marker that I hoped to finish in: 3:15-3:30. I met another gentleman at the beginning who wanted to keep the same pace, so we ended up sticking together. This was his ninth MCM and he grew up in the area, so he actually turned into my tour guide along the route. There's no better way to see the nation's capitol than by running it, and it sure made the time go by faster.

I ended up finishing in 3:23:53. I must keep a pretty consistent pace, because I couldn't seem to finish in anything but the 3:20-somethings. So far this year all my finishing times were within a few minutes of each other.

Utah Valley Marathon: I was planning on running just those three marathons during my year as Miss Utah. I felt like I made the statement I needed to. But then I got a call at the end of March from the Utah

National Guard Headquarters asking me to run on the Utah Guard team at the Lincoln National Guard Marathon in Lincoln, Nebraska. I didn't feel I was in marathon shape at all, since I hadn't really run since that last marathon six months previously, but how could I refuse such an offer?

The marathon was the first weekend in May, so I had about six weeks to prepare. I got training right away and into marathon mode. I was feeling pretty good. My everyday workout was still focused on endurance training, so it's easier to slide into marathon mode whenever the opportunities jump at me.

I happened to discover another marathon three weeks before the National Guard race—the Utah Valley Marathon in Provo, Utah. I saw that they were raising money for the Children's Miracle Network. This just seemed too perfect, and I felt obligated to represent the Miss America Organization at such an event.

I contacted the race director right away and discussed ideas with him of how I could help out, since this was the inaugural race and not many runners knew about it. I got other Miss Utah contestants (the ones vying for my title later in the year) involved to help show our support for the race, as well in helping children. It worked out wonderfully. I ended up finishing in 3:24:55.

Lincoln National Guard Marathon: This was my last race as Miss Utah, and I was ready for it to be. My body was getting worn out. I finished strong, though, in 3:22:18, making the All Guard running team and making this my 14th marathon—thus far.

GI Jill

When you join the military, you are adopted into the biggest family and I couldn't have asked for a better support team from across the world as the word spread about me becoming Miss Utah. Launching the website "GI Jill" became a fun way to capture the unique ties of both the pageant and military world.

The Soldier Media Center wanted me to "blog" at least twice a week about the steps it took to bring out this woman inside of me, and what I was doing to prepare for Miss America. These blogs were well-received, and it was fun to realize how much my life as a soldier prepared me for such events, and I know I would not have made it as far as I had in the pageant world without my Army training and experiences in Afghanistan.

Speaking engagements

My schedule was usually filled with speaking engagements, and most of the groups that I spoke to were youth groups. I love that age! It's just the beginning of the many changes that they will begin to face. Church groups, high schools, leadership conferences, etc. I tend to like speaking in front of the bigger crowds, because you reach more people. Yet I also love meeting each person that may have come to my presentation and visiting with them. I found the individual contact so rewarding.

I traveled to many different states for speaking assignments, but there were a few that stuck out as my favorites. I was one (of the many) keynote speakers at the National Speaking of Women's Health Conference in Cincinnati, Ohio. Speaking to these 1,000 women was the largest group I had spoken in front of to date. I guess it was a success, since I was honored to be invited on their speaking circuit around the nation.

Another state that was a highlight for me was speaking at a pair of hospitals in New Jersey. I felt a little inadequate speaking to professional nurses and doctors when I, myself, hadn't even started working as a nurse yet. They invited me to come speak as part of their Nurses Week in May.

The organizers said they wanted to do something out of the ordinary and decided to connect with a medical unit in Iraq, setting up a buddy system to contribute medical supplies they might need. Well, they thought it would be great to hear from someone who had actually served over there, and that is how my name came up.

The people I met there were a delight to be with, and I had so much fun with them. I had dinner with about 12 of the hospital staff and it turned into a fun, four-hour event with the women. I am already planning on heading out there again, and we are going to do a girls night in New York City.

Miss America Homecoming

Each year after a new Miss America is chosen, she has a big celebration back in her home state during the first chance she gets to go back for a visit. (Miss America will maybe get to go home just a couple of times during her reigning year.) I couldn't believe I was invited to go back with about 10 other contestants in welcoming home Miss America 2008, Kirsten Haglund. It was a great reunion for everyone, just one month after the pageant itself took place.

We were told we could "spice things up a bit" and perform a different number than our actual Miss America talent. After talking with the producer of the show in Michigan and hearing all who were performing—including the top 10 at the Miss Michigan pageant and most of the top 10 at Miss America—I said jokingly, "Wow, do you want me to speak instead and swap war stories on stage?"

"That would be PERFECT," the producer replied enthusiastically.

"Really?" I replied. I had been joking, so her answer took me by surprise.

"That's exactly what we are looking for—something fun and new," she said. So we went with it. Instead of the allotted two minutes for all the performers, she gave me five minutes because, let's face it, by the time you begin your story, it's time to wrap it up if you only have two minutes.

We went through the whole show during dress rehearsal on the afternoon of February 29, 2008. The emcee was hilarious and we had a lot of fun together. Right before I was about to go on, she tripped going up the stage to introduce me. I ran out playing off the funny scene . . .

"It's okay, I'm a medic," I said. "I could change my speech and we could teach the audience some medical skills instead, so that we can fix you up."

We just laughed, and I continued with my "war stories." Later that day, though, she came up to me and said how much my speech meant to her. "Wow, I only spoke for five minutes," I thought. I was flattered that she would even say that. She said she felt I deserved a better introduction at the show, and that just saying "Jill Stevens, Miss Utah" (that's all everyone got) wouldn't do me justice.

I didn't know what she had written about me until the actual show that night when I was about to go on. I stood backstage in my fatigues as she introduced me. She had a family member who also served in the military, and she shared a few funny experiences about him in her humorous way. Then she moved on to me.

"Our next contestant, I'm sure you all know. You are in for a treat tonight as she shares her experiences in combat in the deserts of Afghanistan. Her story motivates all of us to get out and serve better in some way. From combat boots to stiletto heels, she has won the hearts of the American people and at the Miss America Pageant, she ended up as America's Choice . . ."

The crowd started cheering. I was blown away at what she was saying. I was flattered, but nervous at the same time. This was Miss America's home crowd and here the emcee is praising me in such a way when this was Kirsten's night to shine.

". . . And could we ever forget that when she was eliminated, she dropped down and did push-ups? What a true soldier."

The crowd laughed and cheered louder as the emcee added, "So without further ado, please join me in welcoming America's Choice, Miss Utah, Sergeant Jill Stevens!" The crowd continued applauding.

"Let's have fun with this," I thought. I stomped out there with my lapel mic, greeting them with my arms wide open with a big "HELLO!" As I was waving and walking up to the front of the stage, I couldn't believe how loud they were getting.

Then I noticed through the bright lights shining on stage that the whole place was getting on their feet. Was I just getting a standing ovation? I hadn't even started speaking yet! I was at a loss for words and was truly touched. I thanked them and had that much more fun sharing some of my stories. I ended my talk by saluting them. I was truly honored to have been a part of it all!

China

Morris Murdock Travel asked me to host a tour to China the beginning of June 2008. Would anyone turn down such an invitation? There were a few high school students going and I was to be their chaperone. My mom and my little brother Mitch made the trip with me. We spent two days in Hong Kong, spending one day at Hong Kong Disneyland and getting a tour of the city the next. We then flew to Beijing for three days. This was the part of the trip I was most excited about. The first day we hiked part of the Great Wall of China. What a spectacular site! I just love history and learning about how and why things were done. Our tour guide gave us a lot of history as we drove to the different sites.

We visited a few factories to see how the Chinese people harvest pearls and also carve jade. Another highlight was visiting the Temple of Heaven. Not only was the Temple spectacular (and huge) but what I loved was that there was a large park surrounding it. This park was full of older Chinese people. Many come to the area when they are retired and pick up different hobbies, such as Tai Chi, a unique version of foot-bag, dancing, singing, playing musical instruments and many other activities. Our group had a great time joining them in their exercises. The artwork and architecture of the Chinese was so fascinating, especially once you knew the history behind them, like the Forbidden City.

Driving in China is one of the craziest scenes I've ever seen. It is every man for himself. We ended up biking through Beijing one morning to really get a taste of the Chinese people's main mode of transportation. We definitely made a statement with 60 of us on bikes riding through the back roads. I was in awe at how the people lived there. It's such a different culture, but you could tell the people had developed such a strong sense of pride in their community.

We took a night train to Xi'an from Beijing. We were in one sleeper car to ourselves. It was a small corridor with bunk beds, stacked up three beds high. We were on the train for twelve hours, and it wasn't too bad. The only thing that bothered me about the trip was China's sanitation system. It takes a lot to gross me out, and I'm used to 'roughing it' in the Army, but their restrooms really put me over the top. I'll spare you the gory details.

One of the highlights of the trip for me came while we were in Xi'an. We were able to visit an orphanage with close to 100 kids between the ages of 3 and 21. We were told before we left to pack extra school supplies and candy to be able to give out at the orphanage to these kids who needed so much.

When we arrived, all of the kids lined up at the gate, applauding as we came in. Then we went into their auditorium and the kids performed two songs that they had prepared for us. It was wonderful to see these kids and the light in their eyes they carried that would reach out to anyone nearby. You could tell they were so appreciative of the supplies they were getting so that they could get through school easier.

We also gave some of the kids bubbles to blow and they would not put the bottle down. We were able to hang around and play with them for the next couple of hours. It was fun to see the type of sports they love. They seemed to be having so much fun. A lot of them ended up finishing off the bubbles while we were there. We played a lot of catch with some of their balls. This was so worthwhile.

Our last main attraction was the Terracotta Warriors. Wow, there is so much in this world to see and learn. I was grateful for this opportunity.

When all else fails, do push-ups!

After China, I flew straight to DC to emcee the 233rd Army Birthday Ball. I couldn't believe I was asked to host such a big event. Michael Peterson, a country singer, was to co-emcee with me. About 2,500 people were in attendance, mainly dignitaries. Just before I was about to go on, I was standing just three feet away from Vice President Dick Cheney.

The show was starting off with a lot of excitement from entertainers and such. Within five minutes of Michael and I being on stage, it became apparent that we were already *not ready* to move on to the next item on the agenda—the official toast. We had certain dignitaries scheduled to come up and say a line of the toast, yet someone forgot to pull them out of the audience.

So as they were locating the VIPs in the audience, Michael and I had to stall. I wasn't ready for this so early in the show! I tried to go with the flow. Since Michael was a singer, I said, "Hey, why don't we do a duet?"

He must have heard about my questionable singing ability, because he turned me down flat!

"How about a push-up contest?" I countered. The crowd started to react a little to that. Michael's reluctance just got the crowd to encourage us more. He finally agreed to the match, saying that he would do one more push-up than I knocked out.

So I went to center stage (in my evening gown and 5 inch heels) signaling to the audience that I'm going to drop and do 10. As I began, the band behind me and some of the audience in front of me started counting. How could I stop at 10? The competitor in me just had to keep going . . . and going, and going. With the cheers of the audience (now on their feet) I decided to stop at 30. After all, there was still a show that had to go on. Michael, true to his promise, got down and did one more . . . period.

The rest of the evening went smoothly, thank goodness, but it seemed the push-up contest was a definite highlight. I had a blast!

Going out with a bang!

I wanted to finish my "race" as Miss Utah strong and with my head held high. After all, I'm an endurance runner, right? So during the last couple weeks of my reign, I decided to have a little fun. I was in Atlanta filming different "characters" (soldier, nurse, civilian, beauty queen) for some career opportunity DVDs that will be shown in high schools around the nation. I couldn't sleep one evening because I was still recovering from China, and my mind was wandering. The thought of skydiving with the crown and sash entered my mind. How fun that would be!

I got excited just thinking about it and decided to kill some time at 2 a.m. looking up the contact information for Skydive Zion, a place in Hurricane, Utah that I went to in 2002. By the end of the day, I had a jump scheduled for the following week. I got one of my friends, Maddie Brian, who had never jumped before, to come with me and we made it a quick road trip.

I was going to do a tandem jump with the company owner, Rick Eddy, and we knew the sash would be no problem to keep on. It was the crown we were a little concerned about, but we found a way. We used a parachute/bungee cord! The plane was very small, fitting the pilot, another skydiver that tagged along, and Rick and I attached to each other.

On the flight up, I secured the crown to my head. It was kind of giving me a headache with how tight it was. Then I put my goggles over the crown and cord. I tell ya, I was creating a fashion statement with that look.

The view was spectacular from up there, overlooking Zion's National Park in southern Utah. Finally the door opened and a gush of wind hit me. My adrenaline kicked in, and I couldn't believe I was going to be jumping over 11,000 feet. This was too cool! We scooted our way to the edge of the door, where I put my feet on a small platform (less than one square foot) and crouched outside of the plane. There was the ground straight below me.

I gave a little wave to the camera, rolled off to the side and was soon flying or falling, depending how you look at it. What a rush! This second jump was far better than the first one years earlier. I was able to take in more, since I knew what to expect. I did a nose dive, superman dive, and a few turns. I felt free! It was time to pull the cord after about 45 seconds. Gliding through the air with the parachute helped me soak in the thrill of the ride.

Stadium of Fire

While I was still in Atlanta, I also got a call asking me to sing "God Bless America" at the Stadium of Fire on the 4th of July in Provo, Utah. The show is held each year at LaVell Edwards Stadium on the BYU campus and is considered one of the biggest patriotic celebrations in the nation.

I tried to play it casual. "Uh, sure."

"There will be 55,000 people in the stadium and it will be broadcast live to troops deployed across the world," the producer said. "Will that bother you at all?"

I lost my breath as I pictured that many people. I usually sing in front of about 400 people . . . this was a bit more. I can usually handle myself in high pressure situations, but this was going to be a different type of pressure I hadn't faced before.

"Yeah, I believe I can handle it." I surprised myself a little with my bold answer, but I felt up to the challenge. It was only three weeks away. I was really hoping to get the minus track right away, but the producers didn't get one to me until a week before, and I was getting a little nervous.

We had a full dress rehearsal the night before. As I showed up I just had to laugh as they took me to my trailer. I had a trailer! Then my jaw dropped as I saw who the other half of the trailer was occupied by—Glenn Beck from CNN! He was the emcee of the event, and Miley Cyrus' trailer was right next to ours. She was performing that night.

"Whoa! You guys are very nice, but I really don't need a trailer. I'm just singing a song," I said with a laugh.

"No. We wanted you to have this," the talent coordinator said. "It means a lot that you are singing."

The whole experience was surreal: a trailer with my name on it, representing the military singing "God Bless America" to thousands. I even got to chat with Glenn Beck. It was fun to visit with him and his family before the show started. I was able to bring my family back into the VIP area to show them my trailer. We all laughed together, enjoying this unique opportunity.

That whole day I had a knot in my stomach. My rehearsal the night before didn't go as great as I had hoped. My voice was tight and I sounded nervous. I tried to trick myself that I wasn't, but it was hard to hide. My mom gave me some good pointers to help me relax.

The show kicked off at 8 p.m. Skydivers landed on the field, bringing the flag. A few fireworks were shot off. There was so much excitement! We then had an Olympic tribute, bringing out hundreds of athletes, representing all sports (even horses and cyclists came riding out). Right before I was to go out, I got this feeling of excitement and suddenly I felt so honored to be a part of it. "This was going to be fun," I thought.

I stepped out onto the field at my cue. Glenn Beck was on the other side of the field, talking about troops being deployed, but that one unit had just returned home . . .

". . . and here to welcome them home is an outstanding woman," he said before proceeding to give a little bio of me. Wow, I couldn't believe I was doing this! How did I ever get here?

Everyone in the stadium was on their feet as soldiers and family members entered the field. This was all too exciting. I started to sing, and thankfully I did well. I felt so proud to be there and honored to sing such a song. I felt it through the words of "God Bless America"—truly the land that I love.

GI Jive

The 2008 Miss Utah competition began just a few days later. I joined the 50 contestants as we checked into our hotel on Sunday. We kicked off the week with a devotional that evening featuring Mary Kaye Huntsman, the First Lady of Utah, as the keynote speaker.

I had the opportunity to speak for a few minutes, and I shared a few thoughts geared around the book "I Like Myself" and the message that I had shared with each of the Miss America contestants.

What really made the evening powerful was the singer who performed, Jessie Clark Funk. Not only was her voice angelic, but her music and message were so inspiring. The first song that she sang especially touched me. It is entitled "A Million Dreams to Go" and explains that even if one dream doesn't work out, there are still a million dreams to go.

Private interviews kicked off the next morning, as well as dress rehearsals. I was there to introduce the girls as they walked into interview. I warmed up the judges beforehand with a quick interview myself. I walked in with my crown bungee-tied to my head, because the last time I wore it had been when I went skydiving. That broke the judges right in and we got started. Afterward we had our big dress rehearsal, and I got to see for the first time what our producer had put together for the opening number.

I knew it was a "GI Jive" theme but what the choreographer did made it so fun and made a soldier proud. All the contestants were dressed in khaki cargo shorts with the same type of top that had sergeant rank sewn on and military tabs. A khaki female cap was also worn. The girls looked so good up on stage. I wore my Dress Blue uniform for the opening number. It was so much fun.

The preliminary nights kicked off on Tuesday. Each night I performed something different. First was "My New Philosophy" from *You're a Good Man, Charlie Brown*. I had just learned it three days before, but I had such a blast playing the character that it worked out great.

The second night I actually danced! Yep, who would have thought it? Earlier in the year I participated in a fundraiser for a Mental Health Clinic put on through BYU. They had local "stars" teamed up with members of the Ballroom Dance Team in a spin-off of *Dancing with the Stars*. They called it "Dancing for Recovery."

My partner and I did the quick-step and I had so much fun that I asked if he would be willing to do it at Miss Utah, so we performed it during the pageant's second night. The third night, I did my signature piece "Shy." I changed it up just a bit because, hey, I wasn't being judged. I popped up from a different area on stage, behind some stairs and climbed up over them in my gown.

"Hey there! I'm Winnifred. I just came from swimming the moat," I began and then started climbing up, grunting, "I heard you were looking for a new Miss Utah . . ." and then went from there. At the end I was supposed to sit on my stool and then stand up and kick it. Well, I missed and fell off! I changed up my words to just go with the flow and instead of saying, ". . . and despite the impression I give, I confess that I'm living a lie," I concluded with, ". . . I confess (fell off) . . . that I'm literally a blonde!" I then pushed my stool out of the way and stood up for a big finish.

We had my farewell breakfast Saturday morning. My mom spoke for a few minutes and got the crowd laughing and crying. I felt we should have just ended there, but then I was the featured speaker. There was something that I have wanted to do for a long time but I had waited for the right moment. I felt this breakfast was the time. The last few months I had put together a gift to give to those people who had gone well out of their way to help me. I wanted to show my appreciation through a famous military custom . . . "The Coin."

I had my own coin made, representing my different roles. On one side was the military showing digital camouflage with a medical insignia in the middle. Around it were the words, "SGT Jill Stevens" and "Lock 'n Load." On the other side was a wavy American flag with a crown in front. The words "Miss Utah 2007" and "America's Choice" were around it.

I wanted to present the first one at this breakfast to the man that made this whole journey possible for me, DEl Beatty. I made his coin a little differently. I had a rhinestone from my crown placed in the middle of his coin. I had him come up to the front at the beginning of my speech. We both got emotional as I explained all that he had done for me, and for so many other girls. I presented him the coin as you would in the military, through a handshake. After I was done speaking, I shared with them the song that brought me so much strength over the last year, "I Know He Lives."

The big finale

The final night had arrived, and it was going to be a great show! That night my brothers and sisters and I sang a Barber Shop number called "Baby Face," a song we've performed together for more than ten years. I was so excited to be up on stage with them and show everyone one of the many things our family enjoys doing together. They also showed my "year in review" video, but before I went out to do my final walk, our emcee Johnny Revill sang, "Bring Him Home" from *Les Miserables* while a slide show of soldiers was playing.

It was now time to announce our new Miss Utah. I was excited to be a part of this. Kayla Barclay became Miss Utah 2008 and I couldn't have been more honored to crown her. What an incredible women she is—and will be—as Miss Utah. I walked over to her while the crowd was screaming. I grabbed her and we just looked at each other and screamed! I was so excited for her. She truly shined that week.

The following morning, I was about to head off to church but then felt strongly that I should write Kayla a note—one of congratulations and encouragement. I only lived a couple of blocks from the hotel where she was staying, so I decided to drop it by. As I was about to leave it at the front desk, I ran into her dad. Well, that soon turned into me visiting them personally in their room and talking about my year and how she can make it better. Afterward, we said a prayer together. The organization is in good hands.

So many times throughout the week, people had asked, "Is this bittersweet?" or "Are you sad?" or "Is it going to be hard?"

Well, to tell you the truth, I wasn't sad at all. I was Jill Stevens during the year and I'm still going to be afterward. I still have the same goals, the same mission in life. Nothing really changes for me. I will still be traveling the nation speaking. Even two days after Miss Utah, I flew off to Tennessee for an event, with plans to head to Nebraska just two days later.

The crown never defined me, but the service was a part of me and I believe still is. Each happy ending though is a brand new beginning. I look forward to the many dreams ahead thanks to this organization and the genuine people that keep it running.

Finding joy in the journey

Phew! What a year it has been. I have been humbled by what it takes to be at the top of your game 24/7. My soldier training really prepared me for this year-long deployment. My marathon training helped me have the endurance. My nursing skills helped me reach farther with the Children's Miracle Network. And my blood type, B+, helped me stay somewhat optimistic through it all, since it runs naturally through my veins.

I have enjoyed relating my experiences to those around me. It is so rewarding to see the spark light up in a young girl's eyes as she would hear my experiences and turn them inward, finding the courage to reach for her goals and gain a greater belief in herself and her potential. That has made all the difference to me.

But after a few years of being a motivational speaker, and especially with how much it increased this last year, I felt like I was losing my spark a little bit. My body was starting to feel it the last couple of months of my "reign" as Miss Utah. I was getting burned out pretty easily and I wanted to cry every time my cell phone rang. I felt like I was about to explode as I was running through this new minefield trying to handle it all.

Then I understood that each of my challenges in life have only made me stronger, because I have learned from them and made the best of them. But what's the use if I don't put into practice what I have learned as I face more obstacles? I then realized that what I was sharing in my speeches, I needed for myself more than ever . . . so I became my own motivational speaker.

Things started to look up as I reminded myself why I did this in the first place. What was my target? Once I remembered, I made sure to sharpen my focus on that target as things got more hectic. Now I didn't go out and get a pirate patch like I did at Basic Training, and I don't suggest that to you. But I do recommend getting the picture, then getting into it, and getting after it. Those are the gets of life! Get the picture, get into it, and get after it! So what is your target that you are aiming for?

Think about that and once you've got your target, your dream in view, focus in on that, because if you don't—like I didn't while I was trying to shoot for mine—you could end up missing your target completely and missing out on your dreams. You need to keep focused.

There were times where I tripped and fell hard (figuratively and literally). Training for my many marathons may not have seemed worth the pain and long hours I had to put in, especially since I knew that I was probably going to stumble again. But just as I learned while running in those races, I've got to pick myself back up and finish. It's during those hard times that we mustn't give up—we need to plow through it because it will only make us stronger.

There have been many times when I have failed (making my magic shrinking potion as a young girl, my nursing exams, my performance at Miss America, etc.) but I picked myself up then and finished my course, coming away with the "gold," at least as far as my attitude was concerned and the lessons I learned. Why give up now? If you fall down and don't get back on your feet, you'll miss out on so much. Again, sometimes your dreams are shattered and you will fail at times. But don't quit!

Remember my experience with running through a minefield when I first arrived in Afghanistan? Mines can be very ordinary, everyday things. They might be a soda can or a piece of garbage lying on the ground. Something enticing but also dangerous.

Our lives are also full of mines. They are planted everywhere and disguised as ordinary things . . . things that distract or deter us from reaching our potential. During my pageant journey, I found that my standards were constantly being challenged. There was always the temptation to wear a more fashionable evening gown or swimsuit. But I couldn't go that direction. I needed stay on the center of the path that I had set for myself.

When you feel like you're running through minefields of your own, don't let those distractions take you off your path. Be true to who you are and stand strong for what you believe in.

Self-doubt was one of the biggest "mines" that brought me down. Once any small amount of doubt crept into my mind, it soon took over and clouded up my vision, and I lost sight of my target/dream. I wasn't progressing through the course like I should, and my doubts were really holding me back.

I liken this to my experience with my gas mask. Because I doubted the capabilities of my mask, I made my situation much worse during my training. Doubt in our lives works the same way. Taking that risk to follow your dreams can be really scary and make you feel very vulnerable. But if you allow yourself to let any small amount of doubt in, questioning your own capabilities, it can start to cloud up your vision. This could soon take over to the point where you lose your focus and sight of your dream, making your situation much worse. Once you begin to doubt yourself, immediately clear that out of your mind. Remember, get the picture, get into it and get after it. Believe.

Looking ahead

Living through all of these great adventures and challenges has taught me so much. I've learned a lot, and picked up a little here and there to better prepare me for the next adventure. What is that adventure? A very good question indeed.

Bucket list: There are a lot of things that I want and hope to accomplish in life. And knowing my driven nature, I probably will get them done. One thing I will begin right away is my dream of being a nurse. A warning should be put out to all hospitals . . . here I come. I plan on focusing my career on critical care, working in either the Emergency Room, Intensive Care Unit, or even Labor and Delivery. I'm drawn to the fast-paced, think-on-your-feet type of action. I plan on working for the next couple of years and then will consider going on to graduate school somewhere out East. I will take some classes on the side while I'm working, to start learning some foreign languages which will help enhance my career (and life!). I would like to start with Spanish, and maybe even work on sign language at the same time.

As for my plans with the military . . . well, to tell you the truth, I am torn. I can't deny the fact that I love putting on that uniform and representing my country in such a way. The impact of my time in the military has been far greater than I ever thought was possible, and maybe it's time to move on to a new adventure. My 8-year contract ends in March 2009. Wow, I can't believe it! Because I have my Bachelors Degree, though, I can do a direct commission as an officer and become a Lieutenant beginning my career as an Army Nurse. How wonderful that would be! That, however, will also add six more years onto my contract and I know (okay, hope) that I will be getting married and starting my family during that time. My family will be my main focus, as I believe that leads to success for the future. I am still deciding.

Marathons will still continue, but I will probably just average about two a year. Triathlons look very intriguing to me and I will probably begin doing those, although every time I ride my bike I feel I would rather be running. And let's face it, I'm not the best swimmer. In fact when I was trying to teach myself how to swim a few years ago, the lifeguards met me at the other side of the pool (once I finally got there). I looked up in confusion wondering if I was in trouble. They looked down at me and said, "We thought you were drowning." Yep, there is definitely room for improvement in that area.

A lot of people think that great things always happen to me and that, like the saying goes, my life is handed to me "on a silver platter." They don't seem to realize that while I've had some wonderful opportunities, they haven't come without a lot of my own blood, sweat and tears. I highly doubt that most people would want a platter served up to them that said they were going to run 26.2 miles, and I'm pretty sure almost nobody wants a shiny platter handed them that says they're going off to war.

My life has been challenging and I've worked really hard to achieve my goals, but great things have happened to me because of the decisions I have made and my outlook on life. It's as good as you make it and I see the "minefields" of life as a blessing. It's all good.

I am flattered when people say, "You should have been Miss America." Yes, how great that would have been. But what is even greater is that there is still much more to be had in life. I accomplished the mission I set out to do. My mission wasn't necessarily to gain the crown, but to prove that you can be yourself through it all and don't have to be a part of the "mold" to fit in.

I am not necessarily encouraging people to join the military or participate in pageants. But what I do hope is to inspire people to get out and try new things. We are so blessed to live in such a country that makes it possible to go after our dreams.

Only in America could something like this happen, where a woman who had never worn high heels, but preferred combat boots as a soldier, gets talked into competing for a pageant. Where someone who is active military learns the life lessons that also come from embracing the woman that she is by participating in the Miss America Organization.

Although the paths seem different, in many ways they are so similar. Both paths promote education, fitness, leadership, and especially service. The pageant life and the military life have made me who I am, so I guess dreams really do come true . . . because I've lived the life of a soldier, a runner, a volunteer, a nurse, and yes, even a Pageant Girl!

I never grew up thinking that I would ever be a soldier, let alone a beauty queen. Sometimes new dreams land in front of you that you never thought were possible. Step into the unknown and go for it. Believe in your dreams, they are ready and waiting to come true. But most importantly, believe in yourself!

This path has not been a journey of one. There have been many supporting hands along the way: A team of people who have put in countless hours and encouragement as I have braved these new combat zones. But most importantly, I couldn't have lived these dreams without my family. They have supported me in all of my weird adventures in life, and I am forever grateful and feel so blessed.

Everything comes with a price, and my reign as Miss Utah has been no exception.

Miles driven . . . over 30,000.

Protein shakes consumed . . . over 700.

Push-ups completed in contests with school kids across the state of Utah . . . at least 600.

Speaking engagements . . . close to 500.

Media interviews . . . nearly 100.

States traveled to for assignments as Miss Utah . . . over 17.

Different magazines that have written articles about me . . . 15.

Marathons completed as Miss Utah . . . 5. (One more should be added for how much I have walked in high heels!)

 Blenders broken (because I travel with them to have my many protein shakes) . . . 3.

Talented people who helped me discover the woman inside . . . 2 (x 20).

Jumps out of a plane with the crown and sash . . . 1.

But having been true to myself through it all . . . Priceless!

Your biggest challenge isn't someone else. It's the ache in your lungs, the burning in your legs, the voice inside you that yells, "can't." But you don't listen. You push harder and you hear the voice whisper, "can." And you discover that the person you thought you were is no match for the one you really are.

Lock 'n Load!

Stevens/Stephens family, Thanksgiving 2007.

Once I was named Miss Utah, interviews with the media became a part of my everyday life.

An advertisement and billboard that went out when I first became Miss Utah.

I took part in all the different 4th of July parades within my first week as Miss Utah.

My first marathon as Miss Utah when I wasn't allowed to ride in the parade. Some of the local TV stations thought it was a good story.

My mom and I at the end of the race. I'm lucky to have her supporting me through everything.

I ran some of my races as Miss Utah/Elastigirl trying to motivate kids to enjoy fitness. We definitely had a good time.

G.I. JILL
SGT Jill Stevens

Miss Utah 2007

NATIONAL GUARD
UTAH
1-800-GO-GUARD

STEVENS   U.S. ARMY

MISS UTAH

The famous picture that the Army put out there. I wish I'd had a say in choosing it . . . I didn't really like this one as I felt I looked like Bozo the Clown with how my make-up turned out. I'm still learning how to put that stuff on.

My dear friend, Kirsten . . . our Miss America at her homecoming!

A few other state contestants and I having fun with some of the advertisements at the Miss America Homecoming in Michigan.

My mom, Mitch and I at the Temple of Heaven in China.

At the Ming Tombs mimicking the animal statues.

300

Handing out school supplies, candy, and toys to the boys and girls of the orphanage in Xi'an.

This is how you could find me on most of my trips throughout the year. I'm trained to catch sleep wherever I can.

As a keynote speaker at the National Speaking of Women's Health Conference in Ohio.

Posing with my dear friend and second mom, Dorothy Dayton.

My brother Mitch and I with radio and TV personality Glenn Beck outside our trailer before the Stadium of Fire.

Singing in front of 60,000 people at the Stadium of Fire in Provo, Utah on July 4, 2008. Wow!

Mimicking a beauty pageant queen in front of the plane I am about to jump out of 11,500 feet in the air.

Making my fashion statement with the crown tied to my head and the goofy goggles. My adreneline was kickin' as I was about to jump. WOO HOO!

Performing "My New Philosophy" from "You're a Good Man, Charlie Brown" during the 2008 Miss Utah Pageant.

Before a preliminary night at the Miss Utah Pageant where the contestants performed "GI Jive."

The front and back sides of the coin produced by SymbolArts I had made to say thanks to those who helped me throughout the year.

At an event in Tennessee with other soldiers. I loved how the photographer SSG Klika captured us without knowing. To me this picture shows pride in serving.

The Afghanistan Orphanage Project

I have been privileged to be a part of The Afghanistan Orphanage Project. This project was organized by several soldiers that I served with during my deployment to Afghanistan. While there, we saw an overwhelming number of children abandoned, orphaned, abused, and living on the streets.

We had to do something and now have organized this 501(c)3 non-profit organization in hopes to make a difference. The care of these children is among the primary concerns of TAO Project.

We are raising funds to build an orphanage in Khalakan, near Kabul, Afghanistan. Our goal is to fund, build, and sustain one of the largest orphanages in Afghanistan.

This orphanage will provide a safe home and beginning education to 1,000 children (500 girls and 500 boys).

To learn more about this project, please visit **www.taoproject.org**.

Jill enjoys sharing her story at speaking engagements and other events. Contact her at **jill@springcreekbooks.com** to arrange an event in your area.